Baptism with the Spirit
The teaching of Dr Martyn Lloyd-Jones

Baptism with the Spirit

The teaching of
Dr Martyn Lloyd-Jones

Michael A. Eaton

Inter-Varsity Press

INTER-VARSITY PRESS
38 De Montfort Street, Leicester LE1 7GP, England

Unless otherwise stated, quotations from the Bible are from the Authorized
(King James) Version, 1611.

First published 1989
Reprinted 1989

British Library Cataloguing in Publication Data
Eaton, Michael A. *1942–*
    Baptism with the Spirit: the teaching of Dr Martyn Lloyd-Jones.
    1. Christian Doctrine. Assurance. Christian doctrine of assurance. Theories of
Lloyd-Jones, D.M.
    (David Martyn). 1899-1981
    I. Title
    234

ISBN 0-85110-663-3

Set in Linotron Baskerville

Typeset in Great Britain by Parker Typesetting Service, Leicester
Printed and bound in Great Britain by
Biddles Ltd, Guildford and King's Lynn

*Inter-Varsity Press is the book-publishing division of the Universities and Colleges Christian
Fellowship (formerly the Inter-Varsity Fellowship), a student movement linking Christian
Unions in universities and colleges throughout the United Kingdom and the Republic of Ireland,
and a member movement of the International Fellowship of Evangelical Students. For information
about local and national activities write to UCCF, 38 De Montfort Street, Leicester LE1 7GP.*

Contents

Preface

I would like to express my gratitude, without implicating them in any of my opinions, to the Rev. Henry Lederle and Professor Adrio König for their advice and encouragement in the study that underlies this book, to Dr R. T. Kendall for the loan of his doctoral thesis before it was published, and to my wife and children who encouraged me in my writing during our holidays in England and Kenya in 1984.

I am grateful also to the staff of the libraries of the Witwatersrand University, Johannesburg, and the University of South Africa, Pretoria, and to the British Library with its facilities at the British Museum reading room. The Evangelical Library has for many years provided much-appreciated access to the works of English Puritans, and also has back copies of the *Westminster Record*.

I have used a 'short title' method in the footnotes whenever *op. cit.* or *ibid.* would have caused confusion.

This work is a rewritten version of my M.Th. thesis at the University of South Africa, under the supervision of the Rev. Henry Lederle. A copy of my original work is available at the Evangelical Library, London, as well as in UNISA Library, Pretoria.

I am grateful especially to my daughter, Tina, who sacrificed part of her student vacation to edit my manuscript.

I would like to thank the staff of Inter-Varsity Press for their zeal and courtesy in seeing this material through to its final form.

Some readers of this work in its pre-publication form have commented on my remarks concerning 'preparationism'. I could have written more about this but for two reasons chose not to do so. One is that this is primarily a work about Dr Lloyd-Jones's view of the Spirit – and only one aspect of it at that. I have to say *something* about 'preparationism' since it relates to the only point where I am in disagreement with the Doctor in this matter. But this is not a book about preparationism.

A second reason is that I shall soon (August 1989) reach the end of a much fuller research project on the subject of preparationism, the manuscript of which is already twice the length of this book. If ever I go into print on this subject and publish parts or the whole of my work on it, I would like to deal with it more fully than I could within this particular work on Dr Lloyd-Jones. Certainly the introspection of some forms of Calvinism needs looking into. When as great a Christian as Asahel Nettleton can say, 'The most that I have ventured to say respecting myself is, that I think it possible I may get to heaven', we may have come a long way from the New Testament. We need, in my opinion, to analyse the underlying theology that leads to it. But that is another book!

Nor – in this work – am I trying to put forth my own view of the baptism with the Spirit. Readers will glean it from the last chapter, but not in any fullness. Again I have a manuscript on the subject – a transcript of eight broadcasts I once gave in Kenya on 'The Baptism with the Spirit'. But I have deliberately not included any of that here. I have not attempted a general description of Dr Lloyd-Jones's theology. Certainly much more could be written on the corporate aspects of his teaching and its relationship to the doctrine of the church. This aspect of his teaching had a major affect on my own life – an impact I have described elsewhere (see 'Testimony of a Seceder' in J. Peters, *Martyn Lloyd-Jones: Preacher* [Paternoster Press 1986], pp. 150–154). This book will not be the last to be written on Dr Lloyd-Jones's teaching. It will be good – in my opinion – if a number of works pursue different aspects of his theology. His doctrine of the church is already being researched at a doctoral level (not by me). The final synthesis is not being attempted here.

Friendly critics must remember also that Lloyd-Jones's material is still being made public. A yet earlier statement of Lloyd-Jones's view of the baptism of the Spirit (1954) is now available – but does not affect anything I say here. For some time to come anyone who writes about Lloyd-Jones will have to live with the fact that it will be years before everything is published. I have not attempted to mention all the material available. I have in my possession, for example, notes of his sermons on John 6 which rarely receive any mention. Yet with regard to the topic of the baptism with the Spirit there is no reason to think that any further material being made available will substantially change what we already have in the studies of Romans 8:15–16, John 1:26–33, Ephesians 1:13 and the series on revival. (One would like to know, however, if anyone has notes or a transcript of the address once given on Thomas Goodwin.)

Although this work tries to be fairly objective not autobiographical, I have to give thanks to God for Dr Lloyd-Jones's ministry. I recall the day in 1959 when I first went to hear him preaching on revival; and the evening in March 1968 when I sat in Westminster Chapel listening to his last sermon in the Romans series – although I did not know it would be the last. I remember as an Anglican minister taking a group of young people to Westminster Central Hall in October 1966 and telling my vicar beforehand what Lloyd-Jones was going to say. For I knew his view of the church sufficiently well to predict what his line would be. When I got married in 1968 one of my first tasks was to take my newly acquired wife to hear 'William Williams and Welsh Calvinistic Methodism'. As soon as my children were old enough – one of them named after him – I found where 'the Doctor' was preaching and took them to hear him.

I recall the occasion when I was a visiting preacher in a British church and in the middle of the first hymn I saw Dr Lloyd-Jones slip in to the back row. I was disconcerted for a second or two, especially since I was about to preach on Ephesians, but when I began to preach he listened with such agreement on his face that he was easy to preach to.

Once I went to see him to discuss an agonizing problem in theology. He looked at me more as a doctor than as a theologian and refused to discuss the theology until after I had taken a holiday. By the second day of the holiday I no longer had the problem! On another occasion when I was in trouble with an elder in central Africa I took my first opportunity to ask his advice. 'Have they taken your pulpit away from you?' he asked. 'No,' I replied. 'Well then, you are alright. Deal with your problem by seeking the Spirit's power on your preaching.'

I do my own thinking in this book. The Doctor would have commended me for that. I do not agree with every minutiae of the Doctor's teaching. One of my favourite quotations from Lloyd-Jones is his assertion: 'Every preacher should believe strongly in his own method; and if I cannot persuade all of the rightness of mine, I can at least stimulate them to think and to consider other possibilities.' The same is true of writing. If I can persuade some to consider other possibilities with regard to the baptism with the Spirit, I am content.

Michael A. Eaton
December 1988
Nairobi

Part One

Introduction

Part One

Introduction

1

Dr Martyn Lloyd-Jones and charismatic theology

In the twentieth century, since the early 1960s, the charismatic movement has made much of a post-conversion 'experience' of the Spirit, associated with gifts of the Spirit, especially the gift of tongues.[1] A doctrine of a 'baptism with the Spirit' is not, however, an innovation of the charismatic movement, nor even of the Pentecostal movement whose origins date from the turn of the century. Earlier in the history of the church there had been several strands of Christian thinking in which an experience of the Spirit, distinct from and subsequent to Christian conversion, had been taught. There were different ways of expressing the teaching and different points of emphasis; the ramifications of the different views may be expressed diagrammatically (see p. 14).

The concern of the present study is with one line of thought only, that of an 'experience' of assurance, the sealing of salvation, and with its greatest expositor, Dr Martyn Lloyd-Jones, affectionately known in the British Christian world as 'the Doctor'.

Sketch of life

A patriotic Welshman, Lloyd-Jones was brought up in Welsh Calvinistic Methodism but his faith was only nominal until his early twenties, when he came to a vibrant faith in Christ. He left a brilliant medical career in 1926, and in early 1927 became the minister of Bethlehem Forward Movement Mission Hall in

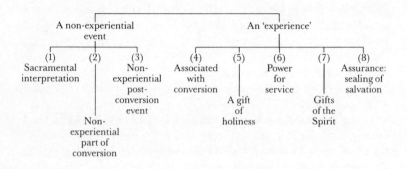

Baptism with the Spirit:
a spectrum of views

Sandfields, a locality in the South Wales mining town of Aberavon. After eleven years of influential ministry at Aberavon Lloyd-Jones, by this time tired and over-worked, accepted an offer by the famous George Campbell-Morgan to share the pulpit at Westminster Chapel for sixth months while recovering from overstrain and considering his future. Within a few months it was clear that Lloyd-Jones was destined to be Campbell-Morgan's successor. The six months stretched out to thirty years. During those years Lloyd-Jones became known as a powerful preacher and influential Christian leader.

After a discouraging period during World War 2, the church at Westminster Chapel began to grow. By 1947 the lower balcony of the church had to be opened. By the time of Lloyd-Jones's retirement in 1968 the congregation had grown perhaps to 1,500 in the mornings and 2,000 on Sunday evenings.[2] The Friday night discussion classes had also grown and during 1953–1955 took the form of expositions of Christian doctrine. This was followed by an exposition of Romans 1:1 – 14:17 which lasted from 1955 to 1968.

Lloyd-Jones's prestige was visible in many areas. He helped

launch the Banner of Truth publishing house and the *Evangelical Magazine*.[3] He provided counsel in the early days of the *Evangelical Times*. He had much to do with the formation of the London Bible College and later with the London Theological Seminary. He was influential in the Inter-Varsity Fellowship (now the Universities and Colleges Christian Fellowship) and helped form the International Fellowship of Evangelical Students, of which he was chairman from 1947 to 1959.[4] He and a few others started a study group within the Tyndale Fellowship for Biblical Research which later became independent and emerged as the Puritan and Reformed Studies Conference and (after its reorganization) the Westminster Conference.[5] It met in December each year for two days of lectures and discussion around Reformed and Puritan interests; it was always chaired by Lloyd-Jones.

From the early 1940s onwards Lloyd-Jones led a monthly ministers' fraternal which increasingly became the focal point of his leadership among evangelical ministers. In the 1960s many of the discussions at the Westminster Fraternal revolved around the doctrine of the church, which had been brought into prominence by the ecumenical movement. This led to Lloyd-Jones's being asked occasionally to speak about church issues. On one notable night in October 1966 he gave his famous appeal at a meeting in Westminster Central Hall, urging evangelical Christians to disengage from doctrinally compromised denominations and come together in closer evangelical fellowship. The appeal was largely unsuccessful but led to a stronger sense of identity among non-Anglican evangelicals.[6]

Although the events of 1966 cast a shadow over the evangelicalism of the late 1960s, Lloyd-Jones continued to enjoy immense prestige among evangelical free church people, especially among the churches attached to the British Evangelical Council[7] and the Fellowship of Independent Evangelical Churches.[8]

In 1968 Lloyd-Jones retired from the ministry at Westminster Chapel. His retirement released him into a wider ministry, and for a further twelve years he continued to preach and to chair the meetings of the Westminster Fraternal and Westminster Conference. He saw through the press thirteen major volumes of sermons, and his lecture series *Preaching and Preachers*.[9]

Lloyd-Jones was never formally a professional scholar. He would often insist that his interest in biblical or historical learning was not merely academic or antiquarian.[10] He was primarily a preacher, and all of his thinking was oriented around his preaching and pastoral interests. He never went to theological college or took a theological degree. Nor did he believe that the taking of examinations on biblical or theological subjects was wise,[11] and for much of his life he was rather reluctant to give support to theological seminaries.[12]

Yet in his own way Lloyd-Jones was a theologian of no mean stature, and over the course of his life-time built up a massive array of theological and historical learning. He taught himself Greek while he was still a consultant in medicine[13] and his interest in theology was kindled in the late 1920s when he was drawn to the reading of P. T. Forsyth, R. W. Dale and James Denney.[14] In his early days he was also attracted to the reading of the Puritans, among whom Bunyan and Baxter were the earliest samples.[15] He was given the complete works of John Owen as a wedding present in addition to some works of Calvin.[16] His reading of A. C. McGiffert's *Protestant Thought Before Kant* led him to Jonathan Edwards, whose complete works he obtained in 1929.[17] The discovery in 1932, while he was in America, of the ten-volume set of works of B. B. Warfield was also a great stimulus to him.[18] These early beginnings led Lloyd-Jones into a lifetime of intense theological and biblical study.

The popular presentation of Lloyd-Jones's work is deceptive. He held that preaching is to be aimed at the 'common man'. Sermons, he would say, 'are not intended for the "experts" but for the "common people" and those who are in need of help'.[19] He also believed that theology should be taught only by preaching: academic 'lectures' on theological subjects were of little interest to him.[20] This practical outlook greatly obscured the breadth of his scholarship, yet it is worth noting that a number of scholars of repute have underlined the need to take Lloyd-Jones's expositions seriously. As one reviewer has pointed out, 'There are very few footnotes, no index, no bibliography, a minimum of documentation. Yet a comprehensive scholarship is discerned.'[21] This, it should be noted, was very much historically oriented. 'I am so indebted', he said to a gathering of supporters of the Evangelical Library in 1965, 'to the reading of history and biography. I like to approach every problem, if I can, histor-ically. I know of no better approach.'[22]

In the following chapters I shall focus on the major influences that contributed to Lloyd-Jones's thinking. Since he gloried in the theology of the Reformation, it is appropriate to begin with Calvin. We shall discover, though, that Lloyd-Jones could not directly quote Calvin in support of his doctrine of the Spirit, however much he admired him.

A greater influence than that of the Reformation was that of the Puritans. Among those who made the greatest contribution to Lloyd-Jones's thinking are Thomas Goodwin (1600–1680), whose doctrine of the Spirit Lloyd-Jones largely reproduces, John Owen (1616–1683), and Richard Sibbes (1577–1635), whose teaching once sustained Lloyd-Jones in a time of weariness and trial.[23] From a later period comes Jonathan Edwards (1703–1758), whose influence Lloyd-Jones confessed was immense. 'I was like the man in our Lord's parable who found a pearl of great price,' he said of the two volumes of Edward's works on one occasion. 'Their influence upon me I cannot put into words.'[24]

Two aspects of Lloyd-Jones's theology are highly significant: his doctrine of the church and his doctrine of the Spirit. The former has yet to be adequately researched; the latter is our concern within these pages. Years before the charismatic move-ment began in the 1960s Lloyd-Jones had been teaching a dis-tinctive view of the work of the Spirit. It was controversial during his earlier years, but since Lloyd-Jones did not publish many major works until after his retirement, his view of the Spirit was not always fully realized outside of Westminster Chapel. Since his death in 1981 and the availability of his teach-ing on tape and in print, his opinions have received much wider consideration. The purpose of this book is to describe and evalu-ate his opinions as a contribution to current thinking about the nature of charismatic experience. One need not agree with every detail of Lloyd-Jones's expositions to profit from him. As he once said about his convictions concerning preaching: 'If I cannot persuade all of the rightness of mine, I can at least stimulate them to think and to consider other possibilities.'[25] Lloyd-Jones would have wanted this book to achieve the same objective.

Overview

It will perhaps help us to get our bearings if some examples of different viewpoints concerning the baptism with the Spirit are first considered. The diagram on page 14 does not represent adequately the entire range of available options. Yet it may be useful in showing where different points of emphasis lie. Nine representative approaches to the 'baptism with the Spirit' may be briefly considered.

We consider first *the sacramental interpretation*. This closely links baptism with the Spirit with water-baptism. From earliest post-apostolic times the work of the Spirit was closely associated with baptism. The particular terms that are of interest in the following study (*e.g.* seal, baptism, earnest, anointing) are closely linked with a sacramental understanding of conversion and the gift of the Spirit. Baptism was almost universally thought of as having regenerating power.

In the *Epistle of Barnabas* baptism 'brings the remission of sins'. Salvation is by hope in the cross and descent into the water. Baptism is the 'vessel of the Spirit'. Baptismal regeneration is clearly implied when the epistle says, 'We go down into the water full of sins and foulness, and we come up bearing the fruit of fear in our hearts, and having hope on Jesus in the Spirit.' Yet this does not happen independently of faith, as is clear from the following: 'Whosoever hears and believes those things spoken shall live for ever.'[26]

In *2 Clement* and the *Shepherd of Hermas* we come across a sacramental use of the term 'seal'. When *2 Clement* speaks of 'those who have not kept the seal', he is referring to sin after baptism, a perennial preoccupation of the early church. Similarly in the *Shepherd of Hermas* there is *one* possibility of restoration in the case of post-baptismal sin. In the description of the third vision, the church appears as a tower. 'Hear then', says the interpreter, 'why the tower has been built upon the water: because your life was saved and shall be saved through water.' Persistent sinners cannot be baptized again, cannot in the Shepherd's words 'be rolled into the water'. In all of this there is a doctrine of baptismal regeneration. The stones of the tower (the church) have 'to come up through the water that they might be made alive'. This is identified with the term 'seal'. 'The seal, then, is the water,' says *Shepherd* 9:16:4. Later, in a part of the *Shepherd* of which only the Latin translation exists, conversion is again described as 'receiving the seal'.[27]

In the writings of Irenaeus[28] the gift of the Spirit seems to be closely linked with baptism. Baptism is 'new birth unto God' (*Adversus omnes Haereses* 1:21:1), a 'laver of regeneration' (*Adv. Haer.* 5:15:3). In commanding his disciples to baptize, the Lord gave them 'power to regenerate' (*Adv. Haer.* 3:17:2). This is linked in Irenaeus's thinking with the outpouring of the Spirit predicted in Joel 2:29 (*Adv. Haer.* 3:17:2). On the other hand, Irenaeus can refer to the apostles' ability (as seen in Acts 8) to fill people with the Holy Spirit by the laying on of hands (*Adv. Haer.* 1:23:1). He speaks of Christ's being anointed with the Spirit (*Adv. Haer.* 3:18:3). Ephesians 1:13–14 is quoted and linked with receiving the Spirit. It is equated with receiving the 'Spirit of adoption' and is taken to refer to the 'earnest' of immortality which Christians receive by the Spirit (*Adv. Haer.* 5:8:1).

In the *Proof of the Apostolic Preaching* we have similar teaching. Baptism gives remission of sins. This baptism '*is* the seal of eternal life and *is* rebirth unto God'.[29] The Holy Spirit is 'given by Him in baptism'.[30] (J.P. Smith links the 'seal' terminology with the later theory of sacramental 'characters'.)[31]

From these early beginnings a sacramentalist approach to baptism and the receiving of the Spirit came into the church and became part of the catholic tradition. It continues to have great influence today. Generally speaking such an approach to the baptism with the Spirit is necessarily non-experiential – it is not consciously experienced, at least, initially. We shall see below, however, an approach which combines sacramentalism with charismatic theology.

We consider next that view of the baptism of the Spirit which regards it as *an inseparable part of Christian conversion, but not a conscious 'experience'*. For Richard Gaffin, the gift of the Spirit is a unique epochal event, 'part of the once-for-all accomplishment of redemption (*historia salutis*) rather than as part of its on-going continual application (*ordo salutis*)'.[32] In his view it is not 'capable of being repeated or serving as a model for individual Christian experience'.[33] The incidents in Acts 8:14ff., 10:44ff., and 19:1ff. are 'elements in the initial, foundational spread of the gospel and so correlate with the events of Acts 2 as part of a

19

unique, nonrepeatable (*i.e.* nontypical, nonmodular) complex of events'.[34] For Gaffin, Christian conversion *is* the baptism of the Spirit for an individual. 'On the individual level, conversion is, among other things, a Pentecostal experience.'[35] Although Gaffin uses the word 'experience' he does not envisage anything other than the event of coming to faith and the enjoyment of forgiveness of sins. An explicit and *conscious* 'experience' of receiving the Spirit is not envisaged. Gaffin believes that even for the disciples Pentecost has been over-emphasized 'as an empowering experience transforming the disciples';[36] he wishes to see 'a shift in accent away from preoccupation with the experiential significance of Pentecost (which tends to lead down a wrong track)'.[37]

A third approach to baptism with the Holy Spirit is that which regards it as *a post-conversion enduement of power which is non-experiential by nature*. Those who regard the baptism of the Spirit as a post-conversion work of grace generally regard it as a matter of conscious experience. Yet such is not always the case, and the experience and teaching of F. B. Meyer provide an illustration of the outlook under consideration.

F. B. Meyer (1847–1929), pastored several churches in Britain between 1868 and his retirement in 1920. He was one of the first ministers to welcome Dwight L. Moody to Britain in 1873, and thereafter was associated with the ministry of Moody in Britain. In the early 1880s two notable Christian student leaders, Stanley Smith and C. T. Studd, conducted meetings at Melbourne Hall, Leicester, where Meyer was then the pastor. His meeting with these men led Meyer to dedicate his life afresh to God. Meyer's biographer, M.J. Street, calls this occasion the 'watershed of his life', and says that from that time onwards Meyer's life was characterized by a power that he had not known before.[38]

This was followed by an event which took place in 1887 at the Keswick Convention. Meyer went to the convention feeling very weary. Many of the Christians he found there were agonizing in prayer for the 'baptism with the Spirit' (viewing it primarily as a work of sanctification). Meyer felt he was too weary to agonize. He prayed: 'My Father, if there is one soul more than another within the circle of these hills that needs the gift of Pentecost, it is I; but I am too weary to think, or feel, or pray intensely. Is it not possible to receive it without the tide of emotion which so often accompanies its advent or renewal in the soul?'

Then, says Meyer, a voice seemed to say, 'Claim and receive it by an act of faith, apart from feeling. As thy share in God's forgiving grace was won for thee by the dying Christ, so thy share in the Pentecostal gift is held for thee by the glorified Christ; and as thou didst take the former, so thou must take the latter, and reckon that it is thine, by a faith which is utterly indifferent to the presence or absence of resulting joy.' Meyer reported: 'It seemed to me as if I took a deep inspiration of wind which bloweth where it listeth. I opened my mouth and panted. I took from the hands of the living Christ my share, or as much of it as I could then receive, of the fulness of the Spirit.'[39]

Meyer's Keswick experience was to become transcribed into his teaching. In March 1896, for example, Meyer gave one of six addresses at a conference in Devonshire Square Baptist Church, London, in which he spoke of 'the enduement of the Holy Ghost'.[40] He taught that although some heroes of the Old Testament (Elijah, Enoch, Samuel and others) had known the baptism with the Holy Spirit, now that gift was within reach of all Christians. 'It is the grand prerogative of every believer to have an equal right to the blessed power and enduement of the Holy Ghost.'[41] This is conceived largely in terms of power for service. When Meyer comes to the end of this address he urges that such a blessing can be *claimed*. 'We have claimed the forgiveness of our sin, but we have never claimed the anointing of the Holy Ghost, and I do exhort you to claim it.'[42] It is evident that Meyer envisages something that may be 'taken' without conscious experience.

Similarly in a book published in 1894 Meyer distances himself from the view that baptism with the Spirit is an emotional experience. There is no reason, he says, why we should not use the term 'baptism with the Spirit' but he fears lest the term 'may lead people to look for something extraordinary, abnormal and emotional'.[43] The Spirit may be received in his fullness 'without rapture or emotion, or any definite experience'.[44]

The three approaches mentioned thus far commonly regard the baptism with the Spirit as non-experiential, as below the level of consciousness. The remaining five approaches agree in thinking of the baptism with the Spirit as very much an 'experience'.

A fourth approach considers the baptism with the Spirit as

21

part of conversion yet as a definite conscious experience without which conversion has not taken place. In the history of the church George Whitefield (1714–1770) and the early John Wesley (1703–1791) illustrate this approach, while more recently it has been urged by James Dunn.

George Whitefield's 'Short Account' of his early life tells the story of his birth in 1714, his early childhood waywardness (as he saw it), his commencement at the university of Oxford in 1732, and his introduction to the 'Holy Club' by Charles Wesley.[45] He tells us 'God worked powerfully upon my soul' through his reading of Law's *Serious Call to a Devout Life*,[46] but it was his reading of Henry Scougal's *The Life of God in the Soul of Man* that led him to say 'I never knew what true religion was, till God sent me that excellent treatise.'[47] The conviction that came through reading Henry Scougal's little book, that there was such a thing as a 'new birth' which was hitherto foreign to him, set him seeking that new birth. For several months he was in considerable distress, until a crisis came one memorable day in 1735. He tells the story as follows:[48]

One day, perceiving an uncommon drought and a disagreeable clamminess in my mouth and using things to allay my thirst but in vain, it was suggested to me, that when Jesus Christ cried out, 'I thirst,' His sufferings were near at an end. Upon which I cast myself down on the bed, crying out, 'I thirst! I thirst!' Soon after this, I found and felt in myself that I was delivered from the burden that had so heavily oppressed me. The spirit of mourning was taken from me, and I knew what it was truly to rejoice in God my Saviour; and, for some time, could not avoid singing psalms wherever I was; but my joy gradually became more settled, and, blessed be God, has abode and increased in my soul, saving a few casual intermissions, ever since.

Thus were the days of my mourning ended. After a long night of desertion and temptation, the Star, which I had seen at a distance before, began to appear again, and the Day Star arose in my heart. Now did the Spirit of God take possession of my soul, and, as I humbly hope, seal me unto the day of redemption.

He speaks of this experience as receiving 'the Spirit of adoption' in his heart,[49] and in a later edition of 1756 he added a fuller description of this experience:[50]

> After having undergone innumerable buffetings of Satan, and many months inexpressible trials by night and day under the spirit of bondage, God was pleased at length to remove the heavy load, to enable me to lay hold on His dear Son by a living faith, and, by giving me the spirit of adoption, to seal me, as I humbly hope, even to the day of everlasting redemption. But oh! with what joy – joy unspeakable – even joy that was full of, and big with glory, was my soul filled, when the weight of sin went off, and an abiding sense of the pardoning love of God, and a full assurance of faith broke in upon my disconsolate soul! Surely it was the day of my espousals, – a day to be had in everlasting remembrance. At first my joys were like a spring tide, and, as it were, overflowed the banks. Go where I would, I could not avoid singing of psalms aloud. . . .

Then in a sermon preached in later life he said:[51]

> I know the place! It may be superstitious, perhaps, but whenever I go to Oxford I cannot help running to that place where Jesus Christ first revealed himself to me and gave me the new birth.

An examination of Whitefield's words reveal that at that time he regarded the 'sealing of the Spirit' as synonymous with receiving the 'Spirit of adoption' and with the 'full assurance of faith'. He also regarded it as the day of his being given faith and the day of his 'new birth'. Thus for Whitefield there is a sealing of the Spirit which is a conscious experience without which conversion has not taken place. (I am *not* suggesting that all his life Whitefield totally identified assurance and saving faith.)

A study of the *Journals* of John Wesley reveals that Wesley held a similar view at first. He regarded his experience on 24 May 1738 as his conversion, yet it was described in strongly experiential terms:[52]

> I felt my heart strangely warmed. I felt I did trust in Christ,
> Christ alone for salvation; and an assurance was given me,
> that he had taken away my sins, even mine, and saved me
> from the law of sin and death.

Subsequently, however, John Wesley changed his views somewhat and taught that it was possible to have saving faith without
having the 'sealing' or 'witness' of the Spirit.[53] In August 1738
he visited the Moravians in Herrnhut where he spent some
hours in conversation with Christian David (1691–1751), the
Moravian exponent of the full assurance of faith. Christian
David distinguished regeneration and the receiving of the Spirit.
It was probably at this time that Wesley first gave thought to
distinguishing regeneration and the witness of the Spirit.[54]

As the years went by he was more willing to allow that a person
might be a Christian yet not experience the direct and assuring
witness of the Spirit. At the age of eighty-five he had come to
accept that salvation was possible without such a subsequent
witness.

> Nearly fifty years ago, when Preachers commonly called
> Methodists, began to preach that grand Scriptural doctrine,
> salvation by faith, they were not sufficiently apprized of the
> difference between a servant and a child of God. They did
> not clearly understand, that even one 'who feareth God,
> and worketh righteousness, is accepted of him.' In con-
> sequence of this, they were apt to make sad the hearts of
> those whom God hath not made sad. For they frequently
> asked those who feared God, 'Do you know that your sins
> are forgiven?' and upon their answering 'No', immediately
> replied, 'Then you are a child of the devil.' No; that does
> not follow. It might have been said (and it is all that can be
> said with propriety), 'Hitherto you are only a *servant*, you
> are not a *child* of God. You have already great reason to
> praise God that He has called you to his honourable ser-
> vice.'[55]

In modern times James Dunn is the most significant expositor of
the view that baptism with the Spirit is the *experience* of becoming
a Christian. Although his work is widely used among those who

wish to reply to Pentecostals and 'charismatics', yet Dunn is in an altogether different category from R. Gaffin, for the heart of his view is that the receiving of the Spirit is a definite *experience*: 'For the writers of the New Testament the baptism in or gift of the spirit was part of the event (or process) of becoming a Christian.' Dunn continues a line or so later: 'The reception of the Spirit was a very definite and often dramatic *experience*.'[56] This puts Dunn closer to Whitefield and the early Wesley than to Gaffin. In Dunn's opinion, 'Jesus can be called a charismatic'[57] because of his *consciousness* of the Spirit's empowering him. For Dunn, someone who is not a charismatic is not a Christian, at least judged by New Testament standards.

A fifth approach is found among those who regard the baptism of the Spirit *as primarily a gift of holiness*. This historically goes back to John Wesley's doctrine of Christian perfection, and is found in the 'holiness churches' of modern times.[58] We take our first example from A. M. Hills's *Holiness and Power*. It is written, the preface tells us, for those 'who are in doubt about the theological and Scriptural standing of the doctrine of the instantaneous "baptism with the Holy Ghost", with its consequent "holiness and power".'[59] Hills says, 'There is a second work of grace which God would have wrought in us all by the Holy Ghost, entirely distinct from regeneration, and subsequent to it.'[60] 'It is a cleansing, purifying act of God himself that sanctifies the heart.'[61] 'Sanctification is not, therefore, reached by a gradual development or growth. Such a notion is a grave and even calamitous error.'[62] 'It is as sudden as Pentecost. Such a work seems great to us and impossible, but not to God. He speaks, and it is done.'[63] 'This blessing, like justification, is obtained by *faith*.'[64]

Another member of this school of thought is Lewis T. Corlett, whose *Holiness in Practical Living* expounds the same viewpoint. Sanctification is, for Corlett, a 'second work of grace' in which the believer is cleansed from all inbred sin. All conflict regarding the will of God is removed.[65] 'Sometimes', says Corlett, 'this experience is known as the baptism of the Holy Ghost.'[66] 'Just as certainly as the disciples were commanded by Jesus to tarry for the promise of the Father, which was the baptism of the Holy Ghost, just as definitely Christians today are commanded to wait for the promise of the Father so that they may have the baptism of the Holy Spirit as well as the birth of the Spirit.'[67] 'In the baptism of the Holy Spirit the Spirit of God cleanses the heart from inbred sin and fills it to the full of man's capacity with himself.'[68]

Corlett deduces this theology from the classic 'Pentecostal' passages of the book of Acts (chapters 2; 8; 9; 10 – 11; 18; 19). Acts 8 relates an evangelistic movement at Samaria thus: 'When the leaders at Jerusalem heard about this revival, they sent Peter and John to help get the people established. They preached unto the people the further work of grace signified by Pentecost, and many were baptized with the Holy Ghost and gave testimony to that fact. This incident clearly outlines God's method in the plan of salvation of directing men in two distinct experiences of Christian grace.'[69]

The best-known exponents of the sixth approach we shall consider are Dwight Lyman Moody (1837–1899) and Reuben A. Torrey (1856–1928). Born in Massachusetts, Moody came to experience an evangelical conversion in 1855. Shortly after his conversion he became involved in the work of a Sunday School in Wells Street, Chicago, and in 1858 started a similar work in a different part of the city. This was highly successful and grew quickly to about 1,500 members. In 1861 he relinquished his employment and gave himself to full-time evangelistic work. Although he had not been formally trained and ordained he was virtually pastor of what was now a large and flourishing church in Chicago. He became well known in Chicago as a successful evangelist, and visited Britain in 1867, during which time he visited the Metropolitan Tabernacle and George Müller's orphanages.[70]

In 1871 something took place in Moody's life which, in Moody's own view, was to give him a measure of power and influence which far transcended anything he had known before that time. He began to feel that he was inadequately fitted for the work he was being called to do. Two women attended his meetings and would sit at the front praying for Moody. W. R. Moody tells the story in his father's words:[71]

'Why don't you pray for the people?' Mr Moody would ask.

'Because you need the power of the Spirit,' they would say.

26

'I need the power! Why,' said he, in relating the incident years after, 'I thought I had power. I had the largest congregation in Chicago, and there were many conversions. I was in a sense satisfied. But right along those two godly women kept praying for me, and their earnest talk about anointing for special service set me thinking. I asked them to come and talk with me, and they poured out their hearts in prayer that I might receive the filling of the Holy Spirit. There came a great hunger into my soul. I did not know what it was. I began to cry out as I never did before. I really felt that I did not want to live if I could not have this power for service.'

During this time the famous Chicago fire of 1871 broke out and the buildings in which Moody's congregation met were burnt to the ground. Moody had to begin to visit Christian churches seeking funds to help rebuild his work. It was during this time that his prayers were answered.

'My heart was not in the begging,' he said. 'I could not appeal. I was crying all the time that God would fill me with His Spirit. Well, one day, in the city of New York – oh, what a day! – I cannot describe it, I seldom refer to it; it is almost too sacred an experience to name. Paul had an experience of which he never spoke for fourteen years. I can only say that God revealed Himself to me, and I had such an experience of His love that I had to ask Him to stay His hand. I went to preaching again. The sermons were not different; I did not present any new truths; and yet hundreds were converted. I would not now be placed back where I was before that blessed experience if you should give me all the world – it would be as the small dust of the balance.'[72]

It will be noted that Moody conceives of this blessing in terms of 'power for service'. From 1871 onwards he taught the need of an experience over and above Christian conversion, *an experience which was an enduement with power to enable Christian service.*

R. A. Torrey continued the teaching that was propagated by D. L. Moody. He begins his chapter 'The Baptism with the Holy Spirit: What It Is and What It Does'[73] by asserting that the

27

blessing is experiential and distinct from conversion. He says that 'the Baptism with the Holy Spirit is a definite experience of which one may know whether he has received it or not'.[74] Acts 19:2 implies as much, thinks Torrey.[75] It is 'distinct from and additional to His regenerating work'.[76] The disciples were regenerate first, argues Torrey, citing John 15:3 and Acts 8:12–16.[77] 'Every regenerate person has the Holy Spirit, but not every regenerate person has what the Bible calls "the gift of the Holy Spirit", or "the baptism with the Holy Spirit", or "the Promise of the Father".'[78] Baptism with the Spirit *may* be virtually simultaneous with conversion but often it is subsequent to it.

Then Torrey defines the essential content of the gift: 'The baptism with the Spirit is a work of the Holy Spirit always connected with and primarily for the purpose of testimony and service.'[79] This Torrey links with Acts 1:8: 'There is not one single passage in the Bible, either in the Old Testament or the New Testament, where the Baptism with the Holy Spirit is spoken of, where it is not connected with testimony or service.'[80] In saying this Torrey is clearly wanting to distinguish his view from the 'holiness' school of thought mentioned above. He makes this clear when in a few sentences below he says, 'The Baptism with the Holy Spirit is not primarily for the purpose of making us individually holy.'[81] Torrey does not cite verses like Romans 8:15–16; 5:5; Ephesians 1:13–14. That is, he does not link his doctrine with the 'sealing' passages or with the theme of assurance. His claim that no text relating to the baptism with the Spirit connects with anything other than service or testimony presupposes that Torrey does not consider the possibility of linking the 'sealing' passages with his doctrine.

Torrey goes on to make a number of denials. The gift of tongues is not part of the gift. Nor will it make anyone an evangelist. The essential matter, in Torrey's view, is power for service: 'Just as surely as anyone here today is baptized with the Holy Spirit, they will have a power in their service that they never had before; they will have power for the work to which God has called them.'[82]

The seventh viewpoint, among those being outlined, is the one which has become extremely influential in the twentieth century. It is that view of the baptism with the Spirit which sees it as *associated with gifts of the Spirit* and generally or, for some at least, inevitably indicated by the manifestation of the gift of tongues.

We may take Don Basham's *A Handbook on Holy Spirit Baptism* as a representative statement. For Basham, 'The baptism in the Holy Spirit is a second encounter with God (the first is conversion) in which the Christian begins to receive the supernatural power of the Holy Spirit into his life.'[83] 'This second experience of the power of God, which we call the baptism in the Holy Spirit, is given for the purpose of equipping the Christian with God's power for service.'[84] It 'opens the way to many wonderful gifts of God, but it does not provide instant holiness or perfection'.[85] (At this point Basham is distinguishing his teaching from that of the older holiness movement.)[86]

Basham goes on to refer to miraculous gifts, and especially the 'initial evidence'[87] of the gift of tongues. Part 2 of the *Handbook* is entitled 'Questions about speaking in tongues'. Basham reluctantly admits that the baptism in the Holy Spirit may be received without the gift of tongues, but he says he encourages 'no one to seek the baptism without expecting tongues'.[88] It is clear, therefore, that the emphasis in Basham (and the twentieth-century charismatic movement) is different from the older view of 'power for service' as taught by Moody and Torrey. The older emphasis was more on powerful preaching and power in lay witness than on the miracle-gifts that have been of interest in Pentecostalism and the charismatic movement.

The remainder of this work is concerned with yet another approach which sees baptism with the Spirit as *primarily a 'sealing' of one's salvation*. It is an intensification of the assurance of salvation, a *direct* assurance from God of one's salvation, not a *syllogistic* assurance (*i.e.* an assurance which one deduces from the fact that one has believed). This view of 'sealing' or direct assurance arose in post-Reformation Calvinism. Its greatest expositor among the English Puritans was Thomas Goodwin. It was taught also by early Methodists. Its greatest expositor in modern times is Martyn Lloyd-Jones.

A representative example is to be seen in the experience of Howell Harris (1714–1773), the Welsh Calvinistic Methodist and one of the leading preachers in the Evangelical Awakening in Wales. Harris was born at Trefecca[89] in south Wales. A dramatic change in his life took place on Palm Sunday 1735 when,

29

through the ministry of the vicar of Talgarth (a village two miles away from Harris' birthplace), Harris was brought to experience Christian conversion. Several weeks later, at a communion service on Whit Sunday, Harris was brought to assurance of his salvation. 'I lost my burden,' he says. 'I went home leaping for joy; and I said to a neighbour that was sad, "Why are you sad? I know my sins have been forgiven".'[90]

Yet these experiences of conversion and assurance were not the all-important ones in Harris' thinking. On 18 June 1735 something happened which Harris was never to forget and to which he would refer in his diaries when the anniversary of the day came. Harris was spending time in prayer in the tower of a church at Llangasty. He describes his experience there as follows:

> June 18, 1735, being in secret prayer, I felt suddenly my heart melting within me like wax before the fire with love to God my Saviour; and also felt not only love, peace, etc. but longing to be dissolved, and to be with Christ; then was a cry in my inmost soul, which I was totally unacquainted with before, Abba Father! Abba Father! I could not help calling God my Father; I knew that I was his child, and that He loved me, and heard me. My soul being filled and satiated, crying, 'Tis enough, I am satisfied. Give me strength, and I will follow thee through fire and water.' I could say I was happy indeed! There was in me a well of water, springing up to everlasting life, Jn. 4:14. The love of God was shed abroad in my heart by the Holy Ghost, Rom. 5:5.

As Evans comments, 'Harris was to refer time and time again to the experience at Llangasty Tal-y-llyn Church as the sealing of the Holy Spirit.'[91] Bennett comments:

> The experience of forgiveness in Talgarth church[92] was sweet. Yet it left a feeling of further need in his soul which he could not define. But when he was at secret prayer in Llangasty church, the sacred spot where he had given himself to God, God now gave Himself to him ... The richest biblical terms are heaped on one another in an attempt to give expression to his experience at that time. He was there

cleansed from all his idols, and the love of God was shed abroad in his heart. Christ had come in previously, but now He began to sup with him; now he recieved the Spirit of adoption, teaching him to cry Abba Father, and with it a desire to depart and be with Christ. All his *fears* vanished for months, and pure love took their place.[93]

Lloyd-Jones held this view of the baptism of the Spirit. He wrote the introduction to the English edition of *The Early Life of Howell Harris*, published in 1962, in which Lloyd-Jones speaks of himself as 'the one primarily responsible for the suggestion that this book should be translated and published'.[94] Later he gave a paper on Howell Harris' view of the Spirit,[95] identifying himself totally with Harris' outlook on the matter.

One more category of thought may be mentioned which does not precisely fit into any of the categories in the diagram proposed above. There are those who do not *precisely* identify the phrase 'baptism with the Spirit' as a post-conversion experience yet who wish to leave room for authentic post-conversion charismatic experience which 'releases' or 'fulfils' that which was given them at conversion. This view therefore sees baptism with the Spirit as *a release of that which has already been given in principle*.

David Watson (1933–1984), the Anglican charismatic leader, provides an illustration of this approach. In the (northern hemisphere) winter of 1962–1963 Watson had an experience which, as he tells the story, he did not entirely understand. 'God met with me in a fresh way: of that I was certain,' he says.[96] He went to see Lloyd-Jones for advice: 'With three friends I went to see a man whose ministry we immensely respected and whose concern for revival was well known, Dr Martyn Lloyd-Jones.'[97] Watson goes on to say how he and his friends were surprised when Lloyd-Jones 'shared a very similar testimony of his own, when the Spirit had come upon him shortly after the Hebrides Revival in 1949. He said that it had given him a new authority in his preaching ministry.' Then Lloyd-Jones told Watson and his friends: 'Gentlemen, I believe that you have been baptized with the Holy Spirit.'

In addition to the interest we have in Lloyd-Jones's own testimony, Watson's reaction is also interesting. He says: 'To be honest I was not happy with that expression, and to some extent

31

have never been, if it refers to something subsequent to conversion.'[98] We are not surprised then to find that Watson, in a book written shortly before his death in 1984, spoke not of the 'baptism with the Spirit' but of a 'release, a fresh experience of the love of God'.[99] Watson relates Romans 8:15 and 2 Corinthians 1:22 to assurance,[100] but is wary of relating this to the baptism with the Spirit. Evidently he prefers to think of the baptism with the Spirit as coming at conversion but its latent potential being 'released' in charismatic experience.

A similar approach is attractive to those Roman Catholics who wish to combine a sacramentalist approach to water-baptism with an openness to charismatic experience. Cardinal Suenens thinks 'we can and indeed must admire classical Pentecostals for their faith in the action of the Holy Spirit', but that 'we cannot follow them on a doctrinal and exegetical level in their interpretation of "baptism in the Spirit".'[101] For Suenens the Spirit 'has already been given us in sacramental baptism'.[102] Charismatic experience is 'an action of the Spirit which releases and frees latent interior energies'.[103] Suenens speaks of 'deeper awareness of the presence and power of the Spirit', 'the grace of actualising gifts already received, a release of the Spirit, a manifestation of baptism, a coming to life of the gift of the Spirit received at confirmation', 'renewal of ... spiritual life accompanied by a feeling of peace and joy of a kind hitherto unknown', 'revitalizing of the sacramental graces they have already received', 'release of the latent potentials of the Spirit'.[104]

It has not been my purpose to survey all possible approaches to charismatic experience.[105] To do this a vast volume would be needed. But our survey has highlighted two crucial issues. First, the divide between those who do and those who do not stress 'experience' draws our attention to a key matter. Some schools of thought have felt it necessary to play down the 'experiential' aspect of the baptism with the Spirit; others have felt this is the vital element. Secondly, the range of possible options is more than one might think. Controversy about the charismatic movement has tended to produce polarized responses. A survey of at least a few of the options available shows the need to be more discriminating and to consider a wider range of possibilities. Similarly Lloyd-Jones cannot be interpreted simplistically as 'for' or 'against' the charismatic movement. To invoke him as foe or friend is pointless. If we will listen to him we shall find he has a carefully nuanced viewpoint that could help us a great deal in our thinking about charismatic experience.

Notes

[1] See the description of early events of the movement in P. Hocken, *Streams of Renewal* (Exeter: Paternoster, 1986); D. J. Bennett, *Nine O'Clock in the Morning* (Plainfield, New Jersey: Logos International, 1970, and Coverdale House, 1974); M. Harper, *As At the Beginning* (Plainfield, New Jersey: Logos International, 1971, Hodder and Stoughton, 1965, part 2, pp. 51–89); E. D. C. O'Connor, *The Pentecostal Movement in the Catholic Church* (Notre Dame, Indiana: Ave Maria, 1971).

[2] This is F. Catherwood's estimate (*Evangelical Times*, April 1981, p.9). I.H. Murray thinks these figures 'cannot be sustained by photographs and are undoubtedly inflated' (Letter, November 1988).

[3] The *Evangelical Magazine* appeared bi-monthly from 1959 to 1975. The managing editor was Elizabeth Braund, a member of Westminster Chapel.

[4] For the story of IFES see P. Lowman, *The Day of His Power* (Leicester: Inter-Varsity Press, 2nd ed. 1988).

[5] See D. M. Lloyd-Jones, *The Puritans* (Edinburgh: Banner of Truth, 1987), pp. vii-xiii.

[6] The definitive account of these events has yet to be written. A brief description is found in J. Peters, *Martyn Lloyd-Jones, Preacher* (Exeter: Paternoster, 1986), pp. 87–94.

[7] The British Evangelical Council was formed in 1952 to draw together churches which are united in their adherence to the fundamentals of the Christian faith and which consciously distance themselves from the Ecumenical Movement.

[8] The Fellowship of Independent Evangelical Churches, founded in 1922, draws together evangelical churches which are outside the main-line Free Church denominations.

[9] The definitive biography is I. H. Murray, *D. M. Lloyd-Jones* (Edinburgh: Banner of Truth, 1982). A further volume is awaited. See also C. Catherwood, *Five Evangelical Leaders* (London: Hodder and Stoughton, 1984), pp. 51–109.

[10] Thus in the earliest of his published addresses to the Puritan Studies Conference he says, 'The ultimate object of this conference is not mere intellectual stimulation, it is that we may have a true and deep concern about the state of the church. If this is not our sole object, then our study becomes just a sort of Puritan scholasticism, a mere barren intellectualism which, though interesting and entertaining, will finally prove to be of no value at all.' This kind of comment was a common occurrence in Lloyd-Jones's preaching. See D. M. Lloyd-Jones, 'Revival: An Historical and Theological Survey', *How Shall They Hear?* (London: Puritan Studies Conference, 1960), p. 38.

[11] See I. H. Murray, *op. cit.*, pp. 65, 75 and especially pp. 84–85; D. M. Lloyd-Jones, *Inaugural Address by D. M. Lloyd-Jones* (London: London Theological Seminary, 1978), *passim*.

[12] This was the point of his remark at the inaugural address of the London Theological Seminary, 'I have a suspicion that many of you feel that the phenomenon by which you are confronted is that of a poacher turned gamekeeper!' (Lloyd-Jones, *Inaugural Address*, p. 1).

[13]See I.H. Murray, *op. cit.*, pp. 81f.

[14]*Ibid.*, pp. 191f.

[15]*Ibid.*, pp. 96–101. The book that started Lloyd-Jones on his life-long interest in Puritanism was F. J. Powicke's *The Life of the Reverend Richard Baxter, 1615–1691* (London: Jonathan Cape, 1924).

[16]See I.H. Murray, *op. cit.*, pp. 155f.

[17]*Ibid.*, pp. 285f.

[18]*Ibid.*, pp. 253; A. C. McGiffert, *Protestant Thought Before Kant* (London: Duckworth, 1919).

[19]See D. M. Lloyd-Jones, *Spiritual Depression* (London: Pickering and Inglis, 1965), p. 5.

[20]See D. M. Lloyd-Jones, 'Preaching', in *Anglican and Puritan Thinking* (Huntingdon: Westminster Conference, 1978), p. 94, 'We must consider once more whether the true way of teaching theology is not through preaching, through exposition of the Word.'

[21]R. Strong, Review of *Sons of God* by D. M. Lloyd-Jones, *Westminster Theological Journal*, Vol. 38 (1975–76), p. 409.

[22]D. M. Lloyd-Jones, 'Address', in *The Annual Meeting of the Evangelical Library* (London: 1965), p. 20.

[23]D. M. Lloyd-Jones, *Preaching and Preachers* (London: Hodder and Stoughton, 1971), p. 175.

[24]D. M. Lloyd-Jones, 'Jonathan Edwards', in *The Puritan Experiment in the New World* (Huntingdon: Westminster Conference, 1977), p. 106.

[25]D. M. Lloyd-Jones, *Preaching and Preachers*, p. 4.

[26]*Epistle of Barnabas* 11:1–10. See *The Apostolic Fathers*, vol. 1, edited by K. Lake (London: Heinemann, 1912; republished 1970), pp. 378–383.

[27]*2 Clement* 7:6; *Shepherd of Hermas*, Visions 3:3:5; 3:7:3; Similitudes 9:16:2; 9:31:1, 4. See *The Apostolic Fathers*, vol. 1, pp. 138–139; vol. 2, pp. 34–35, 44–45, 260–293.

[28]See *Five Books of St Irenaeus Against Heresies with Fragments That Remain of His Other Works*, edited by J. Keble (Oxford: Parker, 1872), pp. 68, 277, 464.

[29]*Proof of the Apostolic Preaching*, paragraph 3. See St Irenaeus, *Proof of the Apostolic Preaching*, edited by J. P. Smith (1952), p. 49.

[30]*Ibid.*, paragraph 42; p. 74.

[31]*Ibid.*, p. 135, footnote 22.

[32]R. Gaffin, *Perspectives On Pentecost* (Phillipsburg, New Jersey: Presbyterian and Reformed, 1979), p. 22.

[33]*Ibid.*, p. 22.

[34]*Ibid.*, p. 24.

[35]*Ibid.*, p. 31.

[36]*Ibid.*, p. 27.

[37]*Ibid.*, pp. 27–28.

[38]See M. J. Street, *F. B. Meyer: His Life and Work* (London: S. W. Patridge, 1902), especially p. 73.

[39]*Ibid.*, p. 74.

[40]See A. C. Brown, W. F. Gooch, E. G. Gouge, W. Cuff, F. B. Meyer and G. P. McKay, *The Glorious Person and Work of the Holy Spirit* (London: Elliot Stock, n.d. [1896?]), p. 38. Meyer's contribution is on pp. 37–47.

[41]*Ibid.*, p. 40.

[42]*Ibid.*, p. 46.

[43]F. B. Meyer, *Calvary to Pentecost* (London: Marshall, 1894), p. 108.

[44]*Ibid.*, p. 109. D. M. Lloyd-Jones alludes to Meyer's teaching in *The Sons of God* (Edinburgh: Banner of Truth, 1974), p. 251, citing in detail Meyer's *The*

Christ-Life for the Self-Life. I have not had access to this work of Meyer's but have made my point from other works by Meyer on the same theme.

[45]See *George Whitefield's Journals*, edited by I. H. Murray (London: Banner of Truth, 1960), pp. 35–49.

[46]*Ibid.*, p. 45. The third edition of Law's work had been published in 1733. See W. Law, *A Serious Call to a Devout and Holy Life*, 3rd ed. (London: Innys and Manby, 1733). A modern edition is W. Law, *A Serious Call to a Devout and Holy Life* (London: Dent 1906, reprinted 1955).

[47]*George Whitefield's Journals*, p. 46. See H. Scougal, *The Life of God in the Soul of Man*, edited with a historical introduction by W. S. Hudson (Philadelphia: Westminster, 1948, London, IVF, 1961).

[48]*George Whitefield's Journals*, p. 58.

[49]*Ibid.*, p. 59.

[50]*Ibid.*, p. 58.

[51]Cited by A. Dallimore, *George Whitefield*, vol. 1 (Edinburgh: Banner of Truth, 1970), p. 77.

[52]J. Wesley, *The Works of the Rev. John Wesley, A M*, vol. 1, (London: Wesleyan-Methodist Bookroom, preface to 3rd edition, 1831), p. 103.

[53]As early as 1733 we find Wesley identifying the 'sealing' and the 'witness'. See Sermon 138 and the comments on it in A. S. Yates, *The Doctrine of Assurance* (London: Epworth, 1952), p. 13.

[54]*Ibid.*, p. 33ff.

[55]*Ibid.*, p. 71.

[56]J. D. G. Dunn, *Baptism in the Holy Spirit* (London: SCM, 1970), p. 4.

[57]J. D. G. Dunn, *Jesus and the Spirit* (London: SCM, 1975), p. 88.

[58]See V. Synan, *The Holiness-Pentecostal Movement in the United States* (Grand Rapids: Eerdmans, 1971), ch. 1, pp. 13–32.

[59]A. M. Hills, *Holiness and Power* (Jamestown: Newby, n.d., [preface 1896]), p. 5. Although the preface is dated 1896 my copy is a modern edition obtained from the Africa Evangelistic Band bookshop, Cape Town.

[60]*Ibid.*, p. 167.

[61]*Ibid.*, p. 167.

[62]*Ibid.*, p. 167.

[63]*Ibid.*, p. 167, 168.

[64]*Ibid.*, p. 168.

[65]L. T. Corlett, *Holiness in Practical Living* (Kansas City: Beacon Hill, 1949), ch. 3.

[66]*Ibid.*, p. 32.

[67]*Ibid.*, p. 32.

[68]*Ibid.*, p. 32.

[69]*Ibid.*, p. 47. L. W. Wood is a modern exponent of this view. See his *Pentecostal Grace* (Wilmore, Kentucky: Francis Asbury, 1980). Another classic statement of this position is Thomas Cook's *New Testament Holiness* (London: Epworth, 1902), in which he said, 'The baptism of the Holy Ghost includes entire cleansing from sin' (p. 64). The Dutch Reformed preacher Andrew Murray (1828–1917) taught a similar view. See W. M. Douglas, *Andrew Murray and His Message* (London: Oliphants, 1926), especially ch. 22, 'The Necessity of the Pentecostal Spirit'. Murray wrote a number of works along this line: *The Spirit of Christ, The Full Blessing of Pentecost, Back to Pentecost, The Divine Indwelling, The Power of the Spirit* (which consists of extracts from the Anglican mystic William Law, 1686–1761). He also wrote several similar works in Dutch. Murray had his own way of putting the matter linked to his trichotomist view of man (*i.e.* the view that body, soul and spirit are distinct entities and the place of the divine indwelling is the human spirit).

[70]For the basic facts of Moody's life, see W. R. Moody, *The Life of Dwight L. Moody* (London: Marshall, Morgan and Scott, n.d., early twentieth century).

[71]*Ibid.*, pp. 132–33.

[72]*Ibid.*, p. 135.

[73]R. A. Torrey, *The Holy Spirit* (London: Revell, 1927), ch. 5.

[74]*Ibid.*, p. 109.

[75]*Ibid.*, p. 110.

[76]*Ibid.*, p. 112.

[77]*Ibid.*, p. 113.

[78]*Ibid.*, p. 115.

[79]*Ibid.*, p. 117.

[80]*Ibid.*, p. 118.

[81]*Ibid.*, p. 119.

[82]*Ibid.*, p. 129.

[83]D. Basham, *A Handbook on Holy Spirit Baptism* (Fort Lauderdale: Whitaker, 1969), p. 21.

[84]*Ibid.*, p. 21.

[85]*Ibid.*, p. 45.

[86]*Ibid.*, ch. 14.

[87]*Ibid.*, p. 62.

[88]*Ibid.*, p. 64

[89]There are several ways in which this word is spelt. In June 1984 I visited the scenes of Howell Harris's ministry; the spelling I adopt is that used in the village today.

[90]Howell Harris's life is related succinctly in E. Evans, *Howell Harris Evangelist: 1714–1773* (Cardiff: Univesity of Wales, 1974). Fuller information about Harris's conversion is found in R. Bennett, *The Early Life of Howell Harris* (London: Banner of truth, 1962). (An earlier edition in Welsh was published in 1909.) See also L. James, *Howell Harris: The Eighteenth Century Exhorter* (London: Protestant Truth, 1972 [dependent on secondary socurces]). The quotation above is found in Bennett, *The Early Life . . .*, p. 26.

[91]Evans, *Howell Harris*, pp. 8–9.

[92]*I.e.* the events of Whit Sunday, May 1735.

[93]Bennett, *The Early Life . . .*, pp. 26–27.

[94]*Ibid.*, p. 7.

[95]D. M. Lloyd-Jones, 'Howell Harris and Revivial', in *Adding to the Church*, Westminster Conference 1973 (Huntingdon, UK: Westminster Conference, 1974), pp. 66–81.

[96]D. Watson, *You Are My God* (London: Hodder and Stroughton, 1983), p. 55.

[97]*Ibid.*, p. 56.

[98]*Ibid.*, p. 57.

[99]D. Watson, *Discipleship* (London: Hodder and Stoughton, 1981), p. 115.

[100]*Ibid.*, pp. 98, 114.

[101]L. Joseph (Cardinal) Suenens, *A New Pentecost?* (Glasgow: Collins Fontana, 1975; reissued in Fount Paperbacks, 1977), p. 79.

[102]*Ibid.*, p. 80.

[103]*Ibid.*, p. 81.

[104]*Ibid.*, p. 81. A similar view of the 'release of the Spirit', although tied to a complex trichotomist view of man with a resultant distinctive doctrine of sanctification, is found in the writings of the Chinese Christian known as Watchman Nee. In his thought it is hard to distinguish between the human spirit and the Holy Spirit, whose activities are intertwined. 'Everyone who has received grace has the Holy Spirit dwelling in his spirit.' In certain spiritual states 'God's Spirit is

imprisoned within man's spirit and is not able to break forth'. See Watchman Nee, *Release of the Spirit* (Bombay: Gospel Literature, 1966; reprinted 1982), pp. 20–21.

[105]Mention might be made of the Pentecostal-Holiness teaching concerning two post-conversion experiences of grace, one connected with holiness and another connected with tongues and the gifts of the Spirit. See V. Synan, *The Holiness-Pentecostal Movement in the United States* (Grand Rapids: Eerdmans, 1971), pp. 47, 63, 76.

Part Two

Lloyd-Jones's theological forerunners

2

John Calvin and the witness of the Spirit

The focus in this chapter is on John Calvin, as this will show the extent to which the Calvinist view of the 'sealing of the Spirit' (as found in Thomas Goodwin and Lloyd-Jones) arose from Calvin's own teaching. Also, since the 'sealing of the Spirit' is an example of *development* of doctrine we shall see what aspects of Calvin's thought were being followed or ignored in this particular doctrinal development. Since Lloyd-Jones himself was vigorously and self-consciously Calvinist it is appropriate to begin at this point.

Calvin's doctrine of the baptism of the Spirit

This section moves (as Calvin would have wished)[1] from Calvin's basic statement of his doctrine of the Spirit in *Institutes* 3:1 to his exposition of key texts concerning the gift of the Spirit.

In Calvin's thinking 'faith is the principal work of the Spirit'.[2] This conviction is reflected in the structure of the *Institutes*. The doctrine of the Spirit does not get a separate major section. Instead Calvin brings in this doctrine as the introductory chapter to Book 3 which deals with the receiving of the benefits of Christ's work through faith. Calvin's major emphasis is on faith, and in chapter 1 he goes *behind* faith to its secret cause, the working of the Spirit. In chapter 3 he speaks not of 'regeneration by the Spirit' but of 'regeneration by faith', and by this chapter faith's hidden source in the working of the Spirit has already been mentioned.

The Holy Spirit is introduced as the bond of union between the believer and Christ. For Calvin, 'as long as Christ remains outside of us, and we are separated from him, all that he has suffered and done for the salvation of the human race remains useless and of no value for us.' Only when we embrace Christ in faith does anything he has done for the human race become effective for us. Yet not all embrace Christ. This leads to the question of why some embrace Christ in faith but not others. Calvin's answer is found in his doctrine of the Spirit. It is the 'secret energy of the Spirit' that enables them to 'come to enjoy Christ and all his benefits'.[3]

Calvin next expounds this view of the Spirit. The deity of the Spirit is assumed, and Calvin refers back to *Institutes* 1:13:14–15 where the subject has been dealt with. He uses various phrases for that work of the Spirit which is prior to faith, and speaks of 'the testimony of the Spirit', 'a testimony we feel engraved like a seal upon our heart', 'the sanctification of the spirit',[4] 'the secret watering of the Spirit', 'his anointing'.[5] Then in the next section of *Institutes* (3:1:2) he speaks of the 'outpouring' of the Spirit and of 'having the Spirit of Christ'.

In the second paragraph of *Institutes* 3:1 Calvin explains a vital matter, namely the difference between the Old Covenant and New Covenant experience of the Spirit. There is not, in his view, a great difference, it is a matter of degree. Calvin assimilates the two covenants and tends to think of them as one covenant. 'To the Kingdom of Christ, then, the prophets give the lofty title of the time when there will be a richer outpouring of the Spirit.' In other words the outpouring of the Spirit was known *before* Pentecost. The only difference Pentecost made was that the gift of the Spirit would be more widely known thereafter. This gift of the Spirit Calvin relates to various texts of Scripture: Joel 2:28–29; Romans 8:9; John 7:37; Ephesians 4:7; 1 Corinthians 15:45; 2 Corinthians 13–14; Romans 5:5.

Calvin's third paragraph in *Institutes* 3:1 takes up the matter of the titles for the Holy Spirit in Scripture. The title 'Spirit of adoption' is related to the witness of the Spirit and associated with Romans 8:15 and Galatians 4:6. The same gift of the Spirit is in view when 'guarantee and seal' or 'life' are used (2

Corinthians 1:22; Ephesians 1:14; Romans 8:10). The Spirit is portrayed as 'water', 'life', 'anointing oil', 'fire' and 'fountain'. All these terms are related to the one-and-only giving of the Spirit without which a person is not a Christian at all.

Calvin's fourth paragraph in *Institutes* 3:1 argues that 'faith is the principal work of the Spirit'. The Spirit is the regenerating agent that enables a person to believe. As 'inner teacher' the Holy Spirit 'seals' the truth of the gospel to our otherwise unbelieving minds. Faith 'has no other source than the Spirit'. In the last few lines of the fourth paragraph Calvin introduces a term that has been highly prominent in the twentieth century. He identifies the gift of the Spirit as he has expounded it with the 'baptism' of the Spirit. 'Accordingly, that we may become partakers of it (salvation) "he baptizes us in the Holy Spirit and fire" (Luke 3:16) bringing us into the light of the gospel and so regenerating us that we become new creatures.'[6]

In the following chapter he pursues his definition of faith. It is not 'mere opinion', not 'common assent to the gospel history'.[7] It is not 'implicit faith' in the teaching of the doctors of the church.[8] 'Faith rests not on ignorance but on knowledge.'[9] In a later section he comes nearer to his definition. Faith is resting on God's Word; it is a 'knowledge of God's will toward us, perceived from His Word'.[10] But even this does not bring Calvin all the way to his definition, for one might subscribe to God's Word yet find there only that which makes us tremble.[11] So finally he comes to his full definition: faith is 'a firm and certain knowledge of God's benevolence toward us, founded upon the truth of the freely given promise in Christ, both revealed to our minds and sealed upon our hearts through the Holy Spirit'.[12] Three points may be emphasized. Firstly, the passivity of faith is stressed. Faith is not doing anything; it is seeing something, it is recognition, knowledge, certainty and a firm conviction. Secondly, faith is inherently assuring. Faith and assurance are synonymous terms for Calvin at this stage. Thirdly, the work of the Spirit enables our faith. The Spirit testifies, seals and anoints the believer. This is saving faith; this, to use a later term, is 'conversion'.

Calvin's New Testament commentaries provide us with detailed exegetical work and serve to confirm and enlarge his teaching concerning this aspect of the work of the Spirit.

According to the commentary on the Epistle to the Romans (1st edition: 1539), the power of Christ is laid hold of 'when it is sealed by the same Spirit in our hearts'. The Spirit takes the glory of Christ and 'imprints it on our hearts'.[13] 'God does not work effectually in all men', writes Calvin, 'but only when the Spirit shines in our hearts as the inward teacher.'[14] He emphasizes the participle 'shed abroad' in Romans 5:5 and says it is 'very emphatic, and means that the revelation of divine love towards us is so plentiful that it fills our hearts. Being thus shed abroad through every part of us, it not only mitigates our sorrow in adversity, but like a sweet seasoning gives a loveliness to our tribulations.'[15]

Romans 8:15–17 refers, in Calvin's view, to a 'special effect produced by the Spirit'. The Spirit allays our disquiet, brings our mind to a state of tranquillity and 'stirs us up to call on God with confidence and freedom'. Calvin links this experience to the expression 'sealing'. 'Our confidence in this forebearance of God, Paul teaches us, is made certain by the Spirit of adoption, who would not bid us be bold in prayer without sealing to us free pardon.'[16] Again Calvin is at pains not to contrast the testaments too much. 'We are not, however, to infer from this either that no one was endowed with the Spirit of adoption before the coming of Christ, or that all who received the law were slaves and not sons.'[17] Though believers under the New Covenant are dealt with by God more liberally, yet even under the law, grace was offered. 'The only difference is that the Spirit is more bountifully and abundantly poured out in the kingdom of Christ.'[18]

Calvin regards Romans 8:16 as an explanation of Paul's previous sentence. The witness of the Spirit is *prior* to our assurance. 'Our mind would not of its own accord convey this assurance to us, unless the testimony of the Spirit preceded it.'[19]

A similar emphasis is found in Calvin's commentary on 1 Corinthians, the first draft of which was written between May 1539 and the end of 1545.[20] Here again the 'inward testimony of the Holy Spirit'[21] is identified with the fact that 'the Spirit of God is the earnest (*arrha*) and seal'. 'The Spirit alone is the faithful and sure witness to each person of his election.'[22]

An important and clear statement is found in Calvin's comments on 1 Corinthians 2:10–13. He says, 'Paul wishes to teach two things here: (i) that the teaching of the Gospel can only be understood by the witness of the Holy Spirit; and (ii) that the assurance of those who have such witness from the Holy Spirit is as strong and firm as if they were actually touching with their hands what they believe, and that is because the Spirit is a faithful and reliable witness.'[23] 'Similarly the purpose and will of God are such that they are hidden from all men; for who was His Counsellor? It is therefore a "Holy of Holies", inaccessible to men. But yet if the Spirit of God Himself brings us into it, that is, if He makes us surer of those things which are otherwise hidden from our perception, there will be no more room for hesitation.'[24]

In Corinthians 12:13 the term 'baptism' is taken to be a reference to ingrafting into the body of Christ by water-baptism, and the phrase 'by one Spirit' is, according to Calvin, added 'so that no-one might suppose that this is effected by the outward symbol'.[25]

Calvin's next New Testament commentary on 2 Corinthians was written in 1546.[26] Commenting on 2 Corinthians 1:21–22 he identifies four terms that say 'the same thing in different words'. 'Anointing' and 'sealing' are first mentioned as terms referring to the same event, and as putting metaphorically what is meant by the word 'establishing'. 'Then', continues Calvin, 'he puts it a fourth way by saying that the Spirit has been given as an "earnest".' All four expressions refer to the inward and secret work of the Spirit testifying to the gospel and bringing man to an assurance of its truth. Such an inward event is the *sine qua non* of salvation; 'all who do not have the witness of the Holy Spirit . . . have no right to be called Christians'.[27]

In the Galatians commentary, written in 1546 and 1547,[28] Calvin takes the 'receiving of the Spirit' in Galatians 3:2 to be 'the grace of regeneration' though he does not disallow the possibility that the phrase refers to 'the special gifts with which the Lord then adorned the preaching of the gospel'.[29]

It is not difficult to see why Calvin hesitates here. He holds that the gift of the Spirit is a *secret* work. Yet here is Paul appealing to a receiving of the Spirit on a definite occasion which may be remembered and recalled as a well-known event, which proves the authenticity of Paul's preaching of justification by faith on that occasion. The *public* nature of the Galatians' reception of the Spirit does not, however, easily cohere with the secrecy-motif of Calvin's teaching. Small wonder then that he allows another interpretation. Furthermore, when he comes to consider Paul's reference to 'ministering the Spirit' (Galatians 3:5), Calvin says, 'He is not now speaking of the grace of regeneration but of other gifts of the Spirit.'[30] Galatians 4:6–7 similarly refers to 'the testimony of a godly conscience which follows the new regeneration'.[31]

Ephesians 1:13–14 is related by Calvin to the assurance of Spirit-created faith (which *is* assurance).[32] The metaphor of a 'seal' is associated with authentication. Elsewhere Calvin thinks of the 'sealing' work of the Spirit as preceding and enabling faith.[33] In this case, however, Calvin takes the aorist tense of *pisteusantes* ('having believed') to imply that the sealing of the Spirit is 'subject' to faith. 'If so', says Calvin, 'faith precedes it.' He then (in effect) reconciles the two viewpoints: 'The commencement of faith is knowledge; its completion is a firm and strong conviction, which admits of no opposing doubt. Each, I have said, is the work of the Spirit.'[34]

Putting Calvin's remarks together then, the truth is 'sealed' upon the heart; it is believed; it is then a steady conviction. The metaphor of sealing may be applied (in Calvin's thinking) to either the preliminary knowledge or to the final steady assurance involved in faith. On the one hand Calvin can think of a *notitia* which precedes faith; on the other hand he can speak of a *cognitio* which is produced by faith. A person may be very familiar with Christian teaching and may feel he understands it; yet he is not convinced by it. This is *notitia* – awareness of an idea. If he were so convinced as to find peace and a changed direction of life it would be *cognitio*-assured conviction. *Notitia* is *bare* knowledge, a 'notion', a concept floating in the mind. *Cognitio* is *assured* knowledge. Both 'bare knowledge' and 'assured knowledge' are the result of the 'sealing' work of the Spirit.[35]

Calvin further points out that the Spirit is called 'the Spirit of promise' because he brings about the Old Testament promise of salvation. The sealing of the Spirit is also to be identified with 'the earnest' of the Spirit, 'the firstfruits' of the Spirit, and 'the testimony' of the Spirit. All three terms are used in his comments on Ephesians 1:14.[36]

After commenting on Paul's epistles,[37] Calvin turned to the 'catholic' epistles. In his comments on James 1:25 he links

46

together a number of themes. The law, he says, can only induce fear. But 'the Spirit of regeneration, printing its message on our inmost being confers in like manner the grace of adoption'. Calvin cites Romans 8:15 at this point; evidently he has Paul's phrase 'the Spirit of adoption' in mind. 'Christ's Spirit never gives us new birth without equally giving testimony and pledge to our adoption, so as to set our hearts free from fear and alarm.'[38]

The commentary on John's Gospel was the next to be published. In commenting on John 1:13 Calvin attributes faith to the illumination of the Spirit. Again there is emphasis on the secrecy of the work of the Spirit: 'When the Lord breathes faith into us He regenerates us in a hidden and secret way that is unknown to us. But when faith has been given, we grasp with a lively awareness not only the grace of adoption but also newness of life and other gifts of the Holy Spirit.'[39] Then in approaching John 1:33 Calvin was compelled for the first time to comment on the expression 'to baptize with the Holy Spirit'. This he interprets sacramentally: 'What it is to baptize with the Spirit' is 'that Christ gives baptism its effect, so that it shall not be vain and invalid, and this He does by the power of His Spirit.'[40]

John 4:10–15 alludes, in Calvin's view, to the 'secret quickening' of the Spirit.[41] Commenting on John 6:40 he clearly identifies the witness and the seal of the Spirit: 'the testimony of the Spirit is nothing but the sealing of adoption.'[42] The secrecy of this work is mentioned a page or so later. The teaching that comes to the believer consists not only in outward word; there is also 'the secret operation of the Holy Spirit', 'the inward illumination of the heart'.[43]

John 7:37–39 refers to the 'power of the Spirit, by which we are born again in Christ and become new creatures'. The phrase 'the Spirit was not yet' refers to the relative paucity of the Spirit's work compared to the revelation that would be 'so bright and clear' after the death of Jesus. 'God promises His Spirit to believers as if He had never given Him to the Fathers. At that time the disciples had undoubtedly already received the firstfruits of the Spirit. For where does faith come from if not from the Spirit?'[44] Here again we note Calvin's familiar playing down of the contrast between the covenants.

Commenting on John 15:26 Calvin identifies the coming of

47

the Spirit predicted by Jesus as an increased empowering to withstand the ungodly fury of opponents of the gospel. The terms 'testimony' and 'sealing' are used side by side to refer to the Spirit's persuasion. It is the Spirit's work to bring people to an assurance of faith: 'faith is by hearing and yet it derives its certainty from the seal and earnest of the Spirit'; 'there is no faith until God's Spirit enlightens our minds and seals our hearts'.[45] Implicit in all of this is Calvin's doctrine of predestination: 'the elect alone profit by the teaching of the Spirit.'[46] John 20 is understood by Calvin as a real bestowal of the Spirit as well as 'an outward symbol'.[47] 'The Spirit was given to the apostles now in such a way that they were only sprinkled with His grace and not saturated with full power.'[48]

Calvin's commentary on Acts provides many occasions for remarks on the Holy Spirit. He continues to maintain the same teaching that was found in the commentaries on the epistles and can say that 'the Lord seals the promises given by Him on the hearts of believers by His Spirit'.[49] Yet he has to face the occasions in Acts when someone already regenerate (as Calvin believes) subsequently receives the Spirit. The first of these occasions is the narrative of the day of Pentecost.

For Calvin the day of Pentecost was chosen by God for the giving of the Spirit because it 'would be more widely talked of in Jerusalem at a season when the Jews were more inclined to give thought to the works of God' and because the news would be 'spread abroad to the remotest lands'. The *visible* element of the day of Pentecost 'was not so much for their benefit as for ours', even as the appearance of the cloven and fiery tongues had its meaning rather for us and for the universal Church than for them.'[50] It accords with what we have seen of Calvin's tendency to assimilate the old and new covenants that Pentecost is not regarded as the day of an entirely new gift of the Spirit. His exposition of Acts 2 is much the same in style as his exposition of any other narrative portion of Scripture, and one does not get any sense that Calvin is expounding a dramatic innovation in the life of the church. No great interest is seen in the gift of tongues. It is a matter concerning which Calvin has 'no desire to engage in long dispute'.[51] Tongues he sees as the ability to speak in an existing foreign language which is a 'special gift with which all are not endowed'.[52]

Calvin evidently regards the day of Pentecost only as the day when visible signs were given to draw the attention of the wider world to what was happening in Jerusalem. The experience itself *could* have been entirely secret. 'God poured out visible graces on His Church in the beginning so that we may know with assurance that He will be present with us by the *secret* virtue of His Spirit, and, furthermore, showed openly by external signs what we realize inwardly by the experience of faith.'[53]

When commenting on Acts 5:32 Calvin raises a problem: 'Since we obtain faith by the revelation of the Holy Spirit, how is he said here to be given after faith?' Here we have the same matter that troubled Calvin when commenting on Ephesians 1:13. He replies: 'What is meant are the gifts of tongues, prophecy, interpretation, healings and similar things', and refers to Galatians 3:2.[54] He now clearly takes Galatians 3:2 this way, although when commenting on the passage in his earlier commentary he had only mentioned it as a possibility. Passages which speak of an *experiential* receiving of the Spirit *after* faith appear to give Calvin some difficulty. His whole emphasis is on a *secret* work of the Spirit *leading* to faith; passages that point to an experiential sealing after faith cause him difficulty.

Acts 8 is interpreted along similar lines. The Samaritan believers 'really had put on Christ in baptism' and 'were also clothed with His Spirit' before the receiving of the Spirit that came with the laying-on of hands. When the Spirit is subsequently received, Luke is not speaking 'about the general grace of the Spirit, by which God regenerates us to be His own sons, but about those special gifts, with which the Lord wished some to be endowed in the first days of the gospel, for the bestowing of honour on the kingdom of Christ'. The Samaritans 'had the Spirit of adoption conferred on them already'.[55]

Similarly the experience of Paul, recorded in Acts 9:17–19, is the occasion when he obtains the gifts of the Spirit.[56] Cornelius, too, had knowledge of Christ before the events recorded in Acts 10: 'his having God well-disposed and favourable to his alms and prayers was already dependent on his faith.'[57] What happened in the events recorded in Acts 10:44–48 was that 'an extraordinary sign of the call of the gentiles' was given. Again, 'these gifts mentioned by Luke are different from the grace of regeneration; nevertheless there is no doubt that in this way God put His seal, not only on the teaching of Peter, but also on the faith and godliness of those who had heard.'[58] This sentence is interesting because it uses the term 'seal' of a post-conversion experience. Such a usage is rare in Calvin.[59] Again he points to Galatians 3:2 as a parallel. Yet he does not seem to expect this kind of post-conversion 'sealing' in the church in his day. 'Certainly', he says, 'the gift of tongues and other things of that kind have long since ceased in the Church, but the spirit of understanding and regeneration thrives and will always thrive.'[60]

Commenting on Acts 15 Calvin underlines again the difference between 'the gifts' and 'the Spirit of regeneration'; God 'sealed his gracious adoption in Cornelius and his relatives with the *visible* grace of the Spirit'.[61]

In his comments on Acts 19 we have the same line of interpretation. The disciples at Ephesus received visible graces. The receiving of the Spirit referred to in Paul's question (Acts 19:2) refers not to 'the Spirit of regeneration but to the "special gifts" which God distributed at the beginning of the Gospel'.[62] The comment on Acts 19 is striking because here Calvin interprets the phrase 'they were baptized into the name of the Lord Jesus' of a post-conversion receiving of gifts of the Spirit. 'I do deny', says Calvin, 'that the baptism of water was repeated, because Luke's words imply nothing else but that they were baptized with the Spirit.' Then he explains: 'It is no new thing for the name of baptism to be transferred to the gifts of the Spirit.' Luke had said earlier that 'when Christ promised that the Spirit would be sent in visible form to the disciples, He called it "baptism"', and again, that when the Spirit descended on Cornelius, Peter remembered the words of the Lord, 'You will be baptized with the Holy Spirit'.[63] This does not quite tally with Calvin's earlier exposition in which the phrase 'to baptize with the Holy Spirit' was related to water-baptism and given a sacramental interpretation. Calvin's difficulty in Acts 19 is that he does not want to admit rebaptism and so give support to the anabaptists, yet the term 'baptism' is used in verse 5. He is driven therefore to interpret the 'baptism' as a metaphor for the post-conversion receiving of the gifts of the Spirit. The laying on of hands and the receiving of the gifts of the Spirit is an *explanation* of the phrase 'they were baptized'.

The assurance of faith in Calvin's teaching

There is an aspect of Calvin's teaching which balances or compensates for the 'secrecy' motif mentioned above: for Calvin the faith that arises in the believer's heart because of the secret work of the Spirit is *immediately* assuring. Indeed, faith *is* assurance. Recently Paul Helm has de-emphasized the note of assurance in Calvin's doctrine of faith, attempting to minimize the difference between Calvin and the later Calvinists. In Helm's view, Calvin's famous definition of faith (*Institutes* 3:2:7) is only a recommendation of what faith should be, and not a definition of what faith is.[64]

That view, however, is unconvincing. There can be little doubt that beginning with Beza, a partial return to pre-Reformation Aristotelianism began to seriously influence Protestant theological methodology.[65] Calvin's successors held to a doctrine of limited atonement and an increasingly voluntaristic conception of faith that were not characteristic of Calvin himself.[66] Helm wishes to maintain that the differences between the Westminster Confession of Faith and Calvin's teaching were minor and that the former was a natural development of the latter. The truth seems to be, however, that certain major changes of direction came in after Calvin, which, mediated through Beza and Perkins, affected the English Puritan and Scottish Presbyterian theology.

There can be little doubt that a steady, jubilant, assurance of salvation is the *sine qua non* of true faith in Calvin's thinking. For Calvin 'faith *consists* in certainty and clear understanding. Wherever, therefore, knowledge of this kind is waiting, faith is unquestionably wanting.'[67] R. T. Kendall's chapter 'John Calvin's Doctrine of Faith' argues this point persuasively[68] but further evidence could easily be advanced. Faith is *assured knowledge* in Calvin's thinking. Believers, urges Calvin, have 'confidence' to 'surmount the heavens'. He rejects decisively the doctrine that Christians are 'in a state of uncertainty concerning our final perseverance'. They have 'constant and unhesitant persuasion for the future'.[69] This is the *sine qua non* of being a Christian; 'there is no true association with the faithful for any who do not believe *for certain* that the Lord is favourable to them, even though they are undeserving and wretched sinners'.[70]

51

There is an assurance, in Calvin's thinking, that 'rests on the promises of God, so that the believer is convinced in his heart that God will never leave him, and relying on this unconquerable conviction he stands up to Satan and sin, cheerful and undaunted. At the same time, however, remembering his own weakness, he falls back on God in fear and humility, and in his anxiety willingly commits himself to Him. *This kind of assurance is a holy thing and cannot be separated from faith*.'[71] Calvin believes that 2 Corinthians 13:5–9 'serves to prove the assurance of faith, a doctrine which the sophists of the Sorbonne have so corrupted for us that it is now almost uprooted from the minds of men . . . those who doubt their possession of Christ and their membership in His body are reprobates. Let us therefore understand that the only true faith is that which allows us to rest in God's grace, not with a dubious opinion but with firm and steadfast assurance.'[72]

What is notable about this passage of Calvin's is the way in which he is deliberately facing the question of the nature of faith. It is not a random remark in the course of biblical commentating but rather a carefully weighed statement over and against scholastic theology.

In Calvin's thinking the 'sealing' of the Spirit and the 'assurance of faith' are correlative concepts: 'the assurance which a man has of his own salvation is very different from what he has as to another. For the Spirit of God is a Witness to *me* of *my* calling, as He is to each of the elect'; 'the assurance of faith remains shut up within, and does not spread to others.'[73] Here we note two things. First, it is the sealing of the Spirit which is the cause of assurance (*i.e.* of faith), and, secondly, that this sealing is a hidden, inner work, known only to the man himself.

Calvin can admit that assurance gets attacked by trials and doubts but in his thinking faith rises triumphant above all such attacks. So *Institutes* 3:2:17 deals with the way in which believers are 'tried with disquiet' and are 'repeatedly shaken by gravest terrors'. These may be so great 'as not to seem quite compatible with that certainty of faith'. He 'cannot imagine any certainty that is not *tinged* with doubt, or any assurance that is not assailed by *some* anxiety'. Some support is given to Helm's view in that Calvin says 'faith *ought* to be certain and assured'. Yet this does not mean that Calvin admits that faith ceases to be assurance:

52

'however much we are shadowed on every side with great darkness, we are nevertheless illumined as much as need be for firm assurance';[74] 'so far is this fear [mentioned in Philippians 2:12] from disturbing tranquillity of conscience and shaking confidence, that it rather confirms it. For distrust of ourselves leads us to lean more boldly upon the mercy of God.'[75] True faith *does* resist attacks of unbelief: 'the elect have been given the Spirit by whose witness they know for a certainty that they have been adopted to the hope of eternal salvation.'[76]

A detailed documentation of the relationship between this view of faith and the extent of the atonement would lead us too far afield and would be a move away from the direct witness of the Spirit which is the particular interest of this study. Yet it should be said that there can be little doubt that R. T. Kendall is correct in saying that the basis of assurance (*i.e.* of faith) in Calvin's thinking is the universal atonement of Christ. No more is needed than to see that Christ has died for the human race. That, in and of itself, is the 'pledge' of God's love. To see, by the Spirit, the death of Christ for the human race is *inherently* assuring. The correlation of atonement with God's secret election so as to produce the Dortian view of 'limited atonement' is a theological subtlety in the thinking of Beza but not of Calvin. Indeed, Calvin's whole position is incompatible with a 'limited atonement'.[77]

Conclusions

We are now in a position to draw some conclusions and make some observations concerning Calvin's teaching.

Firstly, Calvin knows of only *one* gift of the Spirit. In some theologies (Lloyd-Jones's included) a distinction is drawn between regeneration and the sealing of the Spirit, or between the Spirit as a quickener and the Spirit as a consoler (John Owen in particular).[78] No such distinction exists in Calvin's thinking. There is *one* gift of the Spirit. It was known before Pentecost; since Pentecost it has been known in a more profuse manner both intensively (in that the New Covenant believer has greater liberty) and extensively (in that the gift is now an international blessing no longer confined to the theocracy of Israel).

Secondly, the gift of the Spirit is a *secret* donation. The Spirit secretly works in a sinner's heart so as to focus attention on Christ. Calvin calls this action of the Spirit by various names, but the terms 'witness of the Spirit' and 'seal of the Spirit' are common. R. T. Kendall correctly says, 'It should be noted that the spirit is secret and therefore not an emotional feeling, as it were; faith is that which focuses objectively on Christ.'[79] In this respect modern Calvinists who wish to argue that the 'sealing of the Spirit' has no or only minimal 'experiential significance' are following their mentor.[80] L. S. Chafer's statement, 'There is no corresponding experience connected with the sealing of the Spirit' accords with Calvin's teaching in this respect.[81]

Thirdly, however, there is another side to Calvin's teaching which could be said to compensate for his non-experiential view of the sealing of the Spirit. This is the degree of jubilant assurance which Calvin expected to be the immediate and inevitable corollary of saving faith wrought by the Spirit. The Spirit's work in the elect produces *immediate* assurance and jubilation. Faith is not a cold 'notion' or 'the fleeting persuasion of a day';[82] 'it is vain for us to say "We are Christians", when we have only a frivolous opinion',[83] he says. If a person has faith it *must* assure. 'True it is', writes Calvin, 'that if a man have faith, it can not be, but that he hath also a pure conscience, and upright hart.'[84] Admittedly such assurance gets attacked by doubts but such attacks are to be resisted: 'despise all your unbelief, and resolve that, come what may, God will work beyond your expectation, beyond your ideas and your senses'.[85] True faith *does* resist attacks of unbelief. Calvin teaches that 'the elect have been given the Spirit by whose witness they know for a certainty that they have been adopted to the hope of eternal salvation'.[86]

This jubilant assurance is related to the baptism of the Spirit. It is the *immediate* product of the Spirit's work: 'since this office is attributed to Jesus Christ, to baptize with the Holy Spirit, we *must* have the *experience* of Him in us and we *must* be sharers of such a benefit.'[87] Calvin urges that 'the reality of Baptism is not in the water but by the Holy Spirit'; 'if we wish that Baptism may be profitable to us, we must not stop at the water, as if our salvation were enclosed in it, but let us recognize that the Holy Spirit must do the whole thing'.[88] This, for Calvin, is part of conversion, the *sine qua non* of salvation: 'let us recognize that we are all baptized in the Holy Spirit and fire; and that Jesus Christ

54

does not permit His sacraments to be in vain, that is, to believers.'[89] The baptism of the Spirit, though a secret work, has what may be called immediate experiential consequences. The Spirit 'persistently boiling away and burning up our vicious and inordinate desires, he enflames our hearts with the love of God and with zealous devotion. From this effect upon us he is justly called "fire" (Luke 3:16).'[90] It is *this* aspect of Calvin's teaching that is the forerunner of the 'experiential' note in later Calvinists. In this respect Calvin's level of expectation with regard to the *experience* of the Christian accords more with the early Wesley or with George Whitefield's conversion narrative cited above, than with the 'non-experiential' view of some modern forms of Calvinism.

Fourthly, in Calvin's thinking the 'sealing' or 'witness' of the Spirit is prior to faith and produces faith. It is at this point that we shall see a major change in the thinking of Thomas Goodwin and later in the teaching of Lloyd-Jones. Admittedly there are occasions when Calvin wrestles with texts that point in the opposite direction. We have seen his tussles with Ephesians 1:13 and his uncertainty regarding Galatians 3:2. We have already noted his occasional use of the term 'sealing' to refer to a post-conversion bestowal of the gifts of the Spirit. These occasional variations arise because Calvin is seeking to be honest with the text; yet his prevailing view is that the witness of the Spirit is prior to and the cause of saving faith.

In conclusion then, Calvin's view of the baptism of the Spirit must be seen as follows. It is the secret work of the Spirit by which people's attention is focused on Christ. Although it is not in itself an emotional experience, this work of the Spirit *immediately* gives rise to joyful confidence and hope in Christ. Calvin's doctrine of the Spirit does not encourage introspection. There were few things he abhorred more than looking to oneself. The baptism of the Spirit was not something which led a person to feel his spiritual pulse or which drew attention to his own emotional state. Its immediate consequence (and Calvin would envisage no time-gap) is triumphant joy, confidence of victory over death and the devil, and an exuberant expectation of heaven. If the baptism of the Spirit was not a *self-concious* experience it certainly led to hope and joyfulness of which one could not but be immediately aware.[91]

Notes

[1]See J. I. Packer, 'Calvin the Theologian', in *John Calvin*, edited by G. E. Duffield (Abingdon: Sutton Courtenay, 1966), p. 153.

[2]*Calvin: Institutes of the Christian Religion*, edited by J. T. McNeill (London: SCM, 1961), 2 vols. Citations are given in the text by sections. The citation above is from *Institutes* 3:1:4.

[3]*Institutes* 3:1:1.

[4]The phrase refers not to progressive sanctification but to what has been called 'definitive sanctification' (see J. Murray, 'Definitive Sanctification', *Calvin Theological Journal*, vol. 2 (1967), pp. 5–21, now available in J. Murray, *Collected Writings*, vol. 2 (Edinburgh: Banner of Truth, 1977), pp. 277–293.

[5]Here Calvin refers back to his exposition of 'anointing' in *Institutes* 2:15:2.

[6]*Institutes* 3:1:4. Calvin identifies the 'baptism with the Spirit' with regeneration again in 4:16:25.

[7]*Ibid.*, 3:2:1.

[8]*Ibid.*, 3:2:2.

[9]*Ibid.*, 3:2:2.

[10]*Ibid.*, 3:2:6.

[11]*Ibid.*, 3:2:7.

[12]*Ibid.*, 3:2:7.

[13]*Calvin's Commentaries: The Epistles of Paul the Apostle to the Romans and to the Thessalonians*, edited by D. W. Torrance and T. F. Torrance (Edinburgh and London: Oliver and Boyd, 1961), p. 16.

[14]*Ibid.*, p. 27.

[15]*Ibid.*, pp. 107f.

[16]*Ibid.*, pp. 167f.

[17]*Ibid.*, p. 168.

[18]*Ibid.*, p. 169.

[19]*Ibid.*, p. 170.

[20]See T. H. L. Parker, *Calvin's New Testament Commentaries* (London: SCM, 1971), pp. 11f.

[21]*Calvin's Commentaries: The First Epistle of Paul the Apostle to the Corinthians*, edited by D. W. Torrance and T. F. Torrance, (Edinburgh: St Andrew, 1960), p. 21.

[22]*Ibid.*, pp. 21, 23.

[23]*Ibid.*, p. 58.

[24]*Ibid.*, p. 58. On p. 205, Old Testament believers are also said to be given faith by 'the secret work of the Holy Spirit'.

[25]*Ibid.*, p. 265.

[26]See T. H. L. Parker, *Calvin's New Testament Commentaries*, p. 14.

[27]*Calvin's Commentaries: The Second Epistle of Paul the Apostle to the Corinthians and the Epistles to Timothy, Titus and Philemon*, edited by D. W. Torrance and T. F. Torrance (Grand Rapids: Eerdmans and Edinburgh: St Andrew, 1964), pp. 23, 24.

[28]See T. H. L. Parker, *op. cit.*, p. 15f.

[29]*Calvin's Commentaries: The Epistles of Paul the Apostle to the Galatians, Ephesians, Philippians and Colossians*, edited by D. W. Torrance and T. F. Torrance (Grand Rapids: Eerdmans and Edinburgh: St Andrew, 1965), pp. 47f.

[30]*Ibid.*, p. 49.

[31]*Ibid.*, p. 75.

[32]*Ibid.*, pp. 131f.

[33]See his comments on 2 Corinthians 1:21–22 referred to above.

[34]*Calvin's Commentaries: Galatians...*, p. 132.

[35]See T. H. L. Parker, *Calvin's Doctrine of the Knowledge of God* (Edinburgh: Oliver and Boyd, 1969), pp. 132ff.

[36]*Calvin's Commentaries: Galatians...*, p. 132. See significant and similar statements on pp. 134, 194 and 195.

[37]When Calvin comments on the 'outpouring of the Spirit' in Titus 3:5 the verb 'outpoured' is referred not to the Holy Spirit but to the 'washing'. The text is interpreted sacramentally. The gift of the Spirit is described in terms of the Spirit's being 'the earnest and witness of our adoption' and 'the Spirit of regeneration'. Calvin thinks of these as aspects of an undivided unity closely related to baptism, for Paul 'is addressing believers in whom baptism is always efficacious' (*Calvin's Commentaries: Second Corinthians...*, pp. 382f.).

There is not much occasion in the commentary on Hebrews for Calvin to discuss terms like 'seal' or 'earnest' yet there are glimmerings of the same doctrine. See *Calvin's Commentaries: The Epistle of Paul the Apostle to the Hebrews and the First and Second Epistles of St Peter*, edited by D. W. Torrance and T. F. Torrance (Grand Rapids: Eerdmans and Edinburgh: St Andrew, 1963), pp. 112, 149, 157.

[38]*Calvin's Commentaries: A Harmony of the Gospels Matthew, Mark, Luke* (Vol. 3) and *The Epistles of James and Jude*, edited by D. W. Torrance and T. F. Torrance (Edinburgh: St Andrew, 1972), p. 274. Note the by now familiar doctrine also in his comments on 1 Peter and 1 John (*Calvin's Commentaries: Hebrews...*, p. 229; *Calvin's Commentaries: The Gospel According to St John* [part 2] and *The First Epistle of John*, edited by D. W. Torrance and T. F. Torrance [Grand Rapids: Eerdman and Edinburgh: St Andrew, 1959], pp. 263, 278).

[39]*Calvin's Commentaries: The Gospel According to St John*, (part 1), edited by D. W. Torrance and T. F. Torrance (Grand Rapids: Eerdmans and Edinburgh: St Andrew, 1959), p. 19.

[40]*Ibid.*, p. 35.

[41]*Ibid.*, p. 91.

[42]*Ibid.*, p. 162.

[43]*Ibid.*, p. 164.

[44]*Ibid.*, p. 199.

[45]*Calvin's Commentaries: John and First John*, p. 109.

[46]*Ibid.*, p. 139. See his comment elsewhere: 'the elect are enlightened to faith by the special grace of the Spirit', *Calvin's Commentaries: The Acts of the Apostles*, vol. 2, edited by D. W. Torrance and T. F. Torrance (Grand Rapids: Eerdmans 1973), p. 32.

[47]*Calvin's Commentaries: John and First John*, p. 204.

[48]*Ibid.*, p. 205.

[49]*Calvin's Commentaries: The Acts of the Apostles*, vol. 2, p. 237.

[50]*Calvin's Commentaries: The Acts of the Apostles*, vol. 1, edited by D. W. Torrance and T. F. Torrance (Edinburgh and London: Oliver and Boyd, 1965), p. 50.

[51]*Ibid.*, vol. 1, p. 53.

[52]For further comments on Calvin's view of tongues, see L. Sweetman, 'The Gifts of the Spirit: A Study of Calvin's Comments on 1 Corinthians 12:8–10, 28; Romans 12:6–8; Ephesians 4:11', in *Exploring the Heritage of John Calvin*, edited by D. E. Holwerda (Grand Rapids: Baker, 1976), pp. 291–297.

[53]*Calvin's Commentaries: Acts*, vol. 1, p. 135.

[54]*Ibid.*, p. 150

[55]*Ibid.*, p. 236

[56]*Ibid.*, p. 267.

[57] *Ibid.*, p. 289.

[58] *Ibid.*, p. 317.

[59] See however the terminology in *ibid.*, vol. 2, p. 21.

[60] *Ibid.*, vol. 1, p. 317.

[61] *Ibid.*, vol. 2, p. 33.

[62] *Ibid.*, p. 148.

[63] *Ibid.*, p. 151.

[64] P. Helm, *Calvin and the Calvinists* (Edinburgh: Banner of Truth, 1982), p. 29.

[65] See B. G. Armstrong, *Calvinism and the Amyraut Heresy* (Madison, Milwaukee and London: University of Wisconsin, 1969), pp. 127–140.

[66] See R. T. Kendall, *Calvin and English Calvinism to 1649* (Oxford: OUP, 1979), *passim*.

[67] J. Calvin, *Commentary on the Prophecy of Isaiah* (Grand Rapids: Eerdmans, 1956), p. 109.

[68] R. T. Kendall, *op. cit.*, ch. 1.

[69] *Calvin's Commentaries: Romans...*, p. 105.

[70] *Ibid.*, p. 19. See also *Calvin's Commentaries: First Corinthians*, p. 59: 'the elect have been given the Spirit by whose witness they know for certain that they have been adopted to the hope of eternal salvation'.

[71] *Calvin's Commentaries: First Corinthians*, p. 213 (my italics).

[72] *Calvin's Commentaries: Second Corinthians*, p. 173.

[73] *Calvin's Commentaries: Galatians...*, p. 229.

[74] *Institutes* 3:2:19.

[75] *Calvin's Commentaries: Galatians...*, p. 256.

[76] *Calvin's Commentaries: First Corinthians*, p. 59.

[77] For amplification of this point, see B. G. Armstrong, *Calvinism and the Amyraut Heresy*, especially pp. 137–138, 189–191; B. Hall, 'Calvin Against the Calvinists', in *John Calvin*, edited by G. E. Duffield (Abingdon: Sutton Courtenay, 1966), pp. 19–37; H. Rolston III, *John Calvin Versus the Westminster Confession* (Virginia: John Knox, 1972), R. T. Kendall, *Calvin and English Calvinism to 1649*, (1979). I have not had full access to Dr Curt Daniel's doctoral thesis at the university of Edinburgh entitled *Hyper-Calvinism and John Gill*, in which an excursus deals with some difficult passages in Calvin's writings which have been thought to point in the direction of limited atonement. An extract is published in *Westminster Record*, vol. 58, no. 8, August 1983, where Dr Daniel cites Calvin's comments on Galatians 2:20, 'It is not enough to regard Christ as having died for the salvation of the world; each man must claim the effect and possession of this grace personally ... Christ gave himself for the world in common ... but ... every one of us must apply to himself particularly, the virtue of the death and passion of our Lord.' Dr Daniel would agree that for Calvin assurance is 'the very essence of saving faith' (*Westminster Record*, p. 16). Its basis is Christ's completed atonement for the sin of each and every person.

[78] *The Works of John Owen*, vol. 2, edited by W. H. Goold (Edinburgh: Johnstone and Hunter, 1850–53), p. 231.

[79] R. T. Kendall, *Calvin and English Calvinism...*, p. 19, n. 7.

[80] R. B. Gaffin, *Perspectives in Pentecost* (Philippsburg: Presbyterian and Reformed, 1979), p. 28.

[81] L. S. Chafer, *Systematic Theology*, vol. 6, *Pneumatology* (Dallas: Dallas Seminary, 1948), p. 137.

[82] *Calvin's Commentaries: Romans...*, p. 105.

[83] J. Calvin, *Sermons on the Saving Work of Christ*, selected and translated by L. Nixon (Grand Rapids: Baker, 1950), p. 211.

[84]J. Calvin, *Sermons on Timothy and Titus* (Edinburgh: Banner of Truth, 1983), p. 28.

[85]J. Calvin, *Sermons on Isaiah's Prophecy of the Death and Passion of Christ* (London: Clarke, 1956), p. 29.

[86]*Calvin's Commentaries: First Corinthians*, p. 59.

[87]Calvin, *Sermons on the Saving Work. . .*, p. 212 (my italics).

[88]*Ibid.*, p. 217.

[89]*Ibid.*, p. 216.

[90]*Institutes* 3:1:3.

[91]For Calvin's view of charismatic gifts, see P. F. Jensen, 'Calvin, Charismatics and Miracles', *Evangelical Quarterly*, vol. 51 (1979), pp. 131–144.

3

Richard Sibbes and the sealing of the Spirit

The entire Puritan movement was of great interest to Lloyd-Jones. From the days when he first discovered Baxter, Bunyan and George Fox he found a kindred spirit in the men of the late sixteenth and seventeenth centuries. Among the many Puritans whom he read and devoured with eagerness, three stand out as the special background to his doctrine of the Spirit: Richard Sibbes (1577–1635), Thomas Goodwin (1600–1679) and John Owen (1616–1683).

Lloyd-Jones refers to Sibbes when expounding his doctrine of the Spirit[1] and on one opccasion spoke of his special gratitude to Sibbes whose works were a help to him in a time of weariness. 'I shall never cease to be grateful', he said (referring to the Puritans), 'to one of them called Richard Sibbes who was balm to my soul at a period in my life when I was overworked and badly overtired, and therefore subject in an unusual manner to the onslaughts of the devil ... I found at that time that Richard Sibbes ... was an unfailing remedy.'[2]

John Owen was also a source of inspiration in Lloyd-Jones's formulation of a doctrine of the baptism of the Spirit. He is explicitly mentioned in the expositons of Romans 8:15–16 and John 1:26–33.[3] Lloyd-Jones would admit that 'John Owen on the whole is difficult to read; he was a highly intellectual man',[4] but he did admire Owen's theological method.[5]

Thomas Goodwin was also of special interest. On one occasion Lloyd-Jones gave an address to the Puritan and Reformed

Studies Conference on Goodwin's doctrine of assurance (an address which unfortunately was never published).[6] Dr R. T. Kendall also records an incident which reveals the importance of Goodwin's teaching to Lloyd-Jones: 'He once asked me to read Thomas Goodwin's treatment of the "sealing of the Spirit" (Ephesians 1:13). After I had read it, he called me to discuss it at his home. "Well, what do you think?" I responded quite simply, "That's exactly what I believe. I thought it was wonderful." Tears filled his eyes. "That's the greatest thing I have ever heard you say," he replied.'[7]

It is not surprising then to discover once again that Goodwin was quoted with approval during Lloyd-Jones's expositions of the sealing of the Spirit.[8]

Richard Sibbes and 'Preparationism'

The story of Richard Sibbes (1577–1635) may be briefly sketched. Born in Suffolk, he was sent to St John's College, Cambridge, where he graduated with a BA in 1599, commenced an MA in 1602, and was awarded a BD in 1610. He experienced an evangelical conversion about 1602–3, at which time he began preaching. In 1610 a lectureship was set up at Holy Trinity, Cambridge, which Sibbes occupied from 1610 to 1635.[9] In 1615, as a result of the anti-Puritan policy of Archbishop Laud, Sibbes was deprived of his lectureship but in the following year became the preacher of 'Gray's Inne', a chapel in London. In addition Sibbes was appointed master of Catherine Hall, Cambridge, in 1626; he held both positions concurrently until his death in 1635.[10]

Richard Sibbes and his friend John Preston (1587–1628) became the most significant and widely appreciated preachers in Cambridge in the early seventeenth century. Both were 'Puritans',[11] members of the established church of England with a strong desire for the furtherance of reform within the church. In the writings of both Sibbes[12] and Preston there is a strong undercurrent of *experiental* religion. God's people, they thought, would 'see and feel a divine power' and 'feel a powerful work of the Spirit'. Both preachers spoke much of personal communion between the believer and his God.[13] Sibbes was also characterized by a gentle and encouraging manner in his

61

preaching. He was known as the 'heavenly' Dr Sibbes.[14] J. R. Knott rightly says of him that he sought 'to convey the gentler motions of the Spirit, with the primary aim of quieting the doubts and fears of his hearers. He was above all a preacher of assurance'.[15]

In both Preston's and Sibbes's works there is a clear doctrine of the 'sealing of the Spirit'. Our interest is especially with that of Richard Sibbes. There are three occasions within Sibbes's writings where he expounds in detail his view of the 'sealing of the Spirit'. The first occasion is in a single sermon on Romans 8:15–16 entitled *The Witness of the Spirit*, originally published in 1692;[16] the second is found in a series of sermons preached by Sibbes, transcribed by a noblewoman by the name of Lady Elizabeth Brooke, and published in 1637 under the title of *A Fountain Sealed*;[17] and the third in his sermons on 2 Corinthians 1:22–23 which were included in the *Exposition of Second Corinthians Chapter 1*, published in 1655.[18]

Sibbes was a 'preparationist' and a seventeenth-century representative of a line of preachers from Richard Greenham onwards who stressed the need for a definite working of the Holy Spirit to lead someone to faith in Christ. Unlike Calvin the 'preparationists' expected a person to be consciously aware of the work of the Spirit leading him or her to faith. Since this matter of 'preparationism' is of importance in understanding Lloyd-Jones's view of Romans 7:7–25, more should be said about it.

Modern interest in the Puritan analysis of conversion was given a stimulus through the publication in 1939 of Perry Miller's *The New England Mind*.[19] While not beyond criticism[20] Miller's work brought about a new interest in Jonathan Edwards and his Puritan predecessors. Then, in an influential work[21] published in 1966, Norman Pettit distinguished three attitudes towards preparation for grace among the early Protestants. Firstly, the early Reformers, such as Peter Martyr, William Tyndale and Ulrich Zwingli, taught that preparation for grace is impossible: 'if God will, all things are done the moment that he speaks his Word' (Zwingli).[22] A second view was held by Heinrich Bullinger, who may be regarded as the first Protestant preparationist. He put repentance before faith and reverted to some ideas concerning preparation for grace that may be found in Aquinas' *Summa*.[23]

Pettit, however, believes that Calvin took a middle position.

Calvin has no concept of preparatory repentance yet he did allow for 'preparation for faith'.[24] Perhaps it would provide clarification in discussions concerning 'preparation for grace' if a fourfold distinction were made concerning the agent of preparation. Preparation for grace may be conceived as made by God, by the preacher, pastor or counsellor, by the Christian or by the unregenerate potential convert. It is the last-mentioned of the four that was especially offensive to Calvin. Calvin allowed that God's providence and the coming of a 'notion' of the gospel might be preparatory to salvation.[25] In no way at all, however, does the convert prepare *himself*. His only responsibility is to believe the gospel. Great guilt attaches to unbelief precisely because nothing need stand between the sinner and his saviour.[26] Faith is the *only* bond needed.

In England, Richard Greenham (*c*.1535–*c*.1594) was 'the first English divine to deal at length with "afflicted consciences"'.[27] He was the first of a 'spiritual brotherhood' (to use Haller's term)[28] or a 'dynasty' (to use Kendall's term)[29] of preachers who became influential in Cambridge. All of them were in varying degrees and in slightly different ways 'preparationists'. Following Greenham was Richard Rogers (*c*.1550–1618).[30] Contemporary with or immediately following Greenham and Rogers were Lawrence Chadderton (1536–1640), John Dod (*c*.1549–1645), and Arthur Hildersam (1563–1632). These men spoke of a needful work of the Holy Spirit leading to conversion. Rogers called it the 'First Work' of the Spirit.[31] Hildersam called it the 'Spirit of bondage'. 'Ordinarily', he wrote, 'the Lord useth by his Spirit of bondage and legal terrors to prepare men to their conversion'; for Christ was sent to preach the gospel to such as had the 'Spirit of bondage' (Romans 8:15).[32]

The next in this lineage of preachers was William Perkins (1558–1602), the major popularizer of Puritan theology in the late sixteenth century, the 'most widely known theologian of the Elizabeth church' who by the end of the sixteenth century 'had replaced Calvin and Beza near the top of the English religious bestseller list'.[33] Perkins was 'a moderate Puritan, more interested in building up the Church than in worrying about the finer points of Church government'.[34] It was probably Perkins' limited interest in church government that led Lloyd-Jones to call him 'an inconsistent Puritan'.[35] R. T. Kendall has shown that

63

the 'preparationist' type of thinking which gradually emerged in Calvinist theology in sixteenth-century England was consolidated through this leading figure. Perkins himself was not an original thinker but leaned heavily on his Puritan predecessors and on Theodore Beza. He mediated to English theology Beza's supralapsarian doctrine of predestination[36] rather than the milder doctrine of Calvin.[37] The most striking proof of this is the 'Table declaring the order of the causes of salvation and damnation' that is to be found in Perkins' *Golden Chain*.[38] An almost identical chart is to be found in the writing of Beza.[39] Breward rightly says of Perkins that his charts and methods 'owe a good deal to Ramist methods, but also drew on Beza who detested Ramus and his opinions'.[40] Ramus was an educationalist who opposed Aristotelian logic, and made heavy use of analysis by visual diagrams.[41]

For Calvin, however, scarcely any sort of 'preparation' was necessary for faith.[42] Admittedly he knows that certain points must be known before the believer can be persuaded of them, and he occasionally calls this bare knowledge 'preparation for faith'.[43] Other than this Calvin knows of no preparation that is needed. Certainly nothing that could be put in the category of 'works' was allowed to have any significance prior to faith. Repentance follows faith in Calvin's thinking.[44] Assurance is immediate.[45]

A change came with Beza and therefore was introduced into English Puritan thinking via Perkins. Perkins put 2 Peter 1:10 on the frontispiece of his major work on assurance,[46] and took it to be about self-examination to discern one's salvation. Calvin had been careful to exclude an introspective interpretation of this verse. Although godly living helps the believer 'to confirm in themselves' their faith, yet this is 'in such a way that they place their foundation elsewhere'. Calvin said 2 Peter 1:10 'should not be referred to conscience' and partly related it to proving one's Christian sonship *to other people*: 'the faithful ... show to others that they are sons of God'.[47]

It is apparently Perkins and his near contemporaries who are the pioneers in English theology of the concept of the 'seal of the Spirit' which became influential in later Puritan thinking although certain slight changes are noticeable as our consideration moves from Sibbes to Goodwin.

For Perkins it is possible to be a Christian but 'not yet feel the assurance of the forgiveness of his sins'.[48] One has to have a persuasion of the truth of the gospel, a persuasion wrought by the Spirit. But 'This persuasion is and ought to be in every one, even before he have any experience of God's mercies.'[49] In the dialogue between Eusebius and Timotheus (part of the literary form of one of Perkins' works), Timotheus says, 'That is the thing I earnestly desire, to be assured of God's special goodness, even by your experience.'[50] Eusebius replies, first of all, that the 'dealing of God' towards men is an argument in favour of assurance. Then, 'Secondly, when a man is evermore doubting of the promises of God, be they never so certain, God of his infinite mercy, to prevent all occasions of doubtings, promiseth to give his own Spirit as a pledge, pawn, earnest-penny unto his children, of their adoption and election to salvation.'[51]

Here is the doctrine of the 'seal of the Spirit' which will be amplified in Sibbes. Here also is to be seen a preparationist view of the *ordo salutis* in which humbling must precede assurance. In the *Golden Chain*, which describes the stages of salvation, Perkins has a section on the declaration of God's love to men. The declaration of God's love has three major steps. In the first step is 'effectual calling' (*i.e.* being brought by God to salvation). This includes: the saving hearing of God's Word; the mollifying of the heart which is 'bruised in pieces that it may be fit to receive God's saving grace'; and faith. In faith there are five 'motions of the heart'.[52] Here in the writings of Perkins and his predecessors we have the origin of what Sibbes calls the 'spirit of bondage'. It is significant that the terminology of 'bruising' is taken up and expanded in detail in Sibbes's work *The Bruised Reed*.[53]

Preparationism did not begin with Perkins; it has earlier sources in pre-Reformation thought and had been dismissed by Calvin who had written 'Away then with all that "preparation" which many babble about.'[54] Yet it was Perkins who gave preparationism its definitive statement in early English Puritan theology. Such preparationism came to a climax in the seventeenth century and was the cause of the 'antinomian controversy' between John Cotton (1584–1652) and Thomas Shepherd (1605–1649) in New England, America.[55] Cotton was a convert of Richard Sibbes. It was Cotton's breaking away from the Perkins-Baynes-Sibbes-Preston[56] tradition that caused the outbreak of controversy in New England. Within the English domain that is our present sphere of interest, the Puritans of the late sixteenth century must be regarded as the pioneers of the concept that came to be known as the 'spirit of bondage'. We shall meet with this idea again in the teaching of Lloyd-Jones.

Paul Baynes (d. 1617) continued in Cambridge the tradition that he had learnt from Perkins.[57] He too stresses preparation for faith and assurance. God, he says, 'doth by his power often worke some preparative change' in sinners 'before he doth by his power and word worke the spirit of faith in them'.[58] Yet 'these preparations are not absolutely necessary' (*i.e.* to salvation).[59] Such preparations are explicitly called by Baynes 'the spirit of bondage'. It is this 'spirit of bondage' which needs to be replaced by the 'spirit of promise' which seals and assures our adoption into God's family. Again, in Baynes the 'seal' is not direct, for it includes the graces of the Spirit. Here one can see the continuing influence of Perkins.[60]

When summarizing the doctrines taught by Ephesians 1:13, Baynes says, 'The Holy Spirit, and the graces of the Spirit are the seale assuring our redemption.'[61] The Spirit, he says, is both 'the seale and the sealer'.[62] 'How can we receive the Spirit by faith, when we cannot believe before we have the Spirit?' he asks. The Spirit is needed *in order* to believe (Baynes here cites 2 Corinthians 4:13). He maintains that a person's coming to faith, though itself a work of the Spirit, is followed by a fuller receiving of the Spirit: 'we receive it more fully and manifestly, dwelling in us to our sanctification and assurances.'[63] When the Spirit is given he comes to be a sealer. The term 'seal', 'doth figuratively signifie a singular confirmation given to faithful ones touching their redemption.' 'God he doth seale unto the beleever (*sic*), that he shall be infallibly brought to the salvation he hath beleeved.'[64] This is not inexorably part of conversion: 'true beleevers are not alwaies sure of their salvation . . . Let us strive to get ourselves sealed to redemption.'[65] The evidence of sanctification is part of the seal: 'We are confirmed touching salvation, both by the Spirit of God, who is as it were the seale sealing, and by the graces of the Spirit, which is as it were the seal sealed and printed upon us; yea, these two, both of them, are together as a seal.'[66] 'God doth not intend by sealing to make our salvation certain in itself (*sic*), but to us also.'[67]

It is this tradition, then, that Richard Sibbes inherited and developed. For Baynes was succeeded in Cambridge by the two eminent preachers, John Preston and Richard Sibbes. Our interest is especially with the latter. For the purpose of our present studies we may focus on five aspects of Sibbes's teaching: the identity of the 'sealing' and the 'witness' of the Spirit; the sealing of Christ; the preparation needed before the sealing is experienced; the degrees of sealing; the essential nature of the sealing; and the essential nature of the witness of the Spirit.

Interchangeable terms

For Sibbes the term 'witness of the Spirit' and 'seal of the Spirit' have reference to the same spiritual reality. Thus Sibbes can switch from one term to the other in the middle of his exposition. In expounding Romans 8:16 he can use the phrase 'God seals with our spirit the same thing by his Spirit'. He has here replaced the word 'witness' in Romans 8:16 with the word 'seal' in Ephesians 1:13.[68] Later he speaks of 'the sealing of God's Spirit with our spirit' again intermingling the two verses of Scripture.[69]

In *A Fountain Sealed* Sibbes keeps mainly to the language of 'sealing' that is in his text (Ephesians 4:30). However, in the *Exposition of Second Corinthians Chapter One* his text (2 Corinthians 1:21–22) gives him opportunity to point out again the interchangeability of terms. All three terms: anointing, sealing, and the earnest, are explanatory of the establishing grace of God mentioned in 2 Corinthians 1:21. Three metaphors ('three borrowed terms')[70] are used but they all refer to the same spiritual reality. The 'three terms do all argue assurance'. 'He useth four words, implying one and the same thing, 'stablishing', 'anointing', 'sealing', and giving 'earnest'; all of them words used in ratification amongst men'.[71]

This does not mean that the words are entirely identical in meaning. Sibbes brings out the different emphases that he sees in each term used. But each of the four terms have the same denotation. 'Establish' is the main term; 'anointing', 'sealing', and 'earnest' are explanatory metaphors.

The 'sealing' of Christ

In Sibbes's thinking Christ was sealed first and it is this which is the basis and foundation of the sealing of Christians. Sibbes cites in this connection John 6:27 and urges four ways in which Christ was sealed to be the Saviour of mankind by his being predestined by the Father; by his possessing the fullness of the Godhead; by the Father's testimony from heaven, including the miracles Christ was able to perform, and his being installed into office; and by his being raised from the dead. It is evident that Sibbes interprets Christ's sealing comprehensively; in his view it points to *all* that confirms and ensures the saviourhood of Christ.[72]

In the exposition of Ephesians 4:30 Sibbes says no more than that Christ was sealed to secure his saviourhood and that the Christian is sealed in his faith in Christ. In this work (the exposition of Ephesians 4:30) the believer's sealing is not expounded as part of an 'in Christ' relationship. Rather there is just a *likeness* to Christ; as Christ is sealed so the believer is sealed.

There are in fact three ways in which 'sealing' is referred to in this work of Sibbes. There is God's sealing of Christ, the foundation seal or 'the privy seal', as Sibbes puts it. Then when the believer trusts in Christ he is 'setting his seal' to what God has done in Christ. Subesquently the believer himself is 'sealed' in his salvation.[73]

In a later work, the *Exposition of Second Corinthians Chapter One*, Sibbes puts the matter in a slightly different way, and the relation between the anointing of Christ and the anointing of believers is developed as part of the believer's union with Christ. 'Christ himself, as Mediator, is "anointed with the oil of gladness above his fellows," Ps.xlv.7, but *for* his fellows'; 'every Christian, though he be but as the toe or the foot, yet all have communicated by the Spirit, from Christ the head.' 'As there is one Spirit in Christ, and that sacred body he took on him; so there is in the mystical body but one Spirit quickening and enlivening, and moving the head and the members.' 'He is first anointed, and then we are anointed in him.'[74]

As Sibbes develops this theme he relates it to the threefold office of Christ. As in the Old Testament prophets, priests and kings were anointed, so Christ is anointed by the Spirit to be prophet, priest and king. Therefore the Christian who is anointed by the Spirit *in Christ* shares the same threefold office. Each Christian is a prophet to discern the gospel, a priest to stand before God and pray, a king to be lord and master of all things.[75]

Preparation for sealing

As mentioned above, one finds in Sibbes's writing a preparationist strand of thought that is not to be found in Calvin. The background of his thought is more in the introspective trend begun by Perkins and his predecessors. This side of Sibbes's thinking is best considered through a study of Sibbes's sermon on the witness of the Spirit. For, like other Puritans, Sibbes taught that the 'Spirit of bondage' has to precede the 'Spirit of adoption' in the Christian's experience.

In his sermon on the witness of the Spirit, Sibbes summarizes briefly the argument of the letter to the Romans,[76] then comes to his main proposition based on Romans 8:15: 'In this verse he (*i.e.* Paul) opposeth "the spirit of bondage", which doth make a man fear again, unto "the Spirit of adoption", which frees a man from fears, so as boldly to call God Father.'[77] Sibbes wants to emphasize *the order that the Spirit of God keeps*. 'Ere it comforts it shakes and makes us fear.' 'The first work then of the Comforter is to put a man in fear ... until this Spirit doth work this fear, a man doth not fear. The heart holds out. The obstinacy is so great, that if hell's gates were open, a man will not yield till then that the Spirit worketh it.'[78]

What is distinctive in Sibbes's treatment of the 'spirit of bondage' is that he spends time in justifying God's treatment of men in such a way. He faces the objection: 'Why then doth God suffer his children to be terrified first with this fear?' Sibbes divided his reply into two parts. Firstly, it is best for God's glory that the Spirit should deal with people in this way. Secondly, it is for a person's good that the Spirit works in this way.

God's salvation (Sibbes argues) brings praise to God. His wisdom, mercy and justice are displayed in the way God has wrought salvation for mankind and in the way assurance comes to the Christian. Since God's justice is to be declared it is only right (argues Sibbes) that people be brought by the Spirit to face God's justice: 'the Spirit must first become a spirit of bondage and fear for the magnifying of his justice, that God may have the glory thereof'; 'to this end, that a man might pass by, or through, the gates of hell into heaven, the Lord will have his justice extended and spread abroad to the full view.'[79] Similarly it is only when the sinner has seen God's justice that he feels mercy to be indeed mercy. God's mercy 'would never be so sweet, nor relish so well, nor be esteemed of us, if the aweful terrors of justice had not formerly made us smart'.[80]

A second justification for the Spirit's working in this way is that it is for the good of men and women. We will never come to God through Christ, argues Sibbes, 'till we see no other remedy being at the pit's brink, ready to starve, hopeless of all other helps'; 'when men have no mind to come unto Christ, he sends as it were fiery serpents to sting them, that they might look up unto the brazen serpent, or rather unto Christ Jesus, of whom it was a type, for help.'[81] Such a 'spirit of bondage' is also needful for our sanctification. Unless we see 'the law and threatenings of condemnation, the opening of hell, the racking of the conscience, and a sense of wrath present and to come'[82] we shall not really grasp the greatness of sin within us, nor will we be driven to Christ as the only remedy.[83]

Sibbes faces next an obvious objection: Will this doctrine not intimidate those who feel that they have not *sufficiently* experienced the spirit of bondage? Will some not be permanently held back in introspection and fear because they believe that they have not fully experienced the spirit of bondage and therefore cannot hope for the Spirit of adoption. Sibbes's reply to this question is that this work of the Spirit is not 'the principal, sanctifying, and saving work of the Spirit'. The greater work is the Spirit of adoption. What is needed however is sufficient experience of the spirit of bondage to drive the sinner to Christ. 'If I may have so much of it as may bring me to see my danger, and run unto the medicine and city of refuge for help, to hate sin for the time to come, and set myself constantly in the way and practice of holiness, it is sufficient.' He adds the warning also that there are *degrees* of the experience of the spirit of bondage: 'there are indeed diverse measures of it, according unto which the conscience is wounded.'

He also makes the point at the close of this section of his sermon that a person seeking Christ can lessen the terrors of the spirit of bondage. 'The way, then, to avoid these things so harsh and unpleasing to the flesh and blood, is to take up the rod betimes and beat ourselves.'[84]

At this point three comments may be made about Sibbes's teaching. Firstly, much of his exposition revolves around a particular exegesis of the word 'again' in Romans 8:15. The word can be taken either with 'received' or with 'for fear'. Sibbes takes it with 'received'.[85] Secondly, Sibbes regards the conviction of the sinner as something that takes place prior to conversion, and thirdly, Sibbes has thus an introspective note in his exposition. He encourages the sinner to look within for such evidence of a spirit of bondage as will then warrant his or her looking to Christ for salvation. The tendency to introspection is made more acute because Sibbes also teaches that the spirit of bondage may fail of its purpose. Unless one comes through it to assurance it proves nothing. 'No man must think it strange, that God deals with men at first in this harsh manner, as it were to kill them, ere he makes them alive; nor be discouraged, as if God had cast them off for ever as none of his; for this bondage and spirit of fear is a work of God's Spirit, and a preparative to the rest. But it is a common work, and therefore, unless more follow it, it can afford us no comfort.'[86] (By the phrase 'a common work' Sibbes means that it may be found in both converted and unconverted.)

In *A Fountain Sealed* the same points are made, in a different way, when Sibbes is considering how the authenticity of Christian experience is to be established. One may know, says Sibbes, that the sealing work of the Spirit is authentic by what precedes it, what accompanies it, and what are its results. It is in this context that Sibbes again insists that the sealing of the Spirit 'cometh after deep humiliation and abasement'. 'After we have long fasted, and our hearts melted and softened, then God poureth water upon the dry wilderness, and then it comes to pass, through his goodness and mercy, that he comforts and satisfies the desires of the hungry soul.'[87]

The degrees of sealing

An important aspect of Sibbes's teaching is his idea that there are degrees of sealing. In other words Sibbes allows the possibility of various levels of assurance; these various levels of assurance of salvation correspond to different ways by which assurance of salvation comes to the Christian.

In *A Fountain Sealed* Sibbes mentions 'diverse degrees of the Spirit's sealing'. First to be considered is faith itself. 'He that believes hath the witness in himself', he quotes (from 1 John 5:10). Faith is a manifestation of election and the elect cannot be lost. Believing is a 'seed that cannot be lost'.[88] Presumably (although Sibbes does not say so at this point) this is an objective 'seal' possessed by every Christian.

Sibbes next mentions 'sanctifying grace' as a seal (citing 2 Timothy 2:19). 'This seal of sanctification leaves upon the soul the likeness of Jesus Christ.' Sibbes is here suggesting a 'seal' which has an introspective element in it. It involves self-examination. Sibbes admits that the Christian who seeks assurance by means of this 'seal' may well find himself in considerable perplexity: 'We may be sometimes in such a state as Paul and his company was in the ship, Acts xxvii.20, when "they saw neither sun nor stars many days together"; almost past hope.' Yet 'it pleaseth Christ after some trial and exercise to shine upon his own graces in the heart, whereby we may know we believe and know we love; until which time, the heart sees nothing that is good, and seems to be nothing but all objections and doubtings'.[89] This level of assurance may be long delayed.

There is, however, a yet higher level of assurance. 'Joy and strong comfort come from a superadded seal of the Spirit', says Sibbes. 'The works of the Spirit are of a double kind: either *in* us, by imprinting sanctifying grace; or *upon* us, by shining upon our souls in sweet feelings of joy.'[90] It is worth noticing the difference between the three levels of assurance that Sibbes has mentioned in this passage. The first one is inherent in faith itself. The second comes through self-examination and so may be the occasion of a great deal of doubt, and therefore be much delayed. Both of these levels of assurance involve syllogistic reasoning. 'I see that I believe,' says the Christian. 'Believers are saved' is the next step. 'Therefore I am saved' is the final conclusion. However, the third level of assurance does not involve syllogistic reasoning. It is a *direct* witness of the Spirit. It is not 'in us' (as with sanctification); it is 'on us', says Sibbes. It is 'God's "shining upon our souls" in sweet feelings of joy.' His distinction at this point may be thought rather fine. For (it may be said) 'shining upon our souls' is still 'in us'. How could it be otherwise? Yet this is Sibbes's attempt to express the idea that the third level of assurance is a direct witness that is independent of our reasonings. The lower forms of assurance may not involve 'sweet feelings' but the third degree of the sealing of the Spirit is experiential.

At this point Sibbes[91] relates the three degrees of the sealing to 1 John 5:7 which mentions blood, water and the Spirit. This corresponds to the three levels of assurance. Though this is an interpretation which is nowadays universally dismissed, it was common in Puritan times and we shall see it again in the writings of Thomas Goodwin. 'The blood' is correlative to faith because Christ crucified is the object of faith. 'The water' is taken to be the sanctifying work of the Spirit. 'The Spirit' is (as Romans 8:16 puts it) 'the Spirit *Himself*' giving a higher degree of assurance than is available along the previous two lines. The lower forms of assurance are often inadequate. 'Therefore the third, the immediate testimony of the Spirit, is necessary to witness the Father's love to us in particular, saying, "I am thy salvation", Psalm xxxc.3, "thy sins are pardoned", Matthew ix.2.'[92] This is 'a distinct witness by way of enlarging the soul; which is joy in the apprehension of God's fatherly love and Christ's setting the soul at liberty'. Sibbes urges that such a witness may be above syllogism: 'The Spirit doth not always witness unto us our condition by force of argument from sanctification, but sometimes immediately by way of presence;[93] as the sight of a friend comforts without help of discourse. The very joy from the sight prevents[94] the use of discourse.'[95]

The essential nature of the 'witness of the Spirit'

Sibbes analyses Romans 8:16 as having two ingredients. There is first 'The witness of our spirit' and then 'The witness of God's Spirit with our spirit'. 'These be two evidences, not singly but conjoined, wherein you see there must be some work of our spirit.'[96] In Sibbes's teaching concerning the work of *our* spirit we see the continuing influence of Perkins' theology. For as in Perkins' treatise[97] one's *own* spirit comes to assurance by self-examination: 'When I take the candle of the word, and with that

73

bright burning lamp search what is to be done, and therewith lance my corruptions, and so bring it home, then it is mine. This is the groundwork of the witness of our spirit.' 'I must see what is needful to be done to be justified; what free promises of invitation belong thereunto. I must see how God justifies the sinner, what conditions on our part are required in justification, and my interest therein.'[98] (We see here the shift from Calvin that had taken place in Reformed theology. 'Conditions on our part' hardly jibes with a freely-given justification.) The Christian has to *apply* the gospel to himself and come to assurance: 'the witness of our spirit I take to be a sanctified resolution upon deep sorrow and mature judgement both of God's mercies bestowed, and my obedience to the will of God; whence the soul gathers strength to wait and depend on God, and serve him in all holiness, though for the present he hide his face and seem an enemy.'[99]

The witness of *God's* Spirit is over and above this kind of assurance. It is after one has come to assurance in the way outlined above that the seal or witness of God's Spirit is super-added. The former witness was not a matter of conscious experience; it may be known though God 'hide his face'. The witness of God's Spirit is, however, a matter of conscious experience. 'Here is the difference between faith and sense,' says Sibbes.[100] By 'faith' Sibbes means a bare trusting in God's Word. By 'sense' he means a *conscious* and *experiential* feeling of one's sonship to God; it is when God says to the soul 'I am thy salvation'; it is God *manifesting* himself (John 14:21). 'When God hath heard us cry a while until we be thoroughly humbled, then he takes us up in his arms and dandles us, making his Spirit *after a sensible manner unto us* the assurance of our salvation'; 'then comes joy unspeakable and glorious, and in such a measure that the soul is wonderfully pleased. It shall not continue always so, but at some times we shall have it; yet it endures so as that it shall never be quite taken away, as our Saviour's promise is, John xvi.22.'[101]

Another element in Sibbes's doctrine is his principle that 'The Spirit gives no comfort but by the word'.[102] There is a danger, thinks Sibbes, of 'counterfeit illumination'.[103] Even anabaptists and friars may 'now and then have some strange sudden joys, the devil, no question, transforming himself into an angel of light to deceive them'.[104] (One sees here a seventeenth-century

Englishman's dislike of Roman Catholicism on the one side and 'anabaptism' on the other.) Yet there is no need to be deceived. The Word checks the authenticity of the work of the Spirit.

In considering Sibbes we have come a step forward in the history of the doctrine of the Spirit as it moves from Calvin to Lloyd-Jones's view of the baptism with the Spirit. The atmosphere has become more introspective, but the first steps have been taken towards the doctrine of the Spirit that was to be so energetically propounded by Lloyd-Jones.

Notes

[1] D. M. Lloyd-Jones, *Romans: An Exposition of Chapter 8:5–17, The Sons of God* (Edinburgh: Banner of Truth, 1974), pp. 342–344.

[2] D. M. Lloyd-Jones, *Preaching and Preachers*, p. 175. The period referred to is 1949, according to I. H. Murray (Letter, November 1988).

[3] D. M. Lloyd-Jones, *Sons of God*, pp. 319–320; also D. M. Lloyd-Jones, *The Gospel of John* (Barcombe Mills, East Sussex: Martyn Lloyd-Jones Recordings Trust, 1983), sermon no. 1080 (sound recording).

[4] D. M. Lloyd-Jones, *Preaching and Preachers*, pp. 175.

[5] D. M. Lloyd-Jones, 'John Owen on Schism', in *Diversity in Unity* (London: Puritan and Reformed Studies Conference, 1964), pp. 60–61.

[6] This is mentioned by David Fountain in an interview with Erroll Hulse, editor of *Reformation Today*. Fountain said, 'I still have vivid recollections of some early papers. I can recall clearly a paper given by Dr Lloyd-Jones on Thomas Goodwin's exposition of Isaiah 50:10 and 11, on the subject "A Child of Light Walking in Darkness and a Child of Darkness Walking in the Light". It had a stunning effect upon me which lasted for some time. I had not appreciated the biblical doctrine of assurance, and the Puritan view was shattering' ('The Puritan Conference: Twenty Years in Review', *Reformation Today*, no. 6, Summer 1971, p. 22).

[7] R. T. Kendall, 'My Tribute to Dr Lloyd-Jones', *Westminster Record*, vol. 56, no. 6 (June 1981), p. 465.

[8] D. M. Lloyd-Jones, *God's Ultimate Purpose* (Edinburgh: Banner of Truth, 1978), pp. 274, 298.

[9] For Puritan lectureships, see P. S. Seaver, *The Puritan Lectureships: The Politics of Religious Dissent 1560–1662* (Stanford, California: Stanford University, 1970).

[10] See *Works of Richard Sibbes*, 7 vols, edited by A. B. Grosshart, (1862–64; reprinted Edinburgh: Banner of Truth, 1973). A biographical sketch is available in vol. 1, pp. xix-cxxi.

[11] It is well-known that the term 'Puritan' is difficult to define and means different things to different people (see B. Hall, 'Puritanism: The Problem of Definition', in *Studies in Church History*, vol. 2: papers read at the second winter and summer meetings of the Ecclesiastical History Society, ed. by C. J. Cuming [London: Nelson 1965], pp. 283–296). My own view is that it must be accepted that the modern use of the term 'Puritan' does not precisely conform to its use between 1564 (the earliest use of the term) and 1642. I use the term to refer to all British Protestant Christians, between Tyndale and the events of 1662, who wished to see the continuation of the Reformation and a more radical

application of scriptural principles to the churches. See D. M. Lloyd-Jones, 'Puritanism and Its Origins', in *The Good Fight of Faith* (Huntingdon: Westminster Conference, 1972), pp. 72–90.

[12]Sibbes was not extreme in his demands and was more concerned about spiritual life than about ceremonies. His biographer quotes a letter (probably to Thomas Goodwin who was more strictly 'Independent') in which Sibbes urges that to divide the church over ceremonies would be 'a remedy worse than the disease' (*Works of Richard Sibbes*, vol. 1, p. cxv).

[13]J. F. Maclear urges that 'From its earliest beginnings, Puritanism had exhibited a drive towards immediacy in religious experience' (*The New England Puritans*, edited by S. V. James [New York: Harper and Row, 1968], p. 46). This is probably too sweeping a statement. Different types of 'immediacy' are taught and some Puritans excluded 'immediate' workings of the Spirit altogether. The options ranged from mystical Puritans like Morgan Llwyd (see Geraint Gruffydd, 'Morgan Llwyd', in *A Goodly Heritage* [London: Puritan and Reformed Studies Conference, 1959], pp. 52–56), Walter Craddock (see G. F. Nuttall, 'Walter Craddock (1606?–1659): The Man and His Message', in *The Puritan Spirit* [London: Epworth, 1967], pp. 118–129) and Thomas Goodwin, to Puritans with a more moralistic emphasis such as William Perkins and Richard Baxter. Maclear is on stronger grounds when he says that it was Sibbes who more than any other was responsible for the experiential note in Puritan piety in the 1630s (p. 47).

[14]*Works of Richard Sibbes*, vol. 1, p. xix.

[15]J. R. Knott, *The Sword of the Spirit* (London and Chicago: University of Chicago, 1980), p. 44, (The second chapter of this work deals with Sibbes's manner of preaching). Of course, no preacher 'conveys' the Spirit, but Sibbes in his preaching conveyed the idea of the gentler motions of the Spirit.

[16]*Works of Richard Sibbes*, vol. 7, pp. 367–385.

[17]*Ibid.*, vol. 5, p. 409–456.

[18]*Ibid.*, vol. 3, pp. 420–484.

[19]P. Miller, *The New England Mind* (New York: MacMillan, 1939). A survey (including Perry Miller's work) of early American Puritanism is found in *The New England Puritans* (ed. by S. V. James), pp. 1–11.

[20]N. Pettit protests at the interpretation of conversion as a 'rape of the soul' which Miller understood to be Calvin's view of the matter. This gives the impression of violence done to the personality, and the forceful defeat of a person's resistance to God. This is not Calvin's approach. Rather grace removes the *disposition* of enmity towards God. See N. Pettit, *The Heart Prepared* (New Haven and London: Yale University, 1966), p. 40, n. 39.

[21]N. Pettit, *op. cit.*, p. 40.

[22]*Ibid.*, p. 16.

[23]*Ibid.*, pp. 24–27; also D. M. Marshall, 'Becoming a Christian – In the Teaching of Heinrich Bullinger', in *Becoming a Christian* (Huntingdon: Westminster Conference, 1973), p. 50.

[24]R. T. Kendall thinks Calvin's phrase *fidei praeparatio* means 'preparation of faith' (R. T. Kendall, *Calvin and English Calvinism . . .*, p. 19).

[25]See p. 46 above.

[26]See Calvin on John 3:16 (*Calvin's Commentaries: John*, pp. 73–75).

[27]R. T. Kendall, *Calvin and English Calvinism . . .*, p. 45.

[28]W. Haller, *The Rise of Puritanism* (New York: Columbia University, 1938), ch. 2.

[29]R. T. Kendall *Calvin and English Calvinism . . .*, p. 94.

[30]Greenham and Roger's teaching concerning conversion is summarised in

P. E. G. Cook, 'Becoming a Christian – In the Teaching of Richard Rogers and Richard Greenham', in *Becoming a Christian, op. cit.*, pp. 58–67.
[31]See N. Pettit, *op. cit.*, p. 58.
[32]Cited from Hildersam's *'The Doctrine of Fasting'*, in N. Pettit, *The Heart Prepared*, p. 58. J. I. Packer urges that 'By concentrating on this preliminary work of grace, and harping on the need for it to be done thoroughly, these writers discouraged seeking souls from going straight to Christ in their despair.' He quotes also Goodwin's comments on one of his predecessors: 'If you that are now converted had lived in our younger days you would have seen that we were held long under John Baptist's water, of being humbled for sin.' Packer comments: 'This naturally led to much morbidity' (J. I. Packer, 'The Puritan View of Preaching the Gospel', in *How Shall They Hear?* (London: Puritan and Reformed Studies Conference, 1960), p. 20. The quotation from Goodwin is found in *The Works of Thomas Goodwin*, vol. 4, edited by J. C. Miller (Edinburgh: James Nichol, 1861), p. 346.
[33]*The Work of William Perkins*, introduced and edited by I. Breward (Abingdon: Sutton Courtenay, 1970), p. xl.
[34]I. Breward, 'William Perkins and the Origin of Puritan Casuistry', in *Faith and a Good Conscience* (London: Puritan and Reformed Studies Conference, 1963), p. 8.
[35]D. M. Lloyd-Jones, in a personal letter to R. T. Kendall, 22 October 1974, cited by R. T. Kendall, 'Living the Christian Life – in the Teaching of William Perkins and His Followers', in *Living the Christian Life* (Huntingdon: Westminster Conference, 1975), pp. 46, 58.
[36]'Supralapsarianism' is that view of predestination which maintains that the decree to save some men and condemn others has priority in God's plan, and that creation was a means of bringing about this prior plan. 'Infralapsarianism' is less speculative and regards God's predestination as considering men as already created and already fallen. Calvin has supralapsarian statements in his expositions, yet is cautious in his handling of the matter. In the *Institutes*, like Paul in Romans 8–9, Calvin discussed the doctrine only after he had expounded his own doctrine of salvation. Perkins, on the other hand, made predestination central to his system of thought. It is the structural backbone to his theology. Calvin never used predestination in this way. It is of interest to note that Lloyd-Jones's exposition of Romans 9 was vigorously infralapsarian, and his exposition of Romans 9:19–24 repudiated supralapsarian interpretations.
[37]R. T. Kendall, *Calvin and English Calvinism . . .*, chs. 4–9.
[38]A reproduction of the original diagram from Perkins' *A Golden Chain* can be found in *The Work of William Perkins*, edited by I. Breward (Abingdon: Sutton Courtney, 1973). Separate copies of the diagram drawn by June Read are available from the publisher.
[39]A copy of Beza's chart is reproduced in Dr Kendall's Oxford D. Phil. thesis, available in the Bodleian Library, Oxford. Dr Kendall kindly loaned me his own copy in 1977. Unfortunately the published version of Dr Kendall's thesis omits this visual proof of the strong links between Beza and Perkins.
[40]*The Work of William Perkins*, p. 171.
[41]See *New Dictionary of Theology* (Leicester IVP, 1988), article on Ramus, p. 557.
[42]See *Institutes* 2:2:27 ('Away then with all that "preparation" which many babble about!'). Calvin believed, however, that the law *may* prepare for faith (*Institutes* 2:7:11).
[43]*Institutes* 3:2:4. See however footnote 24 above.
[44]*Ibid.*, 3:3:1.
[45]In urging the priority of faith before repentance Calvin takes steps to ensure

77

that he is not read as meaning that repentance is limited to 'a paltry few days'; rather repentance 'for the Christian man ought to extend throughout his life' (*Institutes* 3:3:2). Yet it 'constantly' follows faith (*ibid.*, 3:3:1).

[46]*The Work of William Perkins*, p. 353.

[47]*Calvin's Commentaries: Hebrews . . .*, p. 334.

[48]*The Work of William Perkins*, p. 158. See also p. 229.

[49]*Ibid.*, p. 229.

[50]*Ibid.*, p. 369.

[51]*Ibid.*, p. 369–370. However the *directness* of the assurance of the Spirit is not taught by Perkins. Romans 8:16 and Galatians 4:6 refer to a Christian's *applying* the promise to himself so as to reach full assurance (*The Work of William Perkins*, pp. 155–156). The Christian's spiritual longings *are* the testimonies of the Spirit (*ibid.*, p. 158, citing, among other verses, Galatians 4:6). R. T. Kendall makes a similar observation citing Perkins' last work, his commentary on Galatians, ('Living the Christian Life – in the Teaching of William Perkins and His Followers', in *Living the Christian Life*, p. 59).

[52]*The Work of William Perkins*, pp. 225–229.

[53]M. R. Shaw plays down the legalistic side of Perkins' preparationism ('Drama in the Meeting House: The Concept of Conversion in the Theology of William Perkins', *Westminster Theological Journal*, vol. 45, 1983, pp. 41–72). What cannot be disputed is that Perkins was a clear preparationist. In answer to the question 'How doth God bring men truly to believe in Christ?', the answer is given 'First, he prepareth their hearts that they might be capable of faith and then he worketh faith in them.' In response to the further question 'How doth God prepare men's hearts?', comes the answer 'By bruising them'. Perkins then proceeds to outline the humbling that must take place to prepare the way for faith. See *The Work of William Perkins*, p. 156.

[54]*Institutes* 2:2:27. The standard account of the origins of preparationism is N. Pettit's *The Heart Prepared* (New Haven: Yale, 1966). However, Pettit has little understanding of the doctrine of election or of the relation between preparation for grace and assurance of salvation.

[55]See K. M. Campbell, 'The Antinomian Controversy of the 17th Century', in *Living the Christian Life* (Huntingdon: Westminster Conference, 1975), pp. 61–81; R. T. Kendall, 'John Cotton – First English Calvinist?' in *The Puritan Experiment in the New World* (Huntingdon: Westminster Conference 1977), pp. 38–50.

[56]Peter H. Lewis' paper 'John Preston (1587–1628): Puritan and Court Chaplain', in *Light From John Bunyan* (Huntingdon: Westminster Conference, 1979), pp. 37–52, includes the comment: 'It has, I think, to be confessed, that there is indeed a strong element of preparationism in John Preston's teaching' (p. 39). John Cotton was actually responsible for Preston's conversion, but whereas Cotton broke away from his earlier teaching Preston did not. For an outline of Preston's life and ministry see I. Morgan, *Puritan Spirituality* (London: Epworth Press, 1973); I. Morgan, *Prince Charles's Puritan Chaplain* (London: Allen and Unwin, 1957).

[57]See R. T. Kendall, *Calvin and English Calvinism . . .*, p. 94. The closeness of Baynes and Sibbes is apparent in that Sibbes wrote a commendatory preface which was published in the 1647 edition of Baynes' *Ephesians* (See pp. 4–6 of the pages before page 1, when numbered as in footnote 61 below). In his preface Sibbes stresses the link between Perkins and Baynes ('he succeeds him in opinion whom he succeeded in place', p. 5 when numbered as indicated).

[58]Paul Baynes, *An Entire Commentary Upon the Whole Epistle of the Apostle to the Ephesians* (London: Printed by M. Fletcher for I.B., 1647), p. 174.

[59]Baynes, *Ephesians*, p. 173.

[60]See R. T. Kendall, *Calvin and English Calvinism*, p. 101.

[61]Baynes, *Ephesians*. The British Library copy of Baynes' work has 814 numbered pages, preceded by 12 pages of which 9 contain print. The citation comes from the 8th page of unnumbered prefatory printed pages.

[62]*Ibid.*, p. 137.

[63]*Ibid.*, p. 141.

[64]*Ibid.*, p. 142.

[65]*Ibid.*, p. 143.

[66]*Ibid.*, p. 143. (Romans 8:16 is also quoted in confirmation.)

[67]*Ibid.*, p. 143.

[68]*Works of Richard Sibbes*, edited by A. B. Grosart, 7 vols, 1862–64 (reprinted Edinburgh: Banner of Truth, 1973–83), vol. 7, p. 376.

[69]*Ibid.*, vol. 7, p. 382.

[70]*Ibid.*, vol. 3, p. 442.

[71]*Ibid.*, p. 443.

[72]*Ibid.*, vol. 5, p. 433.

[73]*Ibid.*, pp. 433–434.

[74]*Ibid.*, vol. 3, p. 443.

[75]*Ibid.*, pp. 446–451.

[76]*Ibid.*, vol. 7, pp. 367–370.

[77]*Ibid.*, p. 370. I have corrected the punctuation of this sentence. In the nineteenth-century edition the opening inverted comma is mistakenly put before the 'unto' which is no part of the quotation from Romans.

[78]*Ibid.*, vol. 7, p. 370. The italics are original.

[79]*Ibid.*, p. 371.

[80]*Ibid.*, p. 372.

[81]*Ibid.*, p. 373.

[82]*Ibid.*, p. 374.

[83]*Ibid.*, p. 374

[84]*Ibid.*, p. 375.

[85]*Ibid.*, p. 375.

[86]*Ibid.*, p. 370.

[87]*Ibid.*, vol. 5, p. 441.

[88]*Ibid.*, p. 437.

[89]*Ibid.*, p. 438.

[90]*Ibid.*, p. 439.

[91]*Ibid.*, p. 439.

[92]*Ibid.*, p. 440.

[93]In this remark Sibbes refers to a *felt* presence. He would not have denied that objectively the Spirit is present in every Christian regardless of variation in subjective experience.

[94]'Prevents' is used in its older meaning of 'precedes'.

[95]*Sibbes*, vol. 5, p. 440.

[96]*Ibid.*, vol. 7, p. 376.

[97]See *A Treatise Tending Unto a Declaration Whether a Man be in the Estate of Damnation or in the Estate of Grace* (*The Work of William Perkins*, 1970), pp. 353–385.

[98]*Sibbes.*, vol. 7, p. 377.

[99]*Ibid.*, p. 376.

[100]*Ibid.*, p. 382.

[101]*Ibid.*, p. 382.

[102]*Ibid.*, p. 383.

[103]*Ibid.*, p. 382.

[104]*Ibid.*, p. 382–383.

4

Thomas Goodwin and the
sealing of the Spirit

Thomas Goodwin (1600–1680) was born in Norfolk, a county long known for Puritan opposition to the English religious establishment. He entered Christ's College, Cambridge, just before his thirteenth birthday, earned his BA in 1616, his MA in 1620, and his BD in 1630. Later, in 1653, he was awarded his DD. He writes that from the time he was six years old he 'began to have some slighter workings of the Spirit of God' but in later years he did not think these early religious feelings signified that he was a true Christian. When he went up to Cambridge in 1613 the town was said to be 'a nest of Puritans' and Goodwin later reported that 'the whole town was filled with the discourse of the power of Mr Perkins' ministry', although William Perkins had been dead for ten years. Paul Baynes had continued preaching there after Perkins' death until his own death in 1617. Goodwin thus came under considerable Puritan influence while at Cambridge, having opportunity to hear Baynes and certainly hearing Richard Sibbes and the well-known Puritan, Mr Rogers of Dedham.

In 1619 Goodwin transferred to Catherine Hall, Cambridge. Shortly after, on 2 October 1620, he was persuaded to hear a sermon by a Dr Bainbrigge. It was on this occasion that Goodwin experienced an evangelical conversion, and shortly thereafter attached himself to the Puritan party in Cambridge.[1] The Puritan, Robert Trail (1642–1716), reports that in his early ministry Goodwin was inclined to Arminianism and that it was Richard

80

Sibbes whose teaching brought him to a more Calvinist persuasion. Trail writes: 'I have heard, that Dr Thomas Goodwin was in his youth an Arminian, or at least inclining that way, but was by the Lord's grace brought off, by Sibb's clearing up to him this same point, of Christ's being the head and representative of all his people.'[2]

Goodwin's early ministry brought him into contact with the 'experimental religion' of the type of Perkins, John Rogers and Richard Sibbes. On a famous occasion when he heard John Rogers preaching, the entire congregation dissolved in tears, and Goodwin himself 'was fain to hang a quarter of an hour on the neck of his horse weeping before he had power to mount'.[3] One of his biographers also tells us that he was a great admirer of John Preston and became a regular hearer of his sermons.[4] In 1628 Goodwin succeeded not only to the theological tradition of Perkins, Baynes, Sibbes and Preston but also to Sibbes's old positon as lecturer of Trinity Church, Cambridge.

Goodwin wrote a major book entitled *The Work of the Holy Ghost in our Salvation*, which constitutes volume 6 of his twelve-volumed complete works, edited and published in 1863. It is not this volume, however, that gives us his detailed teaching concerning the 'sealing of the Holy Spirit'; the fullest teaching on the 'seal' is found in his sermons on Ephesians 1:13[5] and (to a lesser extent) in his work entitled *A Child of Light Walking in Darkness*[6] and his sermons on Ephesians 3:16–21.[7] I shall focus on Goodwin's fullest exposition, the sermons on Ephesians 1:13–14, and shall consider in the paragraphs below a number of aspects of his teaching.[8]

Interchangeable terms

In the sermons on Ephesians 1:13–14, Goodwin, like Sibbes, uses more than one expression to designate the direct post-conversion witness of the Spirit. The main term is 'sealing' which is used throughout these sermons. However, Goodwin relates this to other expressions. The sealing is identified with the anointing and the earnest of the Spirit. Goodwin here cites 2 Corinthians 1:21 where there are 'three similitudes used to express what he had said plainly at first'.[9] Goodwin quotes also the expression 'the Holy Ghost fell upon them', from the book of Acts,[10] and later he speaks of the 'witness' or the 'immediate testimony' of the Spirit.[11] He also relates the sealing to the promise of the Spirit in the Johannine discourses of John 14 to 16, and to the Spirit being 'poured out' or 'given' as recorded in Acts.[12] The sealing of Jesus (John 6:27) and the Spirit's coming upon Jesus at his baptism (Matthew 3:17) are both identified with the same spiritual experience. John 1:32 is mentioned in this connection as is Acts 10:38.[13] The term 'promise of the Father' is regarded as an allusion to the same spiritual experience,[14] and Acts 2:4; 2:33; Galatians 3:14; 2 Corinthians 5:5; John 7:38; Luke 24:49; Ephesians 4:30 are correlated with the same spiritual blessing.[15]

At one point, when relating 'the seal' to water baptism, Goodwin urges that we 'shall find it is called "baptizing with the Holy Ghost".'[16] Then in his seventeenth sermon on Ephesians 1, where he is relating the terms 'seal' and 'earnest', he brings in the expression 'first-fruits' which he thinks has the same basic significance as the term 'earnest'.[17] At this point he also mentions that he identifies 'full assurance of understanding' (Colossians 2:2) with the seal (though not exactly with the earnest) of the Spirit.[18] Hebrews 10:22 with its mention of the 'full assurance of faith' refers to the same blessing.[19]

Sealing – negatively considered

There is a clear development in Goodwin's teaching, as compared to that of Richard Sibbes. Goodwin spends some time clearing away misinterpretations of the sealing of the Spirit. Among interpretations dismissed are some of Calvin's and Sibbes's.

Goodwin first dismisses those who interpret the 'sealing' as an integral part of faith. Here Calvin is explicitly mentioned only to be repudiated at this point. Ephesians 1:13 refers, says Goodwin, not to the sealing of the truth but to the sealing of the *person* of the believer. It is also something which happens after believing and therefore cannot refer to the prior work of the Spirit leading to faith.[20]

Goodwin then dismisses the view that takes the sealing to be the work of sanctification. One of Sibbes's 'degrees of sealing' was sanctification, therefore Goodwin is dismissing an interpretation which had been favoured by both Perkins and Sibbes. He excludes it because the principles of sanctification are wrought in the heart with saving faith and are not superadded. One cannot say, 'Having believed, you were sealed' with reference to sanctification. Believing and the image of God and any other holy disposition, are wrought together by the work of the Spirit, and, argues Goodwin, regeneration and sanctification are nowhere called a seal. Expositors have made too much of that aspect of the seal which deals with the stamping of an image.[21]

Sealing as assurance

For Goodwin, the sealing of the Spirit is a work upon the heart of the Christian in which he is given an experiential and direct assurance of his salvation. The Spirit is called a 'seal' only because of his work as a sealer: 'he is not called a seal, but in relation to an act of sealing.'[22] Goodwin refers to the several possibilities in applying the imagery of sealing (ownership, appropriation, evaluation, security) but thinks none of them are relevant to his exposition: 'Let there be never so many uses of a seal, that which is proper to the scope here is sealing of an inheritance'.[23] We must ask, then, what it means to 'seal' an inheritance. Goodwin's answer is twofold: the seal makes the inheritance sure in itself and it makes the persons receiving the inheritance sure of their possesison of it. The first of these is irrelevant ('to make salvation sure there needeth no seal after believing'). It is the second that is of interest in the interpretation of Ephesians 1:13. The 'sealing' makes the recipient of the inheritance sure of his eventual possession of it; it is *to make them sure*, to make their persons sure of their salvation, to persuade their hearts, to put them out of question that this inheritance was theirs'. Goodwin cites illustratively Jeremiah 32:10 and Esther 8:8–10.[24]

It is important for Goodwin that Ephesians 1:13 does not say that the inheritance is sealed but that believers themselves are sealed: 'the *persons* are sealed', 'the end of this sealing is to seal up their personal interest'.[25]

Sealing – the sacramental aspect

Goodwin introduces an unusual piece of sacramental theologizing into his discussion when he argues that the 'sealing of the Spirit' is related to water-baptism. In one respect this was not unusual theology. It was common in the early church to interpret the 'sealing' references of the New Testament as referring to water-baptism. The *Shepherd of Hermas* could say 'the seal . . . is the water'.[26] This interpretation is very common today.[27] What is unusual, however, is that Goodwin relates a *post-conversion* 'sealing of the Spirit' to water-baptism. He makes use of the common Reformation description of the sacraments as 'seals' of grace, and argues that the 'sealing' of the Spirit corresponds *inwardly* to the 'seal' of water-baptism *outwardly*. Water-baptism, he argues, holds the place in the New Covenant that circumcision holds in the Old Covenant (he cites Colossians 2:11–12). If circumcision is called a 'seal' in Romans 4:11 then, in Goodwin's opinion, it is legitimate to call water-baptism a seal. There is therefore an outward seal (water-baptism) and an inner seal (that of the Spirit's witness); the latter is the fruit of the former. Goodwin writes: 'Now then salvation is made sure upon believing; but you are baptized, that is the seal to confirm. Answerably, salvation is made sure upon believing; but the seal of the Spirit cometh as the fruit of baptism, which is the proper work of it. An inward seal answereth to the outward.' (Elsewhere Goodwin says that baptism is not to *work* regeneration but to '*seal* regeneration unto us'.[28] Goodwin now cites the passages (Acts 8:30; 16:33) where the Spirit is given upon water-baptism, which he interprets to refer not to regeneration but to a post-conversion gift of assurance. The 'joy in the Holy Ghost' of the Samaritans and the joy of the Philippian gaoler are the immediate fruit of that gift of the Spirit which followed their baptism. The joy was that of *assured* salvation; such assurance arose immediately from their being baptized.[29]

Immediacy of the Spirit's witness

In Goodwin's thinking, the assurance given by the sealing of the Spirit is direct not syllogistic. In order to clarify yet further the nature of the assurance given in the sealing of the Spirit,

Goodwin distinguishes two types of assurance of salvation. There is firstly a deductive assurance. A person sees, by the knowledge of his own faith and by observing the evidence of a changed life, that he has indeed believed the promises of the gospel and may therefore be sure of his salvation. But there is a second level of assurance which is not deductive; it does not build upon the fact that a man has believed. It is rather 'an *immediate* assurance of the Holy Ghost, by a heavenly and divine light'. The first level of assurance is the result of a syllogism (the promises are for those who believe. I believe; therefore, the promise applies to me). This is '*discoursive*; a man gathereth that God loveth him from the effects, as we gather there is fire because there is smoke'. The sealing of the Spirit, however, is different. It is '*intuitive*'. 'There is a light that cometh and overpowereth a man's soul, and assureth that God is his, and he is God's and that God loveth him from everlasting.'[30]

In this context Goodwin, like Sibbes before him[31] introduces 1 John 5:8 and interprets the blood, the water and the Spirit as three levels of assurance. 'Blood' alludes to an assurance that comes by faith in the death of Christ; 'water' alludes to an assurance that comes through seeing the marks of the sanctified life in oneself, 'the Spirit' alludes to the sealing of the Spirit. The Spirit is indeed involved in the first two levels of assurance but the third level is the exclusive prerogative of the Spirit. At this point Goodwin introduces the phrase 'the immediate testimony' to clarify this point yet further. In the sealing of the Spirit, the Spirit needs no helper. 'When the Holy Ghost cometh to seal up salvation, he will have no witness but himself.'[32]

The distinction of the 'sealing' and faith

For Goodwin, the sealing of the Spirit is subsequent to faith. There is a distinct section of his exposition in which he comments upon the words 'after ye believed' (Ephesians 1:13). He argues that the aorist tense (*pisteusantes*, 'having believed') may be contrasted with the present tense in 1 Peter 1:8 (*pisteuontes*, 'believing'). The aorist tense may be translated 'when ye *had* believed' or 'having believed'. The experience of the apostles mentioned in the context of Ephesians 1 illustrates the point. They 'had faith and the Holy Ghost long before they had assurance and the seal of the Spirit' (John 14:17 is quoted).[33] John 14:16 makes the same point, in Goodwin's thinking, for the world cannot 'receive the Spirit'. In other words, one must have ceased to be part of the 'world' before one is in a position to receive the Spirit. Faith is chronologically prior to the sealing. Acts 15:8–9 is thought to point in the same direction.[34]

Goodwin concludes this sermon thus: 'God should be honoured first by mere trusting, by mere *believing*, before he honoureth your faith with setting to his seal'; 'when you have set to[35] your seal that God is true in his word, God will set his seal after your believing.'[36]

Sealing and union with Christ

Goodwin urges that sealing takes place 'in Christ'. In a further sermon on Ephesians 1:13–14[37] he summarizes what he had said in the previous sermon[38] and then takes up the phrase 'in which' or 'in whom' (the Greek may mean either) in Ephesians 1:13. The allusion could be to the gospel, as the continental reformer Piscator had read it, taking the Greek pronoun to be neuter ('which'). Or it could refer to Christ himself, taking the Greek pronoun to be masculine ('whom'). Goodwin follows the latter option. The implication is that sealing takes place 'in Christ'. This itself has a double meaning and 'both is the meaning and the scope of the place'.[39] It may be read in such a way that the Greek *en* (often translated 'in') is taken to have the force of the Greek *eis* (often translated 'into'). This is an attested phenomenon in Hellenistic Greek although the reverse where *eis* has the force of *en* is more frequent.[40] Thus the believer is sealed *into* Christ, that is, into fellowship with him. Goodwin points out that *eis Christon* ('into Christ') is used in a parallel passage, 2 Corinthians 1:21. The relation of water-baptism to sealing implies something similar, for the Christian is baptized 'into Christ' (Goodwin cites Romans 6:3).

Another equally legitimate way that Goodwin wishes to take 'in which/whom' is to understand that the sealing is bestowed 'by virtue of Christ'. 'The Holy Ghost is the author of it, but Jesus Christ is the virtual cause.' Again 2 Corinthians 1:20 is thought to throw light at this point. All the promises of God have their 'Yes' in Christ. Every blessing comes to people in Christ. 'He, and his virtue, is left out in no work that is done for us'; 'whatsoever work God doth upon us, he doth unto Christ first.'[41] Christ was 'sealed' by the Spirit (*cf.* John 6:27). Union with Christ must lead to our being 'sealed by the Spirit' also.

Here Goodwin is advancing upon the interpretation found in Richard Sibbes. For earlier expositors there was a *similarity* in our being sealed with the Spirit and Christ's being sealed with the Spirit. Goodwin goes further. The sealing of the Spirit is built upon the basis of union with Christ. All that happened to Christ must happen to his people. There will be an identity of experience. Yet Christ is the proto-type; his people receive their experience of the Spirit 'in Him'; 'we are conformed unto Christ'.[42]

Similarly the sacramental aspect of the sealing of the spirit is seen at this point. Just as Christ received his 'seal' at his water-baptism, so the believer must expect the sealing of the Spirit as the fruit of his baptism in water. (However, a time-gap is envisaged; Goodwin believed in infant baptism but can visualize adults receiving the sealing of the Spirit.) As with us so it had been with Christ – what happened at the river Jordan was a sealing of sonship. The accompanying voice declared his unique filial relationship to the Father. Before this sealing Christ had only syllogistic assurance of his Sonship.[43] 'Though he had assurance *of faith* that he was the Son of God, he knew it out of the scriptures by reading all the prophets.' Christ waited till his baptism to have this 'sealed to him with joy unspeakable and glorious'. He was then 'anointed with the Holy Ghost' (see Acts 10:38).[44]

Sealing as the New Covenant promise

Goodwin views the sealing of the Spirit as the climax of the promise of the gospel. He elucidates the phrase 'the Holy Spirit *of promise*' in Ephesians 1:13 as signifying that the gift of the Holy Spirit is the great promise of the New Covenant, just as the coming of Jesus was the great promise of the Old Covenant (*cf.* Acts 1:4; 2:33; Galatians 3:14). The presence of the article in the phrase *tō(i) pneumati tēs epangelias* may be brought out by translating 'the Spirit of *that* promise'. 'There is a special promise, my brethren, unto believers, that they shall have the Spirit to seal them, if they sue it out.' John 14 records the New Covenant promise. Acts 2:38 records that it was offered to those who had just become Christians. It is a promise to 'as many as the Lord our God shall call'. Galatians 3:14 also holds out a promise to those who have already believed.[45]

It is in this context that Goodwin urges Christians to seek the sealing of the Spirit. If such a blessing has been promised, we may seek God's fulfilment of his promise. Believers are to 'sue it out'. Such is the privilege of the ordinary believer under the New Covenant; 'the ordinary saints under the Old Covenant had a spirit of bondage upon them.' The sealing of the Spirit is the fruit of baptism. The Christian has not received the blessing to which baptism points until he or she has known the Spirit in this way. It is called 'baptized with the Spirit' because of this connection with water-baptism.[46] It is for all believers. Paul said it was for 'us with you' (2 Corinthians 1:21) and for both Gentiles and Jews (Ephesians 1:13; 4:30).[47] So at the close of his sixteenth sermon Goodwin gives specific directions for the believer to follow in order to receive the sealing of the Spirit. To the believer he says: 'believe this promise, wait for it by faith, make it the aim of your faith.'

Another reason why the Spirit is called the 'spirit of promise' is that he always seals with a promise from Scripture. The sealing of Christ was that the truth of Isaiah 42:1 was brought home to his heart. Here Goodwin follows the common Puritan view, distinct from that of the contemporary Quakers, that the Spirit is *always* tied to the Word and that there can be no 'immediate revelations'.[48]

The Spirit is also the *Holy* Spirit. We may expect therefore that the seal will come in our meditations upon the promises of God, and that He will come to those who have grown in holiness. Goodwin adds the intimidating comment: 'God doth not give this promise of his Spirit as a sealer till a man be very holy.' This is to be a stimulus in prayer for the Christian. We are to pray to God telling him that the seal will make us holy, and we are to seek the Spirit with this ultimate motivation.[49]

Seal and 'earnest' of the Spirit

The same gift of the Spirit is in one respect the 'sealing' of the

Spirit and in another respect the 'earnest' of the Spirit. This observation of Goodwin's accords well with the inter-changeability of terms that was noted above. That only two of these terms (sealing and earnest) receive major attention arises from the fact that it is these two which occur in Ephesians 1, and the sermons on this chapter were Goodwin's most extended exposition of a section of Scripture.

The particular aspect of the work of the spirit underlined by the term 'earnest' is that in his work of sealing the Spirit imparts some of the heavenly inheritance before the full receiving of it. 'The metaphor of a seal only respecteth the *work* of assurance ... but the similitude of an earnest doth import assuring the *thing*.'[50] It is difficult to distinguish the significance of the two terms. At one time, Goodwin confesses, he had thought that the earnest implied something more than sealing but he tells us that he has changed his mind and now thinks that the two similes are mutually explanatory: 'wherein one simile falleth short the other helpeth it out.' Yet there is a slight difference: 'sealing implieth one thing in assurance, the earnest implieth another.' Sealing is a work especially upon the under-standing; the earnest is a work in the heart. Sealing is not *part* of 'heaven on earth' although it assures of it. The earnest 'works that joy in the heart which the saints shall have in heaven'.[51] Whereas the sealing is to be identified with the 'full assurance of understanding' of Colossians 2:2, the earnest focuses upon the '*taste* of heaven'. 'It is a giving you part in hand, part of that joy and comfort, that taste of heaven. When he thus sealeth he accompanieth it with a taste, with "joy unspeakable and glorious".'[52]

In considering Thomas Goodwin's teaching on the sealing of the Spirit we are watching the process of development in Chris-tian doctrine. For Goodwin's mystical emphasis both builds upon and goes further than the teaching of his predecessors. At the same time we have taken a major step towards our consideration of Lloyd-Jones, for it was Lloyd-Jones supremely who would pick up this emphasis in Goodwin and make it a significant part of his own teaching.

Notes

[1] For these details, see the two memoirs of Goodwin in *The Works of Thomas Goodwin*, vol. 2, edited by J. C. Miller (Edinburgh: James Nichol, 1861), pp. ix–lxxv. 'The lives of Goodwin' in O. C. Watkins, *The Puritan Experience* (London: Routledge and Paul, 1972), pp. 82–91, and B. Freer, 'Thomas Goodwin the Peaceable Puritan', in *Diversities of Gifts* (London: Westminster Conference, 1981), pp. 7–20.

[2] *The Works of Robert Trail*, vol. 1 (Edinburgh, 1810, reprinted Edinburgh: Banner of Truth, 1975), p. 261. (There were several ways of spelling Sibbes's name in the seventeenth-century.)

[3] Cited from the works of John Howe by J. I. Packer, 'Puritanism as a Movement of Revival', *Evangelical Quarterly*, vol. 52 (1980), p.15.

[4] J. Reid, *Memoirs of the Westminster Divines*, vol. 1 (1811, reprinted Edinburgh: Banner of Truth, 1982), p. 331.

[5] See *The Works of Thomas Goodwin*, 12 vols. The sermons on Ephesians are in *Goodwin*, vol. 1, pp. 227–267. These constitute the fifteenth to seventeenth sermons of Goodwin's exposition of Ephesians 1:1–2:10.

[6] *Ibid.*, vol. 3, pp. 231–350. This deals mainly with *lack* of assurance.

[7] *Ibid.*, vol. 2, pp. 391–414.

[8] It is not my purpose to deal in any way with Goodwin's millennialism or his highly articulate defence of congregational independency. It is of interest, however, to note that D. Walker believes that Goodwin's distinctive theology at these points arose from his view of the immediacy of the action of the Holy Spirit (see D. Walker, 'Thomas Goodwin and Church Government', *Journal of Ecclesiastical History*, vol. 34 (1983), pp. 85–99, especially p. 99; see also G. Harrison, 'Thomas Goodwin and Independency', in *Diversities of Gifts* (London: Westminster Conference, 1981), pp. 21–43).

[9] *The Works of Thomas Goodwin*, vol. 1, p. 232.

[10] *Ibid.*, p. 233.

[11] *Ibid.*, p. 234.

[12] *Ibid.*, pp. 238, 242, 245.

[13] *Ibid.*, pp. 244, 245.

[14] *Ibid.*, p. 246.

[15] *Ibid.*, pp. 247, 248, 262.

[16] *Ibid.*, p. 248. See also the phrase 'baptized with the Holy Ghost as a Comforter' on p. 251.

[17] *Ibid.*, p. 258.

[18] *Ibid.*, p. 259.

[19] *Ibid.*, p. 259.

[20] *Ibid.*, p. 228, 229.

[21] *Ibid.*, pp. 229–230.

[22] *Ibid.*, p. 230.

[23] *Ibid.*, p. 231. It should be noted that Goodwin will later apply the 'image' aspect of a seal (*Ibid.*, p. 252).

[24] *Ibid.*, p. 231.

[25] *Ibid.*, p. 232.

[26] *The Shepherd, Similitudes* 9:16:4 (*cf.* 8:6:3 and the whole of 9:16:3–6). Other early references to baptism which use the term 'seal' are *2 Clement* 7:6; 8:6; *Acts of Thomas* 131. The early church's view of 'the seal' is discussed by Gregory Dix ('"The Seal" in the Second Century', *Theology*, 51 (1948), pp. 7–12) and Geoffrey W. H. Lampe, *The Seal of the Spirit* (London: SPCK, 1961).

[27]See W. F. Flemington, *The New Testament Doctrine of Baptism* (London: SPCK, 1964), pp. 66ff.; O. Cullmann, *Baptism in the New Testament* (London: SCM, 1950), p. 46. Markus Barth, *Ephesians*, Anchor Bible, vol. 1 (New York: Doubleday, 1974), pp. 135–144) considers the matter in some detail and concludes 'it is not advisable to limit the meaning and act of sealing exclusively to baptism' (p. 143). See also the discussion in R. E. O. White, *The Biblical Doctrine of Initiation* (Grand Rapids: Eerdmans, 1960), pp. 352–358.

[28]*The Works of Thomas Goodwin*, vol. 1, p. 243, (my italics).

[29]*Ibid.*, pp. 232–233.

[30]*Ibid.*, p. 233.

[31]See above, pp. 71–73.

[32]*The Works of Thomas Goodwin*, vol. 1, pp. 234–235.

[33]*Ibid.*, p. 238. For the grammar of the aorist participle, see E. W. Burton *Syntax of the Moods and Tenses in New Testament Greek* (Edinburgh: T. & T. Clark, 1966) pp. 59–70.

[34]*The Works of Thomas Goodwin*, vol. 1, pp. 238–39.

[35]'Set to' is a two-word verb used in affixing a seal or signature. *Cf. The Shorter Oxford English Dictionary* (Revised and edited by C. T. Onions), 3rd ed., vol. 2, (Oxford: OUP, 1944, reprinted with corrections 1972), p. 1854.
In modern English the sentence would have read 'When you have affixed your seal that God is true, God will affix his seal after your believing.'

[36]*The Works of Thomas Goodwin*, vol. 1, p. 239.

[37]*Ibid.*, pp. 240–252.

[38]*Ibid.*, pp. 240–242.

[39]*Ibid.*, p. 243.

[40]See W. F. Arndt and F. W. Gingrich, *A Greek-English Lexicon*, 2nd edition (Chicago and Cambridge: University of Chicago, 1979), p. 260 (section 1.6), p. 230 (section 9). 'To seal' would, on this understanding, be comparable to a verb of motion. It is interesting that Arndt and Gingrich think 'seal' means 'endue with power from heaven' (*Lexicon*, p. 796, section 2.b).

[41]*The Works of Thomas Goodwin*, vol. 1, p. 244.

[42]*Ibid.*, p. 245.

[43]In itself there is no way of telling, merely by looking at the text of Luke 2:49, how Jesus arrived at the assurance revealed there. Goodwin is not trying to get out of the text more than is there; he is simply trying to show how such a verse would fit into his teaching concerning the sealing of the Spirit.

[44]*The Works of Thomas Goodwin*, vol. 1, p. 245, (my italics). J. D. G. Dunn thinks that to use Jesus' life as a model in this way is mistaken and that 'we are dealing here with events whose significance, at least for those who record them, lies almost totally in the part they play in salvation-history' (*Baptism in the Holy Spirit* [London: SCM, 1970], p. 24). Goodwin might have replied: (i) Salvation-events *are* used in the New Testament as a model of the Christian life (*e.g.* Mark 10:43–45; 2 Corinthians 4:10; Ephesians 5:2). (ii) The humanity of Jesus and the centrality of faith and the Holy Spirit in his life *is* a model for us. In Hebrews 2:13a Jesus' faith is part of his being our 'brother'. There is no reason to think Jesus is not our 'brother' in the enabling of the Spirit also. (iii) To allow salvation-history to swallow up the significance of Jesus' experience is the high-road to denying significance to anything experiential at all. (iv) It is an enabling by the Spirit no matter what epochal significance may be attached to any particular incident. In my opinion J. D. G. Dunn is correct in what he affirms but provides little argumentation for what he denies. Judged by Dunn's criteria, people who have not had an experiential *Pentecostal-type* baptism with the Spirit are not Christians at all. Other objections to Dunn's case are presented by H. M.

Ervin, *Conversion-Initiation and the Baptism in the Holy Spirit* (Peabody, Massachusetts: Hendrickson, 1984), but I do not, however, wholly identify with Ervin.

[45]*The Works of Thomas Goodwin*, vol. 1, pp. 247.

[46]*Ibid.*, p. 248.

[47]*Ibid.*, pp. 248–249.

[48]*Ibid.*, p. 249.

[49]*Ibid.*, p. 252.

[50]*Ibid.*, p. 256. I italicize two words to make Goodwin's meaning clearer. By the 'work of assurance' he means assurance *about* the inheritance. By 'the thing' he means an actual part of the inheritance.

[51]*Ibid.*, p. 259.

[52]*Ibid.*, p. 260.

5

John Owen and the experience of the Spirit

John Owen (1616–1683) was the son of Henry Owen, the vicar of Stadham, Oxfordshire, a man with Puritan leanings. Owen became a student at Queen's college, Oxford, at the unusually early age of twelve years, and he graduated with a BA in 1632, and with an MA in 1635. Later, in 1653, he was awarded a DD degree. It was during the later years of his university life that he experienced an evangelical conversion and, apparently, adopted the Puritan convictions of his father.

After his departure from Oxford in 1637 Owen was chaplain and tutor in the home of Sir Philip Dormer of Ascot for a while, and then chaplain in the family of Lord Lovelace, of Hurley in Berkshire. Owen's Puritan sympathies, however, led inevitably to a breach between himself and the Royalist Lord Lovelace, and Owen moved to London in 1642.

For a number of years after his conversion Owen seems to have been plagued with fears and doubts concerning his salvation (Richard Sibbes would have said he was experiencing the 'Spirit of bondage'). It was through hearing a sermon in 1642, preached by a man whose name Owen never discovered, speaking on Matthew 8:26 ('Why are ye so fearful...?') that Owen was delivered from his fears.

In 1642, Owen's first published work *The Display of Arminianism* appeared, and from then until his death a steady flow of theological works came from his pen. Every year from 1645 to 1662 saw one or more publications, as did most of the subsequent years of his life. About a dozen further works were published posthumously.[1]

Owen produced a large body of written material relating to the person and work of the Holy Spirit. In addition to random remarks, and sections dealing with the Holy Spirit in his various writings, he authored a series of five major writings on the Holy Spirit. They were originally planned as part of one major work, but as with a number of Owen's other works[2] they were published piecemeal rather than as a unified whole. The first part was the *Discourse on the Holy Spirit*, published in 1674. Three years later when Owen published *The Reason of Faith*, he explained in the preface that this was intended to be a further stage in his work on the Holy Spirit: 'About three years since, I published a book about the dispensation and operations of the Spirit of God. That book was one part only of what I designed on that subject.'[3] The next part, published in 1678, was *The Ways and Means of Understanding the Mind of God*. Then came *The Work of the Holy Spirit in Prayer* (1682). Owen still had not finished publishing his material at his death in 1683 but in 1693 *Two Discourses on the Work of the Spirit* appeared, the two parts of which dealt with the Spirit as Comforter and the Spirit's work in prayer.

Lloyd-Jones complained that Owen was 'not very clear in his teaching on this matter of the testimony and witness of the Spirit' and that Owen admitted as much.[4] Certainly Owen's ideas changed over the years. For this reason it is best to treat Owen's teaching not so much thematically as chronologically. I shall deal first with his works before 1674, and then his teaching in the writings published in 1674 and 1698.

Before 1674

In his early years Owen evidently held a view of the sealing of the Spirit similar to that of Thomas Goodwin. Thus in a catechism published in 1645 the question is raised as to how we may know of our adoption as God's sons. Owen's reply is that we may know our sonship, 'By the especial working of the Holy Spirit in our hearts, sealing unto us the promises of God, and raising up our souls to an assured expectation of the promised inheritance.' Romans 8:15 and Ephesians 4:30 are among verses of Scripture cited in support.[5]

Five years later Owen preached sermons in which he again made passing mention of the assuring work of the Spirit. He speaks of the possibility of being a Christian but of having lost one's assurance. He cites in this connection Romans 8:16 and Ephesians 1:13 but warns the Christian, 'Upon our grieving him, he will withdraw as to this also.'[6] In other words, Owen interprets these two verses as referring to a subjective assurance of salvation, not to an objective and irrevocable presence of the Spirit.

The first work of Owen's to have a major section dealing with the Spirit was *The Doctrine of the Saints' Perseverance*, published in 1654. Chapter 1 introduced the controversy concerning perseverance; chapters 2–6 put forward four main arguments in favour of the Christian's security in salvation. Chapters 7–9 consist of supplementary observations concerning Christ's oblation (ch. 7), the work of the Spirit (ch. 8) and Christ's intercession (ch. 9). A further chapter (ch. 10) points to the relevance of the teaching, and the remaining chapters (chs. 11–17) seek to refute objections. In withstanding the Arminian John Goodwin (not to be confused with the Calvinist Thomas Goodwin) Owen insists that John 14:16 ('. . . he will give you another Counsellor to be with you *for ever*') implies the eternal security of the individual believer. Owen will waver on this text, as we shall see, for he sometimes interprets the promises of John 14–16 as referring to the 'comforting' work of the Spirit which may fluctuate, but here he refers it to an irrevocable presence of the Spirit in the beliver's heart.[7]

At this point Owen believes that John 14:16 implies the perseverance of each believer in faith and obedience and thus in salvation.[8] Two paragraphs later, Owen speaks of the testimony of the Spirit and the sealing of the Spirit. The Spirit bears 'a distinct testimony of his own' in giving assurance. The Spirit's sealing of believers is 'his assuring the salvation of believers' (2 Corinthians 1:22 is quoted).[9] In this context Owen explains what sealing implies. It gives privacy and security. However, another use of the seal is to give assurance, and it has this significance in 2 Corinthians 1:22, following mention of the promises (2 Corinthians 1:20): 'To secure believers of their certain and infallible accomplishment unto them, the apostle tells them of this sealing of the Spirit, whereby the promises are irrevocably confirmed unto them to whom they are made.'[10]

Subsequently Owen says, 'their believing is in order of nature antecedent to their sealing'. Then a few paragraphs later: 'It is the intent and purpose of God that the sealing of believers shall abide with them for ever.' Here again is reflection upon John 14:16. It will be noted, however, that Owen's view of John 14:16 has slightly changed. It now refers to a post-conversion sealing which is *intended* to abide for ever. Owen cannot say that the sealing *will* abide for ever because, in line with Goodwin and earlier expositors, he believes this subjective work of the Spirit may fluctuate or even be lost, but the objective presence of the Spirit may not be lost.

It is clear that Owen envisages a sealing of the Spirit subsequent to regeneration and faith. When the disciples are already believers they receive a promise, *with regard to the future* 'to quicken and strengthen their faith'.[11] They already have faith; yet they are looking for the coming of the Spirit. In Owen's view, all graces are objectively bestowed in Christ, but experientially there is sequence in their appropriation by the believer. Owen has a complicated sentence which may be abridged and italicized in order to bring out the contrast which he draws: 'Both faith and sealing and all other mercies, *as to the good will of God bestowing them*, are *at once* granted . . . but *as to our acceptance of them* . . . they have that order which either . . . nature . . . or the will of God hath allocated to them.'[12] In other words, in the mind and plan of God all blessings in Christ are a unit; experientially there may be sequence. Owen goes on to say that sealing is 'a peculiar *improvement* of the grace bestowed on us'[13] – an expression that again implies sequence and development.

On the other hand it must be noted that a *long* time gap is not envisaged. Owen asserts: 'That all believers are so sealed . . . is the plain testimony of Scripture.'[14] Whether there might be an extended delay between the bestowal and the sealing of the Spirit he does not discuss. S. Ferguson rightly notes: 'He was certainly reluctant actually to *deny* that the Holy Spirit might give such full assurance after conversion.'[15] His Puritan background taught him to use the term 'sealing' for this event.

In the next chapter (ch. 8) Owen passingly mentions the same teaching. 'That the Spirit which Christ instructs us to ask for, and which himself promises to send unto us, is the Holy Ghost himself, the Holy Spirit of promise, by whom we are sealed to the day of redemption.'[16]

The next work to deal in any depth with the work of the Spirit was Owen's study of *On Communion with God*, published in 1657. In this work the term 'communion' means more than an experiential fellowship with God. Owen defines 'communion' as 'his communication of himself unto us, with our returnal unto him of that which he requireth and accepteth, flowing from that union which in Jesus Christ we have with him'; it is 'a mutual communication in giving and receiving, after a most holy and spiritual manner, which is between God and the saints, while they walk together in a covenant of peace'.[17] Communion with God is, in J. I. Packer's words, 'a relationship in which Christians receive from, and respond to, all three Persons of the trinity'.[18] 'Communion' is thus a richer term than in modern usage.

Owen maintains that there is a distinct communion between the Christian and each of the three persons of the Trinity. The Christian especially relates to the Father by way of faith and love. He has a *distinct* faith in Jesus (*cf.* John 14:1) and *distinctly* honours the Son (*cf.* 1 John 5:13). Then there is a *distinct* relationship to the Spirit. The Father communicates grace as the origin; the Son provides a 'purchased treasury' of God's grace; the Spirit works grace by 'immediate efficacy'.[19]

It is in part 3 of this work that Owen takes up 'communion with the Holy Ghost' in detail. He makes a distinction between the Spirit's work in the – as yet – unconverted elect person and in one who is already a Christian. In the former case, he is 'a Spirit of sanctification to the elect, to convert them and make them believers'. In the latter, he is 'a Spirit of consolation to believers to give them the privileges of the death and purchase of Christ'. It is the latter ministry that is in view when the Spirit is called the *Paraklētos* (Comforter). Three points are worthy of note. Firstly, 'Our receiving of him as a Spirit of sanctification is a mere passive reception, as a vessel receives water', or like the wind which made the dead bones of Ezekiel's vision live (Ezekiel 37:1–10). When a person has become a Christian, however, his receiving of the Spirit involves his active participation: 'There is an active power to be put forth in his reception for consolation, though not in his reception for regeneration and sanctification.' Thus Owen knows of two 'receptions' of the Spirit. In becoming regenerate a person receives the Spirit passively, but as a believer receives him actively as the 'Spirit of consolation'. 'It is believers that thus receive the Spirit; and they receive him by faith.'[20] Secondly, in receiving the Spirit as the Spirit of consolation, the believer has in view the covenant promise (Galatians 3:14). Owen never mentions Goodwin by name, although he and Goodwin were close friends,[21] and shared the pulpit at St Mary's Church, Oxford.[22] They were allies in the cause of congregationalist church-polity, and on one occasion wrote a joint-preface to the work of another Puritan.[23] Yet it is likely that it is Goodwin's exposition that Owen has in view here because he translates Ephesians 1:13 'the Spirit of *that* promise' exactly as Goodwin had done. 'Faith eyes the promise of God and of Jesus Christ, of sending the Spirit for all those ends that he is desired; thus it depends, waits, mixing the promise with itself, until it receive him.' It must be emphasized that it is the Christian who is exercising this faith, and thus Owen is envisaging a post-conversion receiving of the Spirit.[24] Thirdly, at this point Owen comments on John 14:16, and unlike his rather confused use of this passage in 1654, he now faces the matter squarely, pointing out that it is as a Spirit of sanctification that we think of his permanent indwelling. In John 14:16 'the general notion of it in abiding is ascribed to him as a comforter'. Yet there is a difficulty, he notes, in that although the Comforter abides with us 'for ever', 'we may utterly lose our comfort'. Owen suggests five points to resolve the difficulty he encountered in 1654.

Firstly, it means that although Christ would leave his disciples, the dispensation of the Spirit as Comforter would continue permanently. Owen represents Jesus as saying to his disciples in the Upper Room, 'Fear it not: this is *the last dispensation*; there is to be no alteration. When I am gone, the Comforter is to do all the remaining work: there is not another to be looked for, and I promise you him; nor shall he depart from you, but always abide with you.'

Secondly, the Spirit always abides with us, objectively, although his comfort may not always be apparent. The Comforter may always *abide* with us, though not always *comfort* us.

Thirdly, he is present as Comforter even when he is not at a particular moment doing the work of comforting. Fourthly, the Spirit offers comfort even when through human unbelief the believer refuses to enjoy the sweetness of the Spirit's consolation: 'the well is nigh, and we see it not'.[25] And finally, Owen denies that the Spirit ever leaves the Christian 'absolutely and universally . . . without consolation'.[26]

In chapter 3 of this part of Owen's work, he expounds some of the blessings communicated by the Spirit. Among these he mentions the shedding abroad of the love of God, the witness of the Spirit, the sealing of the Spirit, the earnest of the Spirit, the anointing of the Spirit and the gift of the Spirit of adoption. Romans 5:5 is taken to refer to 'plentiful evidence and persuasion of the love of God to us'.[27] Owen has changed his mind about this text because earlier he interpreted it as referring to the *grace* of Christian love;[28] later he had left open the possibility of interpreting it in two ways;[29] now he understands it to mean the profuse consciousness of God's love towards the Christian.[30]

Romans 8:16 is interpreted in a way that reminds us of Goodwin: 'the Comforter comes, and, by a word of promise or otherwise, overpowers the heart with a comfortable persuasion (and bears down all objections) that his plea is good, and that he is a child of God.' 'When our spirits are pleading their right and title, he comes in and bears witness on our side.' This may take place a long time after a man has begun to seek assurance: 'sometimes the dispute hangs long, – the cause is pleading many years.'[31]

When Owen comes to the phrase 'the sealing of the Spirit' he now hesitates to interpret it as he had done in earlier years. He is no longer so sure of Goodwin's interpretation. 'I am not very clear,' he says, 'in the certain peculiar intendment of this metaphor',[32] and thinks that perhaps the term refers not to a *work* of sealing but to the Spirit's communicating the image of God to believers. He thinks it may denote 'not an act of sense in the heart, but of security to the person'.[33] The earnest is also understood along Goodwin's lines.[34]

Some pages later Owen makes a distinction which Lloyd-Jones would have occasion to refer to, the distinction between a *direct* assurance and an assurance mediated by reflection and argument. There are two ways, says Owen, in which the Spirit can give joy. (In Owen's trend of thought, joy is one of the 'general consequences in the hearts of believers of the effects of the Holy Ghost before mentioned'; he is still pursuing the themes of his previous chapter.) 'He doth it *immediately* by himself; without the consideration of any other acts or words of his, or the interposition of any reasoning, or acts of deductions and conclusions . . . he immediately works the soul and minds of men to a joyful, rejoicing, and spiritual frame, filling them with exultation and gladness: – not that this arises from our reflext considerations of the love of God, but rather gives occasion thereunto.' 'Of this joy there is no account to be given, but that the Spirit worketh it when and how he will.'

Then Owen goes on to describe how the Spirit may work 'mediately'. This is when the Spirit makes use of 'his other works towards us'. The Spirit meditates upon the Spirit's work and 'by the intervenience of these considerations' the Spirit gives joy. Lloyd-Jones would quote this passage *in extenso* using it to support his teaching concerning a direct and unmediated baptism of the Spirit.[35]

From 1674

There was a seventeen-year gap between Owen's *On Communion with God* and the first part of his *magnum opus*, *A Discourse on the Holy Spirit*, published in 1674. It is a work of more than 600 pages (in the Goold edition), yet it was unfinished in 1674 and sections of a second part were published in stages as Owen was able to complete them. Owen tells us in 1677 that 'The consideration of the work of the Spirit as the Spirit of illumination, of supplication, of consolation and as the immediate author of all spiritual offices and gifts, extraordinary and ordinary, is designed unto the second part of it.'[36]

The section which deals with the Spirit as Comforter and seal was never published during Owen's lifetime. It was presumably written in the last years of his life between about 1680 and 1683, but was not published until 1693. By this time Owen seems to have resolved some of the ambiguities and uncertainties about which Lloyd-Jones complained, and makes a clear distinction between the indwelling of the Spirit and the particular acts of the indwelling Spirit, a distinction which to some extent clarifies the confusion which had characterized Owen's earlier works. At the end of his life Owen took more seriously the inhabitation of the Spirit in the believer as the foundation of the New Covenant ministry of the Spirit. 'The first thing which the Comforter is promised for unto believers is, that he should dwell in them; which is their great *fundamental* privilege, and whereon all others do depend.'[37] Owen is concerned to clarify what this means. It is different from the Spirit's omnipresence;[38] it is not used in a transferred sense designating the Spirit's work;[39] it does not refer to the kind of union that existed between the divine and human natures of Christ.[40] It is not independent of Christ but rather is mediated by Christ.[41] It is this that is promised in the Old Testament,[42] what we are to pray for;[43] 'all the principle actings of the Holy Spirit in us and towards us as a comforter do depend on this head, or flow from this spring of his inhabitation'.[44]

Three comments may be made on Owen's teaching at this point. Owen, firstly, makes a sharp distinction concerning the *foundational* fact, the indwelling of the Spirit, and other aspects of the Spirit's ministry which he now calls 'particular actings' of the Spirit. After dealing with the Spirit's indwelling (chapter 4 of *The Spirit as a Comforter*), he then takes three chapters to deal with the three major 'particular actings' of the Spirit, which are connected with the anointing, the seal and the earnest of the Spirit.

Secondly, Owen still distinguishes the inhabitation of the Spirit and regeneration. In the 1674 section of his work he had distinguished the Spirit's work as Comforter and 'his sanctifying work, whereby we are enabled to believe'.[45] The Spirit comes as Comforter to those *already* believers.[46] The world cannot receive him: 'he is neither promised unto them nor can they receive him, until other gracious acts of his have passed on their souls';[47] 'this is not the first saving work of the Holy Spirit on the souls of men. Regeneration and habitual sanctification do always precede it. He comforteth none but those whom he hath before sanctified.'[48] 'If men be not first sanctified by him, they can never be comforted by him';[49] 'none can receive him as a comforter but believers.'[50] This aspect of Owen's thought is confirmed by the fact that Owen expects believers to pray for the Spirit. This is a great mystery, thinks Owen. Christians 'are not able to form any conception in their minds of the manner of his presence and residence in them, yet it is that which they pray for.'[51]

On the other hand, Owen expects that every Christian *will* pray for and enjoy the Spirit as Comforter. He does not envisage any Christian being without the presence of the Comforter. There will be a variation in the Christian's experience of the Comforter. John 14:16 teaches the 'unchangeable continuance' of the Spirit as Comforter within the church.[52] Even when the experiential aspect of the Spirit's work subsides, 'The accomplishment of Christ's promise doth not depend as to its truth upon our experience, at least not on what men sensibly feel in themselves under their distresses, much less on what they express with some mixture of unbelief.'[53] Yet 'if we intend to have experience of his work herein . . . there are sundry things required of ourselves in a way of duty'.[54]

Thirdly, it is helpful to analyse Owen's view of the work of the Spirit before Pentecost. He maintains that 'all light, grace and joy to the souls of believers' was 'no less the immediate work of the Holy Ghost' before Pentecost when Jesus was still with the disciples in the flesh. The difference in experience was partly that the pre-Pentecostal believer did not understand the gift of the Spirit as much as would be possible later. 'They had yet no insight into the mystery of the dispensation of the Spirit.'[55] Also the Spirit was not 'so given or poured out as to *evidence* himself and his operation unto their souls'.[56] Owen explicitly says that 'the Holy Spirit did not then first begin really and effectually to be a comforter of believers upon the departure of Christ'.[57] In other words the indwelling of the Spirit was known before Pentecost. The difference Pentecost brought was that a fuller manifestation and fuller self-evidencing experience of the blessing of the Spirit came to be known.

Having expounded this foundational aspect of the gift of the Spirit, Owen proceeds to consider the terms anointing, sealing and earnest. Each of them is treated along much the same lines. None of these terms refers simply to an activity of the Spirit. Each of them refers to the Spirit *himself*. The Spirit *is* the anointing, he *is* the seal, he *is* the earnest. Each expression refers to the gift of the Spirit to the Christian. 'Our unction, therefore, is the communication of the Holy Spirit, and nothing else';[58] 'it is not said that the Holy Ghost seals us, but that we are sealed with him; he is God's seal unto us';[59] the earnest of the Spirit is 'not any act or work of the Holy Spirit on us or in us that is called his being an "earnest", it is he himself who is this earnest'.[60]

Associated with these terms are particular ministries. Anointing has its force in 'saving illumination of our minds, teaching us to know the truth, and to adhere firmly unto it in love and obedience'.[61] Sealing is connected with assurance 'although the way whereby it doth, it hath not been rightly apprehended'. This last phrase means that Owen has changed his mind and has left aside the approach he had known from Goodwin and earlier Puritans. Owen now says that it is 'not any act of the Spirit in us that is the ground of our assurance, but the communication of the Spirit unto us'.[62] Similarly, the Spirit *is* the earnest; he is that 'whereby we become co-heirs with Christ'.[63]

It will be seen that over the course of his life Owen increasingly broke out of the mould of Thomas Goodwin and the earlier Puritan teaching. The differences and similarities could be outlined as follows: Both Goodwin and Owen maintained throughout their ministry the possibility of wonderful experiences of assurance and joy for the Christian, and both inherited the Puritan tradition of linking such experience with the terms 'sealing', 'earnest', 'witness' and the like. Whereas Goodwin developed such ideas and brought them to sharper and fuller definition, Owen tended to move away from his heritage. It is not that Owen changed his doctrine, but he changed his terminology and his understanding of the terms 'seal', 'earnest' and 'anointing'.

Owen – unlike Goodwin – came to put greater stress on the objective fact of the Spirit being bestowed on the Christian. It was his controversy with John Goodwin the Arminian that led to his greater emphasis on the Christian's perseverence. Texts that Thomas Goodwin used to expound his view of the subjective working of the Spirit (notably Ephesians 1:13) Owen wished – after his controversy with John Goodwin – to expound in support of the Christian's objective security in Christ.

In neither Owen's nor Goodwin's teaching was the gift of the Spirit *precisely* identified with regeneration; it was to be sought by every Christian. Whereas Goodwin tolerated the idea of a time-gap between conversion and sealing, Owen evidently thought of this blessing being given to the Christian soon after his coming to faith. He did not envisage – in his later days – any Christian being without the objective presence, experienced in

103

varying degrees, of the Holy Spirit as Comforter.

Finally, one must remember that Thomas Goodwin and Owen were close friends, although Goodwin was the senior by sixteen years. It is likely that some of Owen's obscurity arises from the fact that he was reluctant to disagree publicly and sharply with his friend. He goes along with Thomas Goodwin as far as he can and never criticises him. Yet a careful reading reveals that while he retained a strongly experiential doctrine, he wishes to emphasize the Christian's final security in Christ as well as the direct witness of the Spirit.

Notes

[1] For these details, see the biographies of Owen in *The Works of John Owen*, vol. 1, edited by W. H. Goold (Edinburgh: Johnstone and Hunter, 1850–53, reprinted Edinburgh: Banner of Truth, 1965), pp. xxi–cxxii; P. Toon, *God's Statesman: The Life and Work of John Owen* (Exeter: Paternoster, 1971); P. Toon (editor) *The Correspondence of John Owen (1618–1683)*, (London: James Clarke, 1970).

[2] Thus the exposition of Hebrews came out in four parts and the material on the Sabbath was yet a further part of the same work. Similarly the two works on the church were intended to be taken together. Other examples could be cited.

[3] See *The Works of John Owen*, vol. 3, edited by W. H. Goold (Edinburgh: Johnstone and Hunter, 1850–53, reprinted Edinburgh: Banner of Truth, 1966), p. 6.

[4] D. M. Lloyd-Jones, *Sons of God* (Edinburgh: Banner of Truth, 1973), p. 325. The allusion is to *The Works of John Owen*, vol. 2, p. 242.

[5] *The Works of John Owen*, vol. 1, p. 489.

[6] *Ibid.*, vol. 8, p. 307.

[7] *Ibid.*, vol. 11, p. 320.

[8] *Ibid.*, pp. 320–322.

[9] *Ibid.*, pp. 322–323.

[10] *Ibid.*, pp. 323–324.

[11] *Ibid.*, p. 319.

[12] *Ibid.*, p. 325.

[13] *Ibid.*, p. 325.

[14] *Ibid.*, p. 328.

[15] S. B. Ferguson, *John Owen on the Christian Life* (Edinburgh: Banner of Truth, 1987), p. 122, citing *The Works of John Owen*, vol. 4, p. 405, 'I do not deny such an especial work of the Spirit'.

[16] *The Works of John Owen*, vol. 11, p. 331.

[17] *Ibid.*, vol. 2, pp. 8–9.

[18] J. I. Packer, 'The Puritan Idea of Communion with God', in *Press Toward the Mark* (London: Puritan and Reformed Studies Conference, 1962), p. 9. (This work focuses mainly on Owen.)

[19] *The Works of John Owen*, vol. 2, ch. 2, pp. 9–17.

[20] *Ibid.*, p. 231.

[21] *Ibid.*, vol. 1, p. lxv.

[22] *Ibid.*, p. liii.

[23]*Ibid.*, p. 550. Owen could refer to Goodwin as 'one among ourselves' (vol. 3, p. 80) or 'my very learned colleague' or 'a very eminent man' (vol. 10, p. 494). On occasions he could disagree with Goodwin's interpretations as he did eventually concerning the seal of the Spirit and as he did in his interpretation of 1 Corinthians 2:11 (see vol. 3, p. 80).

[24]*Ibid.*, vol. 2, pp. 231–232. However, although a sealing after regeneration is envisaged, it is closely linked with the *initial* preaching of the gospel in Owen's view, as his citation of Galatians 3:2 suggests. It is 'the preaching of the gospel, begetting faith in them' which 'enabled them to receive the Spirit'. Again one notes that Owen does not envisage so long a time gap that the connection between justification and the gift of the Spirit is obscured.

[25]*Ibid.*, vol. 2, p. 233.

[26]*Ibid.*, pp. 232–233.

[27]*Ibid.*, p. 240.

[28]*Ibid.*, vol. 8, p. 305 (a sermon preached in 1650).

[29]*Ibid.*, vol. 11, p. 333.

[30]See also the mention of the text in *ibid.*, vol. 2, p. 21, and the sermon on it in 1676 (see *ibid.*, 9, pp. 606–609).

[31]*Ibid.*, vol. 2, p. 241.

[32]*Ibid.*, p. 242.

[33]*Ibid.*, p. 243. Owen does not leave aside the subjective ingredient however, for a few lines later he says 'We are sealed . . . when, from the stamp, image and character of the Spirit upon our souls, we have a fresh *sense* of the love of God given to us, with a comfortable persuasion of our acceptance with him.' There is a slight tension between this and the earlier remark that the seal is 'not an act of *sense* in the heart'. Owen no longer holds that the seal is in and of itself subjective, but he still holds that the objective presence of the Spirit gives rise to experiential blessings.

[34]*Ibid.*, vol. 2, pp. 243–246.

[35]See D. M. Lloyd-Jones, *John* (sound recording), sermon 1085. The passage is in *The Works of John Owen*, vol. 2, pp. 252.

[36]*Ibid.*, vol. 4, p. 6; see also *ibid.*, vol. 3, p. 10.

[37]*Ibid.*, vol. 4, p. 383, my italics.

[38]*Ibid.*, p. 384.

[39]*Ibid.*, p. 384.

[40]*Ibid.*, pp. 384–385.

[41]*Ibid.*, pp. 385–386.

[42]*Ibid.*, p. 386.

[43]*Ibid.*, pp. 386–387.

[44]*Ibid.*, pp. 387–388.

[45]*Ibid.*, vol. 3, p. 154.

[46]*Ibid.*, vol. 4, p. 380.

[47]*Ibid.*, p. 380.

[48]*Ibid.*, p. 382.

[49]*Ibid.*, p. 382.

[50]*Ibid.*, p. 382.

[51]*Ibid.*, p. 386.

[52]*Ibid.*, p. 377.

[53]*Ibid.*, p. 378.

[54]*Ibid.*, p. 379. Owen later refers to not grieving the Spirit (*ibid.*, vol. 4, pp. 413ff.).

[55]*Ibid.*, p. 357.

[56]*Ibid.*, p. 357, my italics.

[57]*Ibid.*, p. 357.
[58]*Ibid.*, p. 393.
[59]*Ibid.*, p. 401, italics omitted.
[60]*Ibid.*, p. 407.
[61]*Ibid.*, p. 394.
[62]*Ibid.*, p. 405.
[63]*Ibid.*, p. 411.

6

Jonathan Edwards and the experience of the Spirit

Just as the seventeenth-century Puritans were a source of inspiration to Lloyd-Jones, so too was the eighteenth-century theologian Jonathan Edwards. Indeed Lloyd-Jones received greater stimulus from the eighteenth century than from the sixteenth or seventeenth centuries. He particularly admired George Whitefield, yet it was Edwards, the theologian *par excellence* of the eighteenth-century awakening, that captivated his interest the most. 'I can simply testify', he said, 'that in my experience the help that I derived in my early years in the ministry from reading the sermons of Jonathan Edwards was immeasurable. And, of course, not only his sermons, but also his account of that Great Awakening, that great religious Revival that took place in America in the eighteenth century, and his great *Religious Affections*.'[1]

In 1976, when speaking to the Westminster Conference, he told of his first encounter with the works of Edwards.

Just before I entered the ministry in 1927 I sought help as regards reading from a friend of mine who not long before had taken first class Honours in Divinity in the university of Oxford. He recommended a large number of books which he had been reading himself for his degree. Among the books was one called *Protestant thought before Kant* by a man called McGiffert. The only thing that impressed me in that book was a chapter on a man called Jonathan

107

Edwards, though he was dealt with mainly as a philosopher. But my interest was aroused immediately. The next time I met my friend I asked 'Could you tell me where I can find out something further about this man Jonathan Edwards?' 'Who is he?' he said! He knew nothing about him, and although I made many enquiries I could not find anybody who could tell me anything about Edwards or about his works. It was not until some two years later, quite by accident, that I found the two volumes of the complete works of Jonathan Edwards which I then purchased for 5/-. I was like the man in our Lord's parable who found a pearl of great price. Their influence upon me I cannot put into words.[2]

Lloyd-Jones used to contrast the seventeenth and eighteenth centuries and expressed his preference for the latter. He disliked the scholasticism of the seventeenth century and felt that the stress on the work of the Spirit in the eighteenth century writers went beyond the seventeenth-century Puritan emphasis, and was an improvement upon their approach. He said:

I believe also that we are entitled to say that with Jonathan Edwards a new element or a new factor can be seen in Puritanism. Most of the great Puritans had a strain or a strand of what one is compelled to describe as scholasticism in them. That led to the involved character of their style, and the divisions and sub-divisions which characterize their works. Edwards is comparatively free from that, and the result is that the element of the Holy Spirit is more prominent in Edwards than in any other of the Puritans.[3]

It was for this reason that Lloyd-Jones preferred eighteenth-century writers over those of the two previous centuries.

Jonathan Edwards was born in October 1703 in Windsor, Connecticut. His father, Timothy Edwards, was the congregational minister there. When still a young boy Edwards 'resolved to make seeking salvation the main business of his life',[4] but it was in 1720–1723 that he experienced conversion and solemnly dedicated himself to God.[5] He was educated first at home, then entered the collegiate school in New Haven (now Yale

University) in 1717, finishing his course there in 1720 before his seventeenth birthday. He continued two further years in preparation for pastoral ministry and in 1722 was licensed to preach. He spent eight months in New York, returned home in 1723, then spent two years teaching at New Haven. In 1727 after five years in the ministry he went to the fashionable congregational church at Northampton, Massachusetts, and it was here that he spent the prime of his life. Initially Edwards was assistant to his grandfather, Solomon Stoddard, who had been the congregational minister since 1669. When Stoddard died in 1729 Edwards continued as the sole pastor.

There were two periods in Edwards' personal ministry, the years 1734–35 and 1739–42, when he saw especially powerful times of revival. After 1743 he found himself immersed in controversy with his congregation, and in 1750 he was dismissed from the pastorate because of his change of view concerning admission to the communion. Thus it was that in 1750 Edwards moved to a mission station in the small town of Stockbridge, where he had increased leisure to write, and there produced the famous works on the *Freedom of the Will* and *Original Sin*.[6]

In 1757 Edwards was appointed the president of Princeton College, but he never really had opportunity to take up the appointment since in February 1758, when he moved to Princeton, he was inoculated against smallpox. The inoculation itself brought on the disease and in March 1758 Edwards died.[7]

Among Protestant evangelicals Edwards is *par excellence* the theologian of revival.[8] His main works which deal with revival and the theology of the Spirit are (in the order in which he wrote them): *A Narrative of Surprising Conversions* (1736); *Distinguishing Marks of a Work of the True Spirit* (1741); *Thoughts on the Revival of Religion* (1742); and *Treatise on the Religious Affections* (1746). These four works each attempted to vindicate the two revivals that Edwards had seen under his own ministry and those being seen in the English-speaking world through the preaching of the Wesley brothers, the Tennant brothers, George Whitefield and others. A fifth work, *A History of the Work of Redemption*, also deals with the history of revivals but from a less controversial angle. One other work of Edwards ought to be specially mentioned, *A Divine and Supernatural Light* (1734), which compactly expresses Edwards' doctrine of spiritual illumination. In the exposition of Edwards' thought, given below, the focus will be on the major theological works which deal with the theme of the Spirit; *Treatise on the Religious Affections*, the *Distinguishing Marks of a Work of the True Spirit* and *A Divine and Supernatural Light*. The emphasis will be on three aspects of Edwards' thought and experience: his caution concerning the direct witness, his positive teaching and his personal experience.

Edwards' caution

There is a tension in Edwards' view of the direct witness and illumination of the Spirit. On the one hand he was very cautious concerning claims to immediate revelation. On the other hand he both experienced himself and taught that others should experience what in one sermon he called 'a divine and supernatural light immediately imparted to the soul by the Spirit of God'.[9] In this section I survey Edwards' cautionary remarks in *The Religious Affections*; in the next section I survey his more positive teaching concerning the illumination of the Spirit.

The Religious Affections, although published in 1746, was initially a series of sermons preached by Edwards to his congregation in 1742 and 1743. In 1740 the second of the two periods of revival commenced in Northampton, yet with the spiritual awakening came religious extremism that both discredited the revival to its enemies and alarmed its friends.[10] Edwards also became alarmed at the fanaticism associated with the revival, but felt, nevertheless, that the movement as a whole was genuinely from God. It was this conviction that revival was a work where true and false could be mixed together that led him to write works seeking to distinguish the true from the false. In *The Religious Affections* he seeks to evaluate what are and what are not true indications that the 'affectionate' or 'emotional' experiences of the Christian are genuine experiences of God.

Edwards begins by urging that the 'affections' are a vital part of religious life (part 1). Then he outlines what are not (part 2) and what are (part 3) signs of genuine Christian experience. However, it is not the concern of this book to outline the whole of his work, rather it is his view of the baptism or sealing of the Spirit that is of interest here.

Early on in *The Religious Affections* Edwards explains what he understands by the baptism with the Spirit. When men 'receive the Spirit of God in his sanctifying and saving influences' they are said to be 'baptized with the Holy Ghost and with fire'.[11] Edwards evidently regards this as synonymous with Christian conversion. Later he says, 'I am bold to assert that there never was any considerable change wrought in the mind or conversation of any person, by anything of a religious nature that ever he read, heard or saw, that had not his affections moved.'[12] Clearly Edwards envisages a gift of the Spirit which is received at conversion and which stirs and rouses the 'affectionate' side of man's nature (using the term in Edwards' sense). The 'earnest' of the Spirit is mentioned later,[13] and although he does not expound his understanding of it in detail, he does seem to identify it with 'having the Spirit'.[14]

It is when Edwards comes to delineate positively the marks of a true work of the Spirit that he explains his view of Romans 8:16, repudiating the view taught by Goodwin. There were evidently those in New England who taught a view of Romans 8:16 similar to that of Goodwin, and on occasions they obviously gave more importance to *direct* 'voices' of the Spirit than Edwards thought was wise or valid. Without mentioning Goodwin by name he says[15] that some Christians:

> . . . imagine a kind of conversation is carried on between God and them; and that God from time to time, as it were, immediately speaks to them, satisfies their doubts, testifies his love to them, promises them support and supplies His blessing in such and such cases, and reveals to them clearly their interest in eternal blessings. And thus they are often elevated, and have a course of a sudden and tumultuous kind of joys, mingled with a strong confidence and high opinion of themselves; when indeed the main ground of these joys and their confidence is not anything contained in or taught by these Scriptures, as they lie in the Bible, but the manner of their coming to them; which is a certain evidence of their delusion.

Edwards does not mean here that the Spirit may not apply Scripture to the human heart. It is simply that the *manner* of its coming home to the Christian is not significant. 'The spiritual application of a promise does not consist in its being immediately suggested to the thoughts by some extrinsic agent, and being borne into the mind with this strong apprehension that it is particularly spoken and directed to them at that time; there is nothing of the evidence of the hand of God in this effect, as events have proved in many notorious instances.'[16] For Edwards there is something much more significant: 'A spiritual application of the Word of God consists in applying it to the heart in spiritually enlightening, sanctifying influences.'[17] The Spirit's work 'consists in enlightening their minds'.[18] 'An application not consisting in this divine sense and enlightening of the mind, but consisting only in the word's being borne into the thoughts, as if immediately then spoken, so making persons believe on no other foundation that the promise is theirs, is a blind application, and belongs to the spirit of darkness and not of light.'[19]

Edwards' conclusion at this point is: 'that what many persons call the witness of the Spirit that they are children of God, has nothing in it spiritual and divine.'[20] 'When the apostle Paul speaks of the Spirit of God bearing witness with our spirit, he is not to be understood of two spirits that are two separate, collateral, independent witnesses; but it is by one that we receive the witness of the other: the Spirit of God gives the evidence by infusing and shedding abroad the love of God, the spirit of a child, in the heart, and our spirit of conscience receives and declares this evidence for our rejoicing.'[21]

What then, in Edwards' view, is the experience described in Romans 8:16? He quotes Solomon Stoddard, his grandfather, to the effect that 'it is the nature of a witness not to make a thing true, but to clear and evidence it'.[22] Romans 8:16 is thus interpreted more along the lines of the syllogistic interpretation of Perkins than the 'direct revelation' taught by Thomas Goodwin. The first 'spirit' in Romans 8:16 is to be identified with the human conscience,[23] the Spirit of God enables one to see the evidence of one's salvation by means of his own love to God. It is 'far from being true that the soul in this case judges by an immediate witness'.[24] Yet the Christian 'stands in no need of multiplied signs, or any long reasoning'.[25] Love, the sign of true salvation, is seen intuitively. When the believer knows he loves God, he knows his own salvation. 'How can he doubt whether he stands in a childlike relation to God when he plainly sees a childlike union between God and his soul, and hence does boldly, and as it were naturally and necessarily, cry, Abba, Father?'[26]

The illumination of the Spirit

The caution of Edwards and his fear of excesses did not prevent him from having a high expectation of what the illumination of the Spirit could do for a believer. In this matter one of Edwards' early works is enlightening. The sermon of 1734, *A Divine and Supernatural Light Immediately Imparted to the Soul by the Spirit of God, Shown to be both a Scriptural and Rational Doctrine*, concisely expresses Edwards' teaching on this matter. Perry Miller thought that 'It is no exaggeration to say that the whole of Edwards' system is contained in miniature within some ten or twelve of the pages in this work.'[27]

The title of the sermon gives Edwards' central proposition which he deduces from his text, Matthew 16:17. His sermon has three sections in which he aims to show what this divine light is, how it is given *immediately* and not by natural means, and thirdly, to show the truth of the doctrine by showing its scripturalness and reasonableness.

The illumination of the Spirit, says Edwards, is not something which men may know by nature; it is not any impression upon the imagination; it is not the suggesting of any proposition *in addition to the Word of God*.[28] This last point distinguishes Edwards' view from any exposition of Romans 8:16 which regards the witness of the spirit as a personal revelation over and above the written scriptures. Nor is this illumination every 'affecting view' that men have of religious things (*i.e.* not everything that men conceive concerning religion which touches their emotions). Positively, this supernatural light is 'a true sense of the excellency of the things revealed in the word of God, and a conviction of the truth and reality of them'. There is a difference, argues Edwards, between having an *opinion* that God is holy and gracious, and having a *sense* of the loveliness and beauty of that holiness and grace. It is the difference between knowing that honey is sweet and *tasting* that honey is sweet. It is the difference between knowing by hearsay that a woman is beautiful and *seeing* that she is beautiful. This sense of the excellency of divine things produces a *conviction* concerning spiritual things. The prejudices of the heart are removed. The doubts of reason are removed and ideas that 'otherwise are dim and obscure are by this means impressed with greater strength'. The 'sense' of things in God's Word 'doth more directly and immediately convince us of their truth'.[29]

In all of this there is a direct activity of the Spirit of God. It is not merely that natural faculties are enhanced. A person's natural faculties are used but there is an illumination that is more than natural. It is not merely that the Word of God is understood. The basic data are conveyed by the Word but the 'due sense of the heart' is 'immediately conveyed by the Spirit'.[30]

Edwards has many texts which he believes teach his doctrine: 1 John 3:6; 3 John 11; John 14:19; 17:3; Matthew 11:25–27; 2 Corinthians 4:6; Galatians 1:15–16; Psalms 119:18; 25:14; John 6:40; 17:6–8; 12:44–46; Luke 12:56–57; 2 Peter 1:16. All of them are given brief exposition.[31] Edwards argues that the doctrine is reasonable; if there is an excellency in God it is reasonable to suppose there is a way of apprehending it by the Spirit.

In all of this Edwards' major concern is not simply with an *individualistic* 'baptism with the Spirit', his greater interest is with the theme of revival in which whole communities are touched by the working of the Spirit of God. At the very beginning of *The Religious Affections* Edwards uses the term 'outpouring of the Spirit' to refer to a communal experience of spiritual awakening.[32] This was a concept he had inherited from his family. Actually the phrase occurs in the earliest datable piece of writing from Edwards. A letter to his sister written on 10 May 1716, when he was twelve years old, describes a 'pouring out of the Spirit of God'.[33]

Personal experience

Special mention should be made of an experience that Edwards once had that Lloyd-Jones would cite in connection with his doctrine of the Spirit.[34] In his memoirs Edwards told of the difficulties he had in coming to an assurance of his salvation. He was much troubled that he had not come to salvation in the stages that were prescribed by the preparationist teaching of the Puritans. In December 1722 he committed to his diary his

114

reasons for having doubts as to his salvation: 'Because I cannot speak so fully to my experience of that preparatory work, of which divines speak'; 'I do not remember that I experienced regeneration, exactly in those steps, in which divines say it is generally wrought';[35] 'I do not feel the Christian graces sensibly enough, particularly faith. I fear they are only such hypocritical outside affections, which wicked men may feel as well as others.'[36]

In May 1723 he wrote that if he were to die he would wish that, 'I had prayed more that God would make me know my estate, whether it be good or bad, and that I had taken more pains and care, to see and narrowly search into the matter.'[37] He resolved 'most nicely and diligently to look into the opinions of our old divines concerning conversion'.

His diary entry of 4 July is another expression of his doubts. He complained about 'want of the Spirit of adoption'[38] on 29 July 1723. Then on 6 November 1724 he noted that he, 'felt sensibly somewhat of that trust and affiance in Christ, and with delight committing of my soul to him, of which our divines used to speak, and about which I have been somewhat in doubt'.[39] Yet he was still in doubt in May 1725.

In 1737 came the experience that Lloyd-Jones used to quote from the pulpit:[40]

Once, as I rode out into the woods for my health, in 1737, having alighted from my horse in a retired place, as my manner commonly has been, to walk for divine contemplation and prayer, I had a view, that for me was extraordinary, of the glory of the Son of God, as Mediator between God and man, and his wonderful, great, full, pure and sweet grace and love, and meek and gentle condescension. This grace that appeared so calm and sweet appeared also great above the heavens. The person of Christ appeared ineffably excellent, with an excellency great enough to swallow up all thought and conception – which continued, as near as I can judge, about an hour; which kept me the greater part of the time in a flood of tears, and weeping aloud. I felt an ardency of soul to be, what I know not otherwise how to express, emptied and annihilated; to lie in the dust, and to be full of Christ alone; to love him

115

with a holy and pure love; to trust in him; to live upon him; to serve and follow him; and to be perfectly sanctified and made pure, with a divine and heavenly purity.

This experience was not the last, for Edwards adds: 'I have several other times had views very much of the same nature, and which have had the same effects.'[41] It will be noted also that this coheres with Edwards' teaching. It was not a new revelation of something other than what could be discovered in Scripture. Nor did it consist of a distinct revelation concerning Edwards' salvation. Rather it was (as Edwards would say) 'a sense of the excellent fullness of Christ'.[42]

So far as I know, Lloyd-Jones never quoted the passage a page later:

On one Saturday night, in particular, I had such a discovery of the excellency of the gospel above all other doctrines that I could not but say to myself, 'This is my chosen light, my chosen doctrine', and of Christ, 'This is my chosen Prophet'. It appeared sweet, beyond all expression, to follow Christ, and to be taught, and enlightened, and instructed by him; to learn of him, and live to him.[43]

Sibbes, Goodwin and Lloyd-Jones would have called this the 'sealing of the Spirit'. In Edwards' own thinking it was part of the supernatural illumination that the Spirit could give. Edwards did not give it an explicit and distinct term such as 'baptism with the Spirit'.

Other influences in Lloyd-Jones's theology

In addition to the crucial figures mentioned, Richard Sibbes, Thomas Goodwin, John Owen and Jonathan Edwards, certain other influences ought to be noted. On the negative side one figure ought to be noted only to be dismissed. Benjamin Breckinridge Warfield (1851–1921) was an influential figure with regard to Lloyd-Jones's Calvinism and his doctrine of Scripture. He first became aware of Warfield's signficance in the late 1920's and then, during a visit to Toronto in 1932, made use of the ten-volumed edition of Warfield's works.[44] However,

Warfield's approach to the doctrine of the Spirit was not acceptable to him. His one reason for disregarding Warfield in this matter was his views on the cessation of the charismata, concerning which Lloyd-Jones once said, 'I am not satisfied by B. B. Warfield's answer to those who have claimed that miracles did continue after the apostolic age.'[45] On other matters Lloyd-Jones commended Warfield.

In addition to the specific Puritans that have been considered (Sibbes, Goodwin and Owen), Lloyd-Jones obviously read very widely in many other Puritan writers. He told the Westminster Conference in 1971 of how he came to make use of their work:[46]

> Brought up as I was in what is called the Welsh Calvinistic Methodist Church, and having become interested in their history, I observed that the leaders of that movement – Daniel Rowland and others – were obviously diligent readers of people called Puritans ... My real interest arose in 1925 when ... I happened to read a new biography of Richard Baxter which had just appeared ... From that time a true and living interest in the Puritans and their works has gripped me, and I am free to confess that my whole ministry has been governed by this.

Thus in *Sons of God* one finds references to John Preston, Thomas Brooks, Thomas Horton, Robert Bruce, William Guthrie, Edward Elton, as well as the three favourites Sibbes, Goodwin and Owen.[47] In the series of sermons on John 1:26, 33 one also finds mention of John Howell, Oliver Cromwell's Puritan chaplain,[48] and John Livingstone, a seventeenth-century preacher.[49]

The influence of a distinctively Welsh Puritanism can also be felt in Lloyd-Jones's theology. His daughter, shortly after his death, reminded her listeners at the Evangelical Library that Lloyd-Jones was supremely a Welshman. He had explored the works of the Methodist fathers of Wales and lectured on both Howell Harris and William Williams. But, as Geoffrey Nuttall reminds us, behind Harris and Williams were the Welsh Puritans Vavasor Powell and Morgan Llwyd.[50] Such men were a great stimulus to Lloyd-Jones although it cannot be said that the eighteenth-century writers were significant theologians. It was

117

the *evangelistic* success of the eighteenth-century revival which attracted Lloyd-Jones at first, leading him in turn to the Puritan tradition which lay behind these men. The stories of Daniel Rowlands, Howell Harris, George Whitefield and the two Wesleys were a constant inspiration. However, among such men only Edwards had any theological eminence.

Lloyd-Jones and his theological forebears

This brief survey of the theological giants whom Lloyd-Jones admired so much brings us to a position where it is helpful to outline what use he made of these predecessors.

Calvin's doctrine of the witness of the Spirit was of little use to Lloyd-Jones who disagreed with the teaching of a non-experiential 'witness of the Spirit'. However, I have suggested above that because faith, for Calvin, was immediately inherently assuring there is a compensating factor. A non-experiential witness that immediately gives rise to assurance is close to becoming an experiential witness! Yet this fact did not help Lloyd-Jones because he disagreed with Calvin's view of immediate assurance as being of the essence of faith. He explicitly criticized the early Protestant reformers for their teaching at this point, and sided with the Westminster Confession: 'a true believer may wait long . . . before he be partaker of it'.[51]

Lloyd-Jones could make no use of these earlier theologians with regard to their teaching concerning the *gifts* of the Spirit. It may be noted that in expounding the views of Sibbes, Goodwin and Owen, little mention has been made of the *gifts* of the Spirit. This is not coincidental; although Owen had written about the gifts of the Spirit, none of the Puritans mentioned so far held that the extraordinary gifts of the Spirit continued. Edwards was also continuing in the Puritan tradition when he wrote, 'I do not expect a restoration of these miraculous gifts in the approaching glorious times of the church, nor do I desire it.'[52] So in this respect Lloyd-Jones seems to have been quite independent of the major theological influences upon him and to have come to his own personal position in the matter.

Lloyd-Jones was, however, in substantial agreement with Richard Sibbes and in almost complete agreement with Thomas Goodwin. As has been seen Goodwin defined the sealing of the

Spirit more sharply and narrowly than Sibbes. Lloyd-Jones took up Goodwin's viewpoint and it is he who is Lloyd-Jones's theological forebear supremely.

Owen's teaching developed in a direction away from that of Goodwin, for he came to believe that the 'sealing of the Spirit' was not a distinct activity of the Spirit but that the 'seal' was the objective presence of the Spirit in the believer. Lloyd-Jones was able to make use of Owen's distinction between mediate and immediate joys imparted by the Spirit but did not wholly agree with Owen's teaching. He reveals an awareness of his position when he says his teaching was maintained by 'Thomas Goodwin, and *to a lesser extent* . . . John Owen'.[53]

In the case of Jonathan Edwards it was not Edwards' explicit teaching concerning Romans 8:16 or the 'baptism with the Spirit' texts which Lloyd-Jones could cite in his support. Rather it was Edwards' more general teaching concerning the experiential 'sense' of spiritual things that Lloyd-Jones delighted in.

In one respect Lloyd-Jones went further than all of these theological forebears, and has a strand of mystical teaching that approximates more to the teaching of George Fox and the early Quakers. It is not surprising that a listener to his early preaching detected both Calvinism and Quakerism.[54] In referring to the debates between Puritans and Quakers, concerning the direct witness of the Spirit, Lloyd-Jones was more sympathetic to the Quakers than to some of the Puritans.[55] Yet he thought the Quakers went too far and that George Fox was too violent in his rejection of the mainstream Puritans.[56]

Finally, it must be remembered that Lloyd-Jones admired those men in history who 'kept their minds open' and 'were not rigid, and set but . . . always ready to listen to new evidence'.[57] 'We are not gramophone records, we are to think originally,' he would say.[58] Talking to ministers he could say, 'There are no popes in Protestantism!' His advice concerning the theological giants of days gone by was: 'Take all you read and masticate it thoroughly. Do not just repeat it as you have received it; deliver it in your own way, let it emerge as part of yourself with your stamp upon it.'[59] In his view of the baptism with the Spirit, he practised what he taught.

Notes

[1]D. M. Lloyd-Jones, *Preaching and Preachers* (London: Hodder and Stoughton, 1971) p. 176.

[2]D. M. Lloyd-Jones, 'Jonathan Edwards and the Crucial Importance of Revival', in *The Puritan Experiment in the New World* (Huntingdon: Westminster Conference, 1977), p. 106.

[3]Lloyd-Jones, 'Jonathan Edwards . . .', p. 104.

[4]*The Works of Jonathan Edwards*, edited by E. Hickman, 2 vols (1834; reprinted Edinburgh: Banner of Truth, 1974), p. xii.

[5]*Ibid.*, vol. 1, p. xiv.

[6]For the place of these works in the history of theology see G. P. Fisher, *History of Christian Doctrine* (Edinburgh, T. & T. Clark, 1908), pp. 394–412.

[7]For the details of Edwards' life, see *The Works of Jonathan Edwards*, vol. 1, pp. xi–cxcvii; P. Miller, *Jonathan Edwards* (New York: William Sloane Associates, 1949 and London: Greenwood Press, 1973); and I. H. Murray, *Jonathan Edwards: A New Biography* (Edinburgh: Banner of Truth, 1987). A succinct outline in E. M. Griffin, *Jonathan Edwards* (Minnesota, University of Minnesota Pamphlets, 1971), summarizes the earlier biographies.

[8]See J. I. Packer, 'Jonathan Edwards and the Theology of Revival', in *Increasing in the Knowledge of God* (London: Puritan and Reformed Studies Conference, 1961), pp. 13–28.

[9]*The Works of Jonathan Edwards*, vol. 2, p. 12.

[10]The excesses of Rev. John Davenport were particularly troublesome. They are related in J. Tracy, *The Great Awakening* (1842, reprinted Edinburgh: Banner of Truth, 1976), ch. 14. Tracy says that Davenport 'embodied in himself and promoted in others, all the unsafe extravagancies into which the revival was running'. In the introduction to the 1898 edition of *The Religious Affections*, Alexander Smellie spoke of the claim to direct revelations and the disparagement of the written Word which troubled the revival movement. (See *Select Works of Jonathan Edwards*, vol. 3 [London: Banner of Truth, 1961], which includes Smellie's introduction. The citation is from p. 11.) The major opponent of the revival was Charles Chauncy (see K. J. Hardman, *The Spiritual Awakeners* [Chicago: Moody Press, 1983], pp. 67, 70, 71).

[11]*Select Works of Jonathan Edwards*, vol. 3, p. 28.

[12]*Ibid.*, p. 30.

[13]*Ibid.*, p. 131.

[14]*Ibid.*, p. 131.

[15]*Ibid.*, pp. 152–153.

[16]*Ibid.*, p. 152.

[17]*Ibid.*, p. 153.

[18]*Ibid.*, p. 153.

[19]*Ibid.*, p. 153.

[20]*Ibid.*, p. 156.

[21]*Ibid.*, p. 165.

[22]*Ibid.*, p. 150.

[23]*Ibid.*, pp. 164–165.

[24]*Ibid.*, p. 164.

[25]*Ibid.*, p. 164.

[26]*Ibid.*, p. 164.

[27]P. Miller, *Jonathan Edwards* (New York: William Sloane Associates, 1949), p. 44. The sermon is found in *The Works of Jonathan Edwards*, vol. 2, pp. 12–17.

[28]*The Works of Jonathan Edwards*, vol. 2, p. 13.

[29]*Ibid.*, p. 14.

[30]*Ibid.*, p. 15.

[31]*Ibid.*, pp. 15–16.

[32]*Select Works of Jonathan Edwards*, vol. 3, p. 17.

[33]P. Miller, *Jonathan Edwards*, p. 37. The letter is quoted in full in I. H. Murray, 'Jonathan Edwards', in *The Banner of Truth*, no. 135 (December 1974), p. 32.

[34]D. M. Lloyd-Jones, *Sons of God*, p. 346.

[35]*I.e.* in conscious experience.

[36]*The Works of Jonathan Edwards*, vol. 1, p. xxiv.

[37]*Ibid.*, p. xxviii.

[38]*Ibid.*, p. xxxv.

[39]*Ibid.*, p. xxxvi.

[40]*Ibid.*, p. xlvii.

[41]*Ibid.*, p. xlvii.

[42]*Ibid.*, p. xlvii.

[43]*Ibid.*, p. xlviii.

[44]For details, see I. H. Murray, *Lloyd-Jones*, pp. 285–287.

[45]D. M. Lloyd-Jones, *The Supernatural in the Practice of Medicine* (London: Christian Medical Fellowship, 1971), p. 10. The allusion is to B. B. Warfield, *Counterfeit Miracles* (1918) reprinted as *Miracles Yesterday and Today, True and False* (Grand Rapids: Eerdmans, 1965).

[46]D. M. Lloyd-Jones, 'Puritanism and Its Origins', in *The Good Fight of Faith* (Huntingdon: Westminster Conference, 1972), p. 72.

[47]D. M. Lloyd-Jones, *Sons of God* (Edinburgh: Banner of Truth, 1973), pp. 315, 321, 333, 339, 342, 344.

[48]D. M. Lloyd-Jones, *The Gospel of John* (sound recording [Barcombe Mills, East Sussex: Martyn Lloyd-Jones Recordings Trust, 1983]), sermon no. 1087.

[49]D. M. Lloyd-Jones, *John* (sound recording), sermon no. 1088.

[50]See G. F. Nuttall, 'The Healing Herb and the Rose of Love: The Piety of Two Welsh Puritans' [Vavasor Powell and Morgan Llwyd], in *Reformation, Conformity and Dissent*, edited by R. B. Knox (London: Epworth, 1977), pp. 154–179. Dr Nuttall's last sentences are: 'William Williams, Pantycelyn, and Howell Harris were indebted to both Powell and Llwyd. And so, therefore, are the Welsh Christians of today.'

[51]D. M. Lloyd-Jones, *John* (sound recording), no. 1083; D. M. Lloyd-Jones, *The Christian Warfare* (Edinburgh: Banner of Truth, 1976), p. 238.

[52]*The Select Works of Jonathan Edwards*, vol. 2, (London: Banner of Truth, 1965), p. 40.

[53]D. M. Lloyd-Jones, *God's Ultimate Purpose* (Edinburgh: Banner of Truth, 1978), p. 249.

[54]I. H. Murray, *Lloyd-Jones*, p. 190.

[55]D. M. Lloyd-Jones, *Sons of God*, p. 307. I do not mean Lloyd-Jones sympathized with Quakerism as a whole. He was too Calvinist for that. But his view of the Spirit leaned that way.

[56]*Ibid.*, p. 307; also sermon on Romans 12:6–8, 18 March 1966.

[57]D. M. Lloyd-Jones, 'Henry Jacob and the First Congregational Church', in *One Steadfast High Intent* (London: Puritan and Reformed Studies Conference, 1966), p. 59.

[58]D. M. Lloyd-Jones, *Preaching and Preachers* (London: Hodder and Stoughton, 1971), p. 181.

[59]*Ibid.*

Part Three

Lloyd-Jones's teaching on the Spirit

7

A preliminary survey

Lloyd-Jones's teaching on the Spirit is the subject of the next four chapters of this book. In this chapter we survey the material which deals with the direct witness of the Spirit, followed in the next chapter by an analysis of the three occasions in his ministry when he preached on Ephesians 1:13, Romans 8:16 and John 1:33. In chapter 9 I seek to pinpoint matters of interpretation and to give an outline of his teaching; an outline which draws on all his mature expositions. Then in chapter 10 I shall indicate how Lloyd-Jones's teaching on this subject coheres with other aspects of his teaching in general.

The years 1927–1954

The only published materials available for an assessment of Lloyd-Jones's teaching from 1927 to 1938 are the twenty-one sermons published in 1983 as *Evangelistic Sermons at Aberavon*. Since there is little mention of a post-conversion 'sealing of the Spirit' in these sermons they are largely outside the area of our interest. What is worth noting, however, is that the emphasis of the early sermons is on the work of the Spirit, rather than on the objective work of Christ. In the earliest of the twenty-one sermons[1] there is no mention of the death of Jesus at all. Conversion is thought of as 'submitting to Jesus' power'.[2] There is mention of the subjective aspect of conversion but not of the objective basis of faith. In coming to Christ the convert will say 'I will *feel*, not pretend, that I am helpless'.[3] Referring to new converts in his congregation Lloyd-Jones would comment:

> Look at some of these men here. You know how they once were. See the change. What has done it? The power of God and nothing else. Ask them how it happened. They cannot tell you. They felt a power dealing with them and shaking them and changing them. You feel you are a desperate case. So were we all, but with God 'All things are possible'. He can change you and recreate you.[4]

This was typical of Lloyd-Jones's preaching at this stage of his life. His evangelistic preaching focused more on regeneration than on the atonement.

In another sermon, while there is no mention of atonement, there is mention of the Spirit's direct voice. 'At some time or other the Spirit of God visits each one of us and moves us and disturbs us.' 'We become conscious of a power and a presence that we have never felt before. We become melted and softened for the time being.' 'What is the meaning of such an experience? It is the voice of God calling us from sin to salvation.'[5] It is clear that this is what Lloyd-Jones would later call the 'Spirit of bondage', the work of the Spirit prior to faith, leading men to faith.

It was this particular combination of Calvinism and the experiential note that led an early listener to consider Lloyd-Jones a combination of a Quaker and a Calvinist. A change came in 1929, however, when he was challenged about the lack of centrality of the atonement in his preaching. Thereafter, while the experiential element continued, the atonement also played a major part in his thinking and preaching.[6]

In a sermon written in about 1931 we have what is (among works published to date) the first reference to the baptism of the Spirit in Lloyd-Jones's writings. 'If only we believe Christ and trust ourselves to Him', says Lloyd-Jones, 'we shall be baptized with the Spirit and clothed with His power.'[7] The point is not developed and is capable of more than one interpretation.

In some ways the years 1938–1946 form a distinct period in the ministry of Lloyd-Jones. In 1938 the pressures of the work at Sandfields, Aberavon, were becoming increasingly arduous. Lloyd-Jones was finding his ministry there too great a strain,[8] so he resigned from the pastorate of Sandfields and for some months his future was uncertain.[9] He then joined Dr G. Campbell-Morgan at Westminster Chapel initially on an open-ended basis. After a somewhat unsettled period of seven months, other possible avenues of service were left aside and he continued at Westminster Chapel. Then in September 1939 the second world war broke out and, as Westminster Chapel was in the heart of London, it seemed that his ministry was once again uncertain. Lloyd-Jones was convinced that the German bombing would not destroy Westminster Chapel[10] yet he did not give himself to lengthy series of sermons. After the war had ended in 1945 Lloyd-Jones commenced his first major series of sermons, the exposition of 2 Peter, during October 1946 to March 1947.

Apart from some minor single sermons,[11] Lloyd-Jones's first major published work was a series of sermons under the heading *Why Does God Allow War?* published in 1939.[12] Most of the book is again unrelated to our particular theme. The priority of repentance over blessing is stressed in the first sermon; the second points out the danger of a religion which is no more than an 'intellectual hobby' and is 'purely objective'.[13] Lloyd-Jones's initial interest in Barth is apparent for Barth's work is described as a 'theological revival'.[14] Though the Holy Spirit is mentioned in the fifth sermon as one who 'gives us the assurance of salvation, testifying with our spirits that we are children of God, and therefore heirs and joint-heirs with Christ', the point is not developed.[15]

Other single sermons from this period were printed in the *Westminster Record*. In five of them that I have had access to[16] there is scarcely any mention of the Holy Spirit. Only in *Gospel Power* (preached in the late 1930s but unpublished till 1940) is there mention of the Spirit's work. This sermon contains, however, an interesting couple of sentences concerning conversion. 'I remember', says Lloyd-Jones, 'the ancient discussion that used to occupy time and attention in the Sunday School and Bible Class, as to whether conversion was sudden or gradual; there were always the two sides. But I would point out that the wrong question was being discussed. The question was not so much whether conversion was sudden or gradual. The vital question surely is, "Have you been converted"'?[17] In this remark Lloyd-Jones reveals that the *speed* at which conversion may take place was not a matter of any interest to him. He believed that conversion was a process; he also believed that that process could take place so swiftly as to be a sudden event. He could analyse the 'steps' in conversion[18] yet at the same time he could believe in a virtually instantaneous conversion.

In 1939 Lloyd-Jones spoke at an International Conference of Evangelical Students, convened by the Inter-Varsity Fellowship.[19] One particular address, 'Christ our Sanctification' (published in the report of the conference and then in 1948 in a separate booklet), reveals several aspects of Lloyd-Jones's views at this time. The main theme of the address concerns sanctification; it criticizes the idea that sanctification is an 'experience' to be received by faith on an occasion subsequent to conversion.[20]

The address also reveals Lloyd-Jones's concern with the *ordo salutis* ('order of salvation', the ordering of the various elements in personal salvation), which will be of interest to us later in this study. Some rather contradictory statements concerning the *ordo salutis* may be gathered. 'We cannot determine the exact order or sequence but we know that regeneration and justification go together,' he said in 1939.[21] In 1967 he urges that regeneration is prior to faith in the *ordo salutis*.[22] In 1957 he could argue that justification takes place in the life of one who is ungodly.[23] These statements are not easily harmonized. However, when it is realized that in Lloyd-Jones's view regeneration is a *process* (no matter how short a space of time it may take) which leads to faith and yet full regeneration takes place through faith, then his seeming contradictions may be harmonized. The whole subject of the *ordo salutis* is one which may lead to the most subtle and hair-splitting distinctions. It was not often alluded to by Lloyd-Jones and was rejected altogether by G. C. Berkouwer.[24] One point, however, of Lloyd-Jones's teaching in 1939 was to change. In his address to students in that year he interpreted Acts 19:2 by dismissing the AV ('since ye believed') and referring to the RSV ('when ye believed'). Later, in 1955, he still recommended the RSV translation but did not think it settled the matter of the timing of the receiving of the Spirit. 'I confess that at one time I myself fell into error on the matter,' he says. 'A little booklet bearing my name, entitled "Christ our Sanctification", includes the argument that if we but follow the RSV instead of the AV we shall see that there is no time interval between the believing and the sealing. I confess my error ... I was mistaken at that time with regard to the "sealing".'[25]

In 1942 Lloyd-Jones's second book was published, *The Plight of Man and the Power of God*.[26] This was a transcription of lectures given in Edinburgh in the early years of the second world war. It focuses on the biblical teaching concerning people and sin, and the relevance of the Christian message for all in such a plight. The Spirit is mentioned only passingly.

It was also at about this time that an address on evangelistic methods was given to a meeting of the 'Crusaders' Union' (an organisation for evangelism among young people). It was published by the Crusaders' Union in 1942, although the 1949 edition published by the Inter-Varsity Fellowship is better known.[27]

In this address Lloyd-Jones's admiration of Jonathan Edwards is apparent:

> There are some who seem to think that evangelistic work in Great Britain was unknown until Moody came to this country ... Go back to the eighteenth century. Go back to the time of the Puritans, and even farther back to the Protestant Reformation. And go back even beyond that, and study the history of those groups of Evangelical people who lived on the Continent at the time when Roman Catholicism held supreme sway ... Go right back to the time of the Early Fathers who held Evangelical ideas.

Then Lloyd-Jones mentions his great hero:

> I would commend to you a very thorough study of that great American divine, Jonathan Edwards. It was a great revelation to me to discover that a man who preached in the way he did could be honoured of God as he was, and could have such great results in his ministry.[28]

In this address Lloyd-Jones emphasizes the need of the Spirit's work in evangelism. Two principles concerning the Spirit's work are mentioned.[29] Firstly, 'The only power that can really do this work is the Holy Spirit ...', and secondly, 'The one and only medium through which the Holy Spirit works is the Word of God.' According to Lloyd-Jones, on the day of

Pentecost Peter expounded the Scriptures. Likewise the apostle Paul 'reasoned out of the Scriptures'. 'The medium which is used by the Holy Spirit is the truth.'

In the decade following the close of World War 2, Lloyd-Jones's ministry began to be exceedingly influential. The move from Wales to London put him at the centre of a wide sphere of influence. Major series of sermons were preached at Westminster Chapel, the most notable of which were the sixty sermons on the Sermon on the Mount, sermons on Habakkuk, eleven sermons on Psalm 73, and the series on Spiritual Depression. All of these were published subsequently. Yet the longest series (Ephesians; Romans; Acts 1–8; John 1–4) had not yet commenced. It was only in the closing fourteen years of his work at Westminster Chapel that these lengthy series were attempted. At this stage (1946–1954) we still find relatively little by way of detailed exposition of the baptism with the Spirit.

In the 1930s Lloyd-Jones came into increasing contact with the English (as opposed to the Welsh) religious scene, and was very slowly drawn into English religious life. His first impression of the English-speaking Inter-Varsity Fellowship was one of dislike of their anti-intellectualism.[30] Because he felt that the major problem was doctrinal indifference he spent much of his time seeking to persuade evangelicals to think through their faith doctrinally. Later, however, he came to believe that the situation had changed and intellectual pride and self-confidence had become the major snare of British evangelicalism. Lloyd-Jones's teaching reacts to these trends. In the early years of his ministry he was countering anti-intellectualism. But in the 1960s and the 1970s he was countering 'dead orthodoxy'. His *major* emphasis on the Spirit's baptism seemed to commence in the 1950s (although he had held his view from the earliest days of his theological thinking). He moved from an interest in apologetics to an interest in the direct work of the Spirit. In 1952 he could report: 'For very many years now, although I would not for a moment have chosen such a course for myself, a great deal of my time has been taken up with the task of maintaining and defending the evangelical faith.'[31]

Among the series of sermons on 2 Peter there is one sermon which deals with 'Assurance of Salvation'. Here we find the characteristic teaching of Lloyd-Jones concerning the Spirit's witness. Towards the end of the sermon he asks how certainty of salvation is to be obtained. The primary way is to look directly to Jesus Christ. A second way is to fill out one's faith. 'The more we do the work of the Lord and practise the Christian life, the more certain we are of the Lord.'[32] Then comes a third mode of assurance: 'We do everything we can to please Him and to fill out our faith, as we do so the Holy Spirit will "testify with our spirit that we are children of God".'[33]

No significant mention of the Spirit is found in *The Mirage Shall Become a Pool*[34] or in *Truth Unchanged Unchanging*[35] or *Faith on Trial*.[36]

In the sermons on Matthew 5–7 no occasion arose when it was appropriate to mention the baptism with the Spirit. In the published version[37] one finds occasional mention of the direct leading of the Spirit in guidance,[38] the danger of counterfeit experiences,[39] and of over-interest in phenomena such as elated feelings and physical healings.[40] D. L. Moody's experience of the 'baptism of the Spirit' is mentioned[41] but not by that name and without receiving any detailed exposition. The 'preparationism' of Lloyd-Jones is seen in his exposition of Matthew 5:3–4 especially.[42] However his later preparationist view of Romans 7:14–25 is not found here. At this stage in his ministry (1950–52) he regards the 'wretched man' of Romans 7:14–25 as a Christian.[43] Later he would change his mind.[44]

In preaching on Habakkuk he tells us that 'God sometimes answers directly in our spirits'.[45] In the context of his sermon Lloyd-Jones is speaking about prayer. An answer may come, he maintains, by God's speaking directly.

The eleven sermons on Psalm 73, preached between October 1953 and January 1954, contain little of relevance to this work.

The sermons on *Spiritual Depression*, preached during 1954 included a sermon on Romans 8:15–16, preached on the morning of 28 March and given the title 'The Spirit of Bondage'. These two verses were the subject of fifteen sermons in the Romans series during November 1960 to March 1961, and Lloyd-Jones's special interest in them was evident in the 1954 sermon: 'No greater words than these have ever been written.'[46] A careful study of this sermon, however, reveals that Lloyd-Jones did not interpret Paul's words in precisely the same way as he would do in the more detailed series over six years later. He speaks of a Christian having a 'spirit of bondage',[47] and denies that this is from God: 'God hath not given us a spirit of bondage.'[48] Accordingly the word 'Spirit' is not given a capital 'S'. In these respects he either changed his views or he was merely 'using' Romans 8:15–16 to address himself to one aspect of spiritual depression. Later he would deny that the *Christian* ever has a 'spirit of bondage'. He would regard the 'Spirit of bondage' as a preliminary to full regeneration. He would give the word 'Spirit' a capital 'S' because he believed the phrase alluded to the work of the Holy Spirit.[49]

Similarly the exposition of the phrase 'Spirit of adoption' falls short of the meaning that Lloyd-Jones gave it in his later exposition. In all probability Lloyd-Jones was only 'using' Romans 8:15–16, something he could do and concerning which at least one reviewer complained.[50] Evidence has already been presented to suggest that Lloyd-Jones held to a richer exposition of Romans 8:15–16 long before 1954 when this particular sermon was preached.

The years 1954–1968

The year 1954 saw the beginning of the series on Ephesians, the second longest exposition of a complete book of the Bible that Lloyd-Jones ever gave (the longest was Romans). On return from his summer recess (mid-July to mid-September) he commenced the series which was to continue until July 1962 with occasional breaks during Christmas, Easter and summer, and with occasional digressions on other themes.[51] This mammoth series was printed in eight volumes during 1972–1982.[52] Not all the sermons that were preached, however, are to be found in the published version. In addition, a further thirty-two sermons of the Ephesians series may be found in *Westminster Records* or on cassette tape. It is in these sources that we have Lloyd-Jones's teaching on the direct witness of the Spirit in its fullest form. We find five sermons on Ephesians 1:13,[53] a sermon on Ephesians 2:19 which interestingly alludes to the Christian's 'passport or birth certificate', the sealing of the Spirit.[54] Then in connection with Ephesians 3:16–19 there are fifteen sermons of 'Puritan mysticism'.[55] The volume on Ephesians 4:1–16 contains a sermon on revival.[56] In the next volume a sermon on Ephesians

132

4:30 again contains comments on the relationship of the sealing of the Spirit and the grieving of the Spirit.[57] The volume dealing with marriage, home and work commences with five sermons on being 'full of the Spirit' which greatly clarify Lloyd-Jones's view of the differences between various aspects of the Spirit's work.[58] (Four sermons were omitted from the published version, which is unfortunate because they contain the only full statement of the *musical* aspects of the charismatic dimension of church life).[59]

The volume on Ephesians 6:10–13 contains five sermons on assurance and on quenching the Spirit.[60] The eighth and final volume (on Ephesians 6:10–20, especially 6:14–20) contains little on our theme. However the sermon 'Praying in the Spirit' is of interest.[61]

One year after the commencement of the Sunday morning series on Ephesians, Lloyd-Jones began a series of expositions of the epistle to the Romans on Friday evenings. He tells us[62] that from at least 1943 he had been held up by the feeling that he did not really understand Romans 6. While preaching the series on 'Spiritual Depression' during 1954 he felt he had come to a satisfactory understanding of that chapter. So after the summer break of 1955 he commenced to preach on Romans from October to May each year, taking short breaks at Christmas and Easter. He continued this way until February 1968 when sudden illness precipitated his abrupt resignation from the pastorate of Westminster Chapel. He had reached Romans 14:17. During the years 1970–1975 six volumes of these sermons appeared in print (covering Romans 3:21 – 8:39), and a seventh volume (covering Romans 1:1–32) was published in 1985.[63] I have some personal notes on the sermons on Romans 2:1 – 3:20 and 9:1 – 14:17 in my files, and much of this material is available on tape.[64]

There are, however, a number of sermons on the 'baptism of the Spirit' to be found in the published material. In addition to the significant sermon on Romans 5:5 there are fifteen sermons on Romans 8:15–16. The still unpublished sermons on Romans 9:1 – 14:17 do not contain any comparable treatment of the baptism of the Spirit. What are of interest are the sermons on Romans 12 where once again the charismatic dimension of the church is very evident, and material is presented which (like the

133

unpublished sermons on Ephesians 5:19–20) reveals that Lloyd-Jones's view of the charismatic life of the church was closer to Pentecostalism than to traditional Reformed church life.[65] Lloyd-Jones never made any attempt, however, to introduce changes in the direction of a Pentecostal style of worship into the Sunday Services at Westminster Chapel.

After the Ephesians series had finished in July 1962, and on returning from his summer break (July–September), Lloyd-Jones commenced a new series of sermons on John's Gospel in October 1962. This series was to continue until February 1968 when it was abruptly terminated by Lloyd-Jones's illness. He had by this time reached John 4:30. Although these sermons have never been published, 184 of them are available from the Martyn Lloyd-Jones Recordings Trust in Britain.[66] The majority of these sermons are strongly experiential in flavour; the mystical element in Lloyd-Jones's thinking reached its peak in this series. Even visual appearances of Jesus to the believer are not excluded[67] (sermon 1178, following the enumeration of the Lloyd-Jones recordings trust). These sermons contain what must surely be the richest exposition of the baptism with the Spirit, from a Puritan viewpoint,[68] since the days of Thomas Goodwin's sermons on Ephesians 1:13.

Our main concern will be with the 24 sermons[69] which deal fully with the more restricted topic of the direct witness of the Spirit. They include a sermon entitled 'What Baptism Did You Receive?', six sermons entitled 'The Baptism of the Spirit', two entitled 'The Gifts of the Spirit', five entitled 'Testing the Spirits', one entitled 'The Gift of Tongues', three entitled 'Seeking Baptism in the Spirit'. These sermons, along with those on Ephesians 1:13 and Romans 8:15–16 constitute the fullest exposition of Lloyd-Jones's teaching on these themes. Alongside the three major series of sermons being preached during 1954 to 1968, a steady flow of other sermonic material continued to come from Lloyd-Jones, much of which is not of major importance for our particular purpose.[70] A series of nine evangelistic sermons on Galatians 6:14, and another similar series of eleven sermons on 2 Timothy 1:12 were published in 1986.[71]

Other works during this period contain significant material on the work of the Spirit. In 1957 Lloyd-Jones gave a series of three lectures to students in Canada under the heading of 'Authority'.

The third, on the 'Authority of the Holy Spirit', contains a statement of Lloyd-Jones's view of the baptism of the Spirit in which Romans 8:15–16, 2 Corinthians 1:22 and Ephesians 1:13–14 are briefly expounded.[72]

In 1959 Lloyd-Jones broke off from his Ephesians series to preach a series of sermons on revival in order to mark the centenary of the 1859 revival.[73]

He continued this theme at the Puritan and Reformed Studies Conference in December 1959 by giving a lecture on 'Revival – An Historical and Theological Survey'.[74]

The following year (1960), Lloyd-Jones, as was his custom, again gave the closing address at the Puritan and Reformed Studies Conference. His theme was 'Knowledge – False and True'. The sermon, an exposition of 1 Corinthians 8:1–3, is replete with historical allusions to the charismatic experiences of church history. He evidently felt it necessary to call the conference to an experiential emphasis in the closing address.[75]

Seven years later, again at the Puritan and Reformed Studies Conference, Lloyd-Jones spoke on the theme of 'Sandemanianism'. Robert Sandeman was an eighteenth-century Scotsman who taught what Lloyd-Jones thought was a very dry and non-experiential view of Christian faith. The opening words of this lecture shares his conviction that 'Sandemanianism' was becoming a major threat in evangelical life. 'I have had an increasing conviction', he said, 'that it is in many ways the most urgent matter for us to consider at the present time.'[76] His closing words echo the same conviction: 'Is Sandemanianism merely a matter of antiquarian or historical interest, or is it our major problem today – Calvinists as well as Arminians?'[77]

The years 1968–1981

As we have seen, Lloyd-Jones retired from his pastoral ministry at Westminster Chapel in February 1968. His retirement was precipitated by an illness which required a sudden operation. He soon recovered from the illness and made a complete surgical recovery. His convalescence went on till the time of his summer break (July–September) but he did not return in October as he had done every previous year since 1939.

His years of retirement, however, were productive ones. He

went on preaching almost every week and chairing the Westminster Fraternal Meetings on the first Monday of the month, speaking at the Puritan and Reformed Studies Conferences of 1968 and 1969, and then (after the conference had been reorganized as the Westminster Conference) every year from 1971 to 1978. He also gave himself to the task of publishing what he had been preaching in earlier years. *Atonement and Justification* (1970) was the first of many volumes that have been published under Lloyd-Jones's name since that date.

Many of the lectures and addresses published during these years are not of particular relevance to us.[78] Others, however, continued to focus on the topic of great interest to Lloyd-Jones, that of the power of the Holy Spirit. Shortly after his retirement he did something that he had refrained from doing through his four decades of preaching. He accepted the opportunity to lecture on preaching. His lecture series at Westminster Theological College, USA, during the spring of 1969, was published under the title *Preaching and Preachers* in 1971. The last lecture was given over to the topic of the power of the Spirit in preaching.[79]

In his retirement years Lloyd-Jones continued to emphasize the need of an experiential side to the Christian life. His address on 'William Williams and Welsh Calvinistic Methodism, was virtually a definitive statement of his position on these matters.[80] The combination of the two words 'Calvinistic' and 'Methodism' perfectly expressed his background and the source of his distinctive view of the Spirit. Likewise the address on Howell Harris in 1973[81] was a restatement of his view of the baptism of the Spirit, as was the lecture on Jonathan Edwards in 1976.[82] His lecture on 'Preaching' at the Westminster Conference on the theme of 'Anglican and Puritan Thinking' contained many allusions to the need of the Spirit's power.[83]

Several of Lloyd-Jones's addresses at the Puritan and Westminster Conferences compress much of his thinking into a short space. 'Puritanism and Its Origins' is his definitive statement concerning Puritanism and how he came to be influenced by it. 'Revival: An Historical and Theological Survey' was perhaps his most definitive statement concerning revival. 'Ecclesiola in Ecclesia' is possibly his most concise statement concerning his view of the church. His address on 'Preaching' gave his final statement on what he called 'a climax in any consideration of the Puritan view of worship and of the conduct of the Christian church'. Four addresses bring out his view of experience and the Holy Spirit: 'Knowledge – False and True', 'Sandemanianism', 'William Williams and Welsh Calvinistic Methodism' and 'Howell Harris and Revival'. Anyone wishing to understand the teaching of Lloyd-Jones could scarcely do better than to begin with these addresses, especially his consideration of 'William Williams and Welsh Calvinistic Methodism', which in the compass of one address contains many of the themes which were central in his thinking.[84]

Lloyd-Jones was still preaching in the spring of 1980 in his 81st year, but a visit to Charing Cross Hospital in May of that year revealed that his illness demanded such severe treatment that further preaching would be impossible. By the following February he knew that his life was drawing to a close. He died on 1 March 1981, St David's day, a day most appropriate in the career of a nationalistically-minded Welshman.[85]

Notes

[1]D. M. Lloyd-Jones, *Evangelistic Sermons at Aberavon* (Edinburgh: Banner of Truth, 1983), pp. 1–51, 65–77.

[2]*Ibid.*, p. 11.

[3]*Ibid.*, p. 7.

[4]*Ibid.*, p. 11.

[5]*Ibid.*, p. 26.

[6]I. H. Murray, *David Martyn Lloyd-Jones* (Edinburgh: Banner of Truth, 1982), pp. 190–191.

[7]D. M. Lloyd-Jones, *Evangelistic Sermons at Averavon*, p. 72.

[8]See I. H. Murray, *op, cit.*, p. 331.

[9]*Ibid.*, chs. 16, 17.

[10]D. M. Lloyd-Jones, *Westminster Chapel 1865–1965: Centenary Address* (London: Westminster Chapel, 1965), p. 17.

[11]I leave aside 'The Shunammite Woman', a sermon on 2 Kings 4:8, printed in the *Westminster Record*, the magazine of Westminster Chapel, in December 1938. No doubt other single sermons had been reported.

[12]D. M. Lloyd-Jones, *Why Does God Allow War?* (London: Hodder and Stoughton, 1939). Lloyd-Jones had also contributed to C. B. Perry, *Bacterial Endocarditis* (Bristol: John Wright, 1936), a scientific report entitled 'An Experimental Study in Malignant Carditis' (pp. 111–137).

[13]D. M. Lloyd-Jones, *Why Does God Allow War?* p. 40.

[14]*Ibid.*, p. 97.

[15]*Ibid.*, pp. 103–104.

[16]I refer to 'A Little Maid's Testimony', 2 Kings 5:1–3 (*Westminster Record*, December 1940), 'Conquest of the Fear of Death', Matthew 10:28 (*Westminster*

Record, October–December 1975; originally preached on 14 July 1940), 'The Divine Wisdom', James 1:5–8 (*Westminster Record*, July 1940), 'The Nature of Sin', Numbers 11:4–6 (*Westminster Record*, August 1941), 'Gospel Power', Acts 9:32–35 (*Westminster Record*, April 1940, reprinted in *Westminster Record*, August 1976).

[17]*Westminster Record*, August 1976, p. 96.

[18]See the tenth and twelfth sermons in D. M. Lloyd-Jones, *Evangelistic Sermons at Aberavon.*

[19]Murray, *Lloyd-Jones*, p. 375.

[20]D. M. Lloyd-Jones, *Christ our Sanctification* (London: IVF, 1948), p. 14.

[21]*Ibid.*, p. 10.

[22]D. M. Lloyd-Jones, 'Sandemanianism' in *Profitable for Doctrine and Reproof* (London: Puritan and Reformed Studies Conference, 1968), p. 64.

[23]D. M. Lloyd-Jones, *Romans: An Exposition of Chapters 3:20–4:25; Atonement and Justification* (Edinburgh: Banner of Truth, 1970), pp. 171–173.

[24]G. C. Berkouwer, *Faith and Justification* (Grand Rapids: Eerdmans, 1954), ch. 2.

[25]D. M. Lloyd-Jones, *God's Ultimate Purpose: An Exposition of Ephesians 1:1–23* (Edinburgh: Banner of Truth, 1978), p. 252.

[26]D. M. Lloyd-Jones, *The Plight of Man and the Power of God* (London: Hodder and Stoughton, 1942).

[27]D. M. Lloyd-Jones, *The Presentation of the Gospel* (London: IVF, 1949).

[28]This is a reference to the fact that in his early years Edwards would read from a manuscript, holding it in one hand and a candle in the other. Lloyd-Jones held that such a style was crippling. (I have access only to an unpaginated transcript of this work and therefore cannot cite the page number of the original.)

[29]Other principles are mentioned but they do not directly concern the work of the Spirit.

[30]This is recorded in I. H. Murray, *Lloyd-Jones*, pp. 293, 296, 297, 366f., 375. I recall occasions in the Westminster fraternal in London when Lloyd-Jones would mention his first visit to the IVF conference at Swanwick in 1935: 'It was a conference suitable for washerwomen!' he would say. In the 1970s, however, he would complain that the major problem of evangelicalism was no longer anti-intellectualism but intellectual pride.

[31]D. M. Lloyd-Jones, *Maintaining the Evangelical Faith Today* (London: IVF, 1968 [a different format but not a different text compared to the original 1952 edition]), p. 3.

[32]D. M. Lloyd-Jones, *Expository Sermons on 2 Peter* (Edinburgh: Banner of Truth, 1983), pp. 39–40.

[33]*Ibid.*, p. 40.

[34]D. M. Lloyd-Jones, *The Mirage Shall Become a Pool* (Welwyn: Evangelical Press, 1965).

[35]D. M. Lloyd-Jones, *Truth Unchanged Unchanging* (London: James Clarke, 1951).

[36]D. M. Lloyd-Jones, *Faith on Trial* (London: IVF, 1965; reprinted in *Faith Tried and Triumphant* [Leicester: IVP, 1987]).

[37]D. M. Lloyd-Jones, *Studies in the Sermon on the Mount*, 2 vols. (London: IVF, 1959–60 [combined volume with same pagination, Grand Rapids: Eerdmans, 1971]).

[38]*Ibid.*, vol. 1, p. 9; *ibid.*, vol. 2, p. 19.

[39]*Ibid.*, vol. 1, p. 10.

[40]*Ibid.*, vol. 2, p. 285.

[41]*Ibid.*, pp. 31–32.

[42]*Ibid.*, vol. 1, chs. 4–5.

[43]*Ibid.*, p. 57.

[44]See D. M. Lloyd-Jones, *Romans: An Exposition of Chapter 7:1 – 8:4, The Law: Its Function and Limits* (Edinburgh: Banner of Truth, 1973), *passim.*

[45]D. M. Lloyd-Jones, *From Fear to Faith* (London: IVF, 1953; reprinted in *Faith Tried and Triumphant* [Leicester: IVP, 1987]), p. 33.

[46]D. M. Lloyd-Jones, *Spiritual Depression: its Causes and Cure* (London: Pickering and Inglis, 1965), p. 165.

[47]*Ibid.*, p. 167.

[48]*Ibid.*, p. 167. The words are attributed to the epistle to the Galatians. Although some reference to 'bondage' is made in Galatians (4:24; 5:1), Lloyd-Jones was clearly quoting from memory at this point in the sermon (of which chapter 12 of *Spiritual Depression* is an almost word-for-word transcript) and conflated the concerns of the epistle to the Galatians with the wording of 2 Timothy 1:7 and Romans 8:15.

[49]See D. M. Lloyd-Jones, *Romans: An Exposition of Chapter 8:5–17, Sons of God* (Edinburgh: Banner of Truth, 1974), chs. 16–30.

[50]*E.g.* A. T. Lincoln, Review of *Life in the Spirit in Marriage, Home and Work*, in *Westminster Theological Journal*, vol. 39 (1976), p. 146.

[51]The longest digression was in the sermons on Revival, during 1959. These have now been published in D. M. Lloyd-Jones, *Revival* (Basingstoke: Marshall Pickering, 1986).

[52]D. M. Lloyd-Jones, *God's Ultimate Purpose: An Exposition of Ephesians 1:1 to 23* (Edinburgh: Banner of Truth, 1978); *God's Way of Reconciliation: An Exposition of Ephesians 2:1 to 22* (Edinburgh: Banner of Truth, 1979 [an earlier edition was published by Evangelical Press in 1972]); *The Unsearchable Riches of Christ: An Exposition of Ephesians 3:1 to 21* (Edinburgh: Banner of Truth, 1979); *Christian Unity: An Exposition of Ephesians 4:1 to 16* (Edinburgh: Banner of Truth, 1980); *Darkness and Light: An Exposition of Ephesians 4:17–5:17* (Edinburgh: Banner of Truth, 1982); *Life in the Spirit in Marriage, Home and Work: An Exposition of Ephesians 5:18 to 6:9* (Edinburgh: Banner of Truth, 1974); *The Christian Warfare: An Exposition of Ephesians 6:10 to 13* (Edinburgh: Banner of Truth, 1976); *The Christian Soldier: An Exposition of Ephesians 6:10 to 20* (Edinburgh: Banner of Truth, 1977).

[53]D. M. Lloyd-Jones, *God's Ultimate Purpose*, chs. 21–25.

[54]D. M. Lloyd-Jones, *God's Way of Reconciliation*, pp. 378–379.

[55]D. M. Lloyd-Jones, *Unsearchable Riches . . .* , chs. 9–23.

[56]D. M. Lloyd-Jones, *Christian Unity*, ch. 6.

[57]D. M. Lloyd-Jones, *Darkness and Light*, ch. 21.

[58]D. M. Lloyd-Jones, *Life in the Spirit . . .* , chs. 1–5.

[59]Lloyd-Jones had a large following among Scottish Presbyterians who sang only biblical psalms in worship. His sermons on Ephesians 5:19–20 would have been offensive to such readers, for they contained criticisms of the psalm-only viewpoint. Probably for this reason they were omitted in the published form. Yet they are illuminating in that they reveal Lloyd-Jones's views concerning New Testament worship. However, the tradition at Westminster Chapel was far removed *in practice* from the charismatic worship envisaged in the sermons on Ephesians 5:19–20. M. C. Ramsay read these sermons in the *Westminster Record* and sought to refute them (and two other hymn-singing writers) in *Psalms Only* (Sydney: Presbyterian Church of East Australia, 1971).

[60]D. M. Lloyd-Jones, *The Christian Warfare*, chs. 16–20.

[61]D. M. Lloyd-Jones, *The Christian Soldier*, ch. 25.

62D. M. Lloyd-Jones, *Romans: An Exposition of Chapter 6, The New Man* (London: Banner of Truth, 1972), p. xi.

63D. M. Lloyd-Jones, *Romans*, 6 vols. (London and Edinburgh: Banner of Truth, 1970–1975). The sub-titles are *Atonement and Justification* (Romans 3:20–4:25); *Assurance* (Romans 5:1–21); *The New Man* (Romans: 6:1–23); *The Law: Its Functions and Limits* (Romans 7:1–8:4); *The Sons of God* (Romans: 8:5–17); *The Final Perseverance of the Saints* (Romans 8:17–39). The seventh, published in 1985, is *The Gospel of God* (Romans 1:1–32), by the same publishers. These works will be referred to in abbreviated form by their sub-titles.

64See D. M. Lloyd-Jones, *The Letter to the Romans* (sound recordings [Barcombe Mills, East Sussex: Martyn Lloyd-Jones Recordings Trust, 1983]), sermons 3032–3048 have not been published in *printed* form. Two sermons are omitted from *The Gospel of God*.

65See D. M. Lloyd-Jones, *The Letter to the Romans* (sound recording), sermons 3318–3319.

66D. M. Lloyd-Jones *The Gospel of John* (sound recordings [Barcombe Mills, East Sussex: Martyn Lloyd-Jones Recording Trust, 1983]), sermons 1001–1184.

67*Ibid.*, sermon 1178.

68By 'a Puritan viewpoint' I refer to the tradition which is characteristic of Thomas Goodwin. It is not the only Puritan view.

69D. M. Lloyd-Jones, *John* (sound recordings), sermons 1082–1105.

70*I.e.* 'Stock-taking', a sermon on 2 Corinthians 13:5, in *Westminster Record*, February 1957; *Sound an Alarm*, a sermon preached in Cardiff in 1957 (London: Westminster Chapel, 1957); 'A New Heaven and a New Earth', a sermon on Revelations 21:1, *Westminster Record*, January 1959; various medical addresses reprinted in *The Doctor Himself* (London: Christian Medical Fellowship, 1982); 'A Christmas Message', a sermon on John 1:17, *Westminster Record*, December 1958; several addresses at the Puritan and Reformed Studies Conference, 'Puritan Perplexities, Some Lessons From 1640–1662', in *Faith and a Good Conscience* (London: Puritan and Reformed Studies Conference, 1963), pp. 64–80; 'John Owen on Schism', in *Diversity in Unity* (London: Puritan and Reformed Studies Conference, 1964), pp. 59–80; 'John Calvin and George Whitefield', in *Able Ministers of the New Testament* (London: Puritan and Reformed Studies Conference, 1965), pp. 75–96; 'Ecclesiola in Ecclesia', in *Approaches to Reformation of the Church* (London: Puritan and Reformed Studies Conference, 1966), pp. 57–72; 'Henry Jacob and the First Congregational Church', in *One Steadfast High Intent* (London: Puritan and Reformed Studies Conference, 1967), pp. 56–72; the lecture in 1962 at the Evangelical Library, *1662–1962 – From Puritanism to Nonconformity* ((London: Evangelical Library, 1962); two addresses on the nature of the church given in 1962, see *The Basis of Christian Unity: An Exposition of John 17 and Ephesians 4* (London: IVF, 1962); 'Weight of Glory', a sermon on 2 Corinthians 4: 17–18, *The Evangelical Magazine of Wales*, April 1981,); the address at the British Evangelical Council annual meeting celebrating the Reformation events of 1517, see *Luther and His Message for Today* (Welwyn: Evangelical Press, 1968).

71D. M. Lloyd-Jones, *The Cross: God's Way of Salvation*, ed. C. Catherwood (Eastbourne: Kingsway 1986); D. M. Lloyd-Jones, *I Am Not Ashamed: Advice to Timothy*, ed. C. Catherwood (London: Hodder and Stoughton, 1986).

72D. M. Lloyd-Jones, *Authority* (London: IVP, 1958).

73D. M. Lloyd-Jones, *Revival* (sound recordings [Barcombe Mills, East Sussex: Martyn Lloyd-Jones Recordings Trust, 1983]). These are two albums each with eight cassettes.

74Published in *How Shall They Hear?* (London: Puritan and Reformed Studies Conference, 1960), pp. 38–56.

[75]Published in *Increasing in the Knowledge of God* (London: Puritan and Reformed Studies Conference, 1961), pp. 47–63.

[76]Published in *Profitable for Doctrine and Reproof* (London: Puritan and Reformed Studies Conference, 1968), pp. 54–71.

[77]*Ibid.*, p. 71.

[78]*E.g.* the addresses at the British Evangelical Council meeting in 1968; see *What is the Church?* (London: British Evangelical Council, 1969); various addresses to medical students or to doctors (see *Will The Hospital Replace The Church?* [London: Christian Medical Fellowship, 1968]; *The Doctor Himself*, chs. 4 and 6); the lectures at the Puritan and Reformed Studies Conference of 1969, 'Can We Learn From History?' in *By Schisms Rent Asunder* (London: Puritan and Reformed Studies Conference, 1970), pp. 69–86, and at the Westminster Conference in 1971, 1972, 1974, 1975 and 1978, 'Puritanism and Its Origins', in *The Good Fight of Faith* (Huntingdon: Westminster Conference, 1972), pp. 72–90; 'John Knox – the Founder of Puritanism', in *Becoming a Christian* (Huntingdon: Westminster Conference 1973), pp. 95–111; 'New Developments in the Eighteenth-and Nineteenth-Century Teaching', in *Living the Christian Life* (Huntingdon: Westminster Conference, 1975), pp. 82–99; 'The French Revolution and After', in *The Christian and the State in Revolutionary Times* (Huntingdon: Westminster Conference 1976), pp. 94–110; 'John Bunyan: Church Union', in *Light from John Bunyan* (Huntingdon: Westminster Conference, 1979), pp. 86–102); the address at the British Evangelical Council rally in October 1970 (see *The State of the Nation* [Welwyn: British Evangelical Council and Evangelical Press, 1971]); the address given to ministers in Wales in June 1971 (in *The Evangelical Magazine of Wales*, April 1981, pp. 16–22); the sermon at the fiftieth anniversary of his first visit to Aberavon (published in *The Evangelical Magazine of Wales*, April 1981, pp. 4–13); the sermon on Genesis 3:22–24 preached in Wales in 1978 (*The Evangelical Magazine of Wales*, April 1981, pp. 27–35).

[79]D. M. Lloyd-Jones, *Preaching and Preachers* (London: Hodder and Stoughton, 1971), ch. 16.

[80]See D. M. Lloyd-Jones, *The Manifold Grace of God* (London: Puritan and Reformed Studies Conference, 1969), pp 76–95.

[81]'Howell Harris and Revival', in *Adding to the Church* (Huntingdon: Westminster Conference, 1974), pp. 66–81.

[82]'Jonathan Edwards and the Crucial Importance of Revival', in *The Puritan Experiment in the New World* (Huntingdon: Westminster Conference, 1977), pp. 103–121.

[83]D. M. Lloyd-Jones, 'Preaching', in *Anglican and Puritan Thinking* (Huntingdon: Westminster Conference, 1978), pp. 89–102.

[84]*Inaugural Address by D. M. Lloyd-Jones* (London: London Theological Seminary, 1978).

[85]See *Evangelical Times*, April 1981, p. 10, column 2.

8

Three significant expositions

There were three occasions in the ministry of Lloyd-Jones when he set out his understanding of the baptism with the Spirit in considerable detail: the five sermons on Ephesians 1:13b preached in 1955, the fifteen sermons on Romans 8:15–16 preached at the end of 1960 and the beginning of 1961, and the twenty-four sermons on John 1:26, 33 preached in late 1964 and early 1965. These have all been published, but the third of them has been rearranged for the purpose of publication.[1] I base my analysis upon the printed versions of the first two series but upon the recordings of the third series.

The material which Lloyd-Jones expounded when preaching on Ephesians 1:13, Romans 8:16 and John 1:33 contains a large amount of duplication and overlap. There would be no point in giving a separate exposition of each. I intend rather to present an analysis of each set of sermons and then in the next chapter consider the teaching that arises from all three.

Ephesians 1:13

There were five sermons on Ephesians 1:13b.[2] The structure of the sermons may be analysed as follows. (I include page numbers in the text for convenience of reference.)

I. **'Sealed with the Spirit'**, the first sermon, unfolds as follows:

A. The context of Ephesians 1:13b is introduced and the subject of the sealing of the Spirit is generally introduced (p. 244).

B. Meanings of the term 'seal' are considered. The term may point to (1) Authentication, (2) Ownership or (3) Security (pp. 244–245).

C. Scriptural usage of the term 'seal' is next considered, focusing on (1) John 3:33 and (2) John 6.27. The latter, which refers to Jesus' being 'sealed' is elucidated with reference to a) Jesus' baptism, b) the voice from heaven attesting Jesus, c) Jesus' understanding of Scripture, d) Jesus' works. Bishop Westcott's summary is cited (pp. 245–248).

D. The question is discussed: when in the Christian life does the 'sealing' take place? (1) The translations of the AV and RSV are considered. (2) Goodwin, Owen and Hodge are quoted in support. (3) The scriptural evidence is cited (John 14; Acts 2, 8, 9, 15, 19) and is said to support a post-conversion sealing of the Spirit (pp. 240–254).

II. **'The Nature of Sealing (I)'**, unfolds as follows:

A. The topic is again introduced (pp. 255–256).

B. The significance of the term 'promise' is explored by considering the theme of the promise of the Spirit in (1) Isaiah, (2) Ezekiel, (3) Joel, (4) the predictions of John the Baptist, (5) the teaching of Jesus as found in Luke 11, John 7, 14–16 and in Acts 1 and 2; 'the promise' in Galatians 3:14 is considered (pp. 256–259).

C. A third section asks the question: in what sense is the Spirit received in the baptism with the Spirit? (1) The Spirit was known by Old Testament believers. (2) The Spirit was experienced by the disciples before Pentecost (pp. 259–260).

D. This leads to some negative conclusions. The baptism of the Spirit is *not* (1) regeneration, (2) the unction of the Spirit to give saving knowledge, (3) sanctification, (4) the fruit of the Spirit, (5) syllogistic assurance or (6) the fullness of the Spirit (pp. 260–263).

E. At the end of the sermon the baptism of the Spirit is positively described (pp. 264–265).

III. **'The Nature of the Sealing (II)'**, unfolds as follows:
  A. The matter is again introduced (p. 266).
  B. Now the 'sealing of the Spirit' is positively described as an experiential blessing. (1) The predominant view is mentioned. (2) The difficulty arising from varying uses of the term 'baptism' is considered. (3) The context of Ephesians 1:13b is thought to support an experiential interpretation. So also is (4) the identity of the 'sealing' and the 'baptism' of the Spirit and (5) the scriptural parallels which are again cited: Acts 1, 2, 8, 19; Galatians 3 (pp. 267–271).
  C. The 'sealing of the Spirit' is positively described by referring to (1) Romans 8:16 and (2) Galatians 4:6 (pp. 271–274).
  D. Supportive material is presented from the lives and writings of Goodwin, Wesley, Flavel, Edwards, Evans and Whitefield (pp. 274–278).

IV. **'True and Counterfeit Experiences'** begins to take up subsidiary questions as follows:
  A. The matter is introduced (pp. 279–280).
  B. The relation of sealing to the gifts of the Spirit is discussed (pp. 280–283).
  C. The relation of sealing to conversion is explored (pp. 283–284).
  D. So also is the relationship between sealing and sanctification (pp. 284–286).
  E. The question of the intensity of the experience is briefly covered (p. 286).
  F. The place of true emotion is assessed (pp. 286–287).
  G. The tests of true experience of the Spirit are mentioned (pp. 287–288).

V. **'Problems and Difficulties'** continues to deal with subsidiary questions, and unfolds as follows:
  A. The subject is, as always, briefly introduced (pp. 289–290).
  B. The questions are now considered and answered.
    (1) Did all Christians have this experience in New Testament times? Lloyd-Jones replies by urging that a) the New Testament assumes that this is the

144

norm for every Christian, b) most Christians were
given it, c) it was the standard at the inauguration of
the church (pp. 290–292).

(2) Is it for every Christian? Lloyd-Jones thinks it is.

(3) Are we to seek it? Lloyd-Jones replies with both
negative and positive answers. a) Negatively: it is
not to be 'taken' by faith; tarrying meetings are not
to be held. b) Positively: the Christian is to seek the
promise of God; he is to seek God himself not
experiences; he is to prepare the way by holy living;
he is to seek in prayer the sealing of the Spirit
(pp. 292–300).

Romans 8:15–16

On 7 October 1960, after a four-month recess, the Friday Bible-
exposition at Westminster Chapel recommenced. From then
until March 1961 Lloyd-Jones preached every Friday (apart
from a short break at Christmas) on three verses of Scripture,
Romans 8:14–16. Three sermons focused on the 'Spirit of bondage', four on the 'Spirit of adoption'; another eight dealt with
'the witness of the Spirit'; the opening paragraphs of the first
sermon on Romans 8:17 considered the relation between the
'sealing' and the 'earnest' of the Spirit. All of these sermons were
published thirteen years later, in 1974, as part of the volume
entitled *Sons of God*.[3]

Since there was a four-month gap between the sermons which
now constitute chapters 11 and 12 of *Sons of God*, we are not
surprised to find that chapter 12 commences with a summary of
the argument of Romans 5–8. Lloyd-Jones was putting Romans
8:14–17 into the context of the whole letter before coming to the
detailed exposition. Lloyd-Jones argues that the theme of the
verses is 'the assurance and absolute certainty of our final salvation in terms of our divine sonship'.[4] He rejects that analysis of
chapters 5–8 which saw them as a section dealing with 'Sanctification'.[5]

In the first of these sermons, chapter 12 in *Sons of God*, Lloyd-
Jones summarized five points he would be proceeding to
expound in detail.

Negatively, he tells us that every man is not a son of God. Then he reminds us that only Christians are sons of God. Thirdly he explains what this sonship means. Next he shows how we may be sure of our sonship; and in the fifth and last place, he points to the consequences and results of our sonship.[6]

The first of these points is expounded on pages 152–154, the second on pages 154–156, the third begins on page 156 and continues to the end of the sermon. The third point is picked up again in the next sermon (chapter 14) and continues until page 165. Thereafter the fourth point is given immensely detailed attention, running from the middle of this sermon (page 165), through the next seventeen sermons (chapters 14–30), and into the opening paragraphs of the first sermon on Romans 8:17 (chapter 31). At this point Lloyd-Jones loses sight of the five points mentioned earlier. Beginning in the sermon preached on 14 October 1960 (chapter 13) he launched into such a detailed exposition of the leading of the Spirit, the Spirit of bondage, the Spirit of adoption and the witness of the Spirit, that the fifth point was never enumerated. Presumably, by the time Lloyd-Jones got to the end of his fourth point, five months later, the congregation would have forgotten the original enumeration. The fifth point was no doubt covered in what he said concerning the Christian as an heir of glory (in his sermons on Romans 8:17).

Lloyd-Jones did not generally announce to the congregation the enumeration and sub-divisions of his material. Nevertheless he almost invariably had an outline in his notes of what he wanted to say. It is possible to extract from his sermons the key divisions of his material and to reconstruct the schema. The divisions of Lloyd-Jones's material at this point are outlined in the next paragraph. Of course such a schema has never been published and is a subjective reconstruction of my own. Its justification lies in the fact that Lloyd-Jones explicitly urged preachers to have such an outline in their notes when preaching, but that they should not share such enumerations with the congregation. The reason for not announcing the divisions is that the preacher should always remain free to develop or change any particular point in the inspiration of the moment.[7]

There are certain inelegancies in the lay-out and occasions where Lloyd-Jones inserts material in the 'wrong' place, or takes up again something dealt with earlier. It is likely therefore that he was constructing his outline as he went along from week to week. Certainly those who sat under his ministry, heard him talking to ministers, or spoke with him, know that this was in keeping with his method and style. The reconstruction of a schema below is partly an objective analysis of what the sermons turned out to be; it will also partly reflect the kind of outline Lloyd-Jones had in his notes. The sermons on Romans 8:15–16 may be analysed as follows:

I.   **'Assurance that arises from the leading of the Spirit'** (pp. 165–196; chs. 13 [in part], 14, 15, 16 [in part]).
     A. Assurance that comes by being led by the Spirit (pp. 165–169).
     B. Question: 'leading' or 'driving'? (pp. 170–175).
     C. How is the Christian led? (pp. 175–180).
        1. In connection with the truth (pp. 175–177).
           (a) In contrast to Roman Catholicism (p. 176).
           (b) In contrast to 'the secret rapture' teaching (p. 177).
           (c) In contrast to teaching concerning elders (p. 177).
        2. By the illumination of our minds (pp. 177–180).
           (a) Illumination concerning God, (p. 178).
           (b) Illumination concerning the soul (p. 178).
           (c) Illumination concerning Jesus (p. 178–179).
           (d) Illumination concerning the purpose of God (p. 179–180).
        3. The Spirit's action on our desires (p. 180).
        4. The Spirit's action on our wills (p. 180).
     D. The marks of being led by the Spirit (pp. 181–193).
        1. Determination of one's outlook (pp. 183–185).
           (a) A spiritual outlook (p. 183).
           (b) A taste for spiritual things (pp. 183–184).
           (c) Love of the brethren (pp. 184).
           (d) Concern for the soul (p. 184).
           (e) One's view of life (p. 184–185).
        2. Desire to live to God's glory (pp. 185–187).

147

IV. **'The witness of the Spirit'** (pp. 285–402)
   A. Introduction (pp. 285–287).
   B. Exegesis (pp. 287–290).
       1. 'Itself' (p. 287).
       2. 'Bears witness' (pp. 287–288).
       3. 'Children' (pp. 288–290).
   C. Basic interpretation (pp. 290–301).
       1. Negatives (pp. 290–294).
           (a) Not Denney's view (pp. 290–291).
           (b) Not Moule's view (p. 291).
           (c) Not Alford's view (p. 292).
           (d) Not Olshausen's view (p. 292).
           (e) Not Hamilton's view (p. 293).
           (f) Not Chalmer's view (pp. 292–293).
           (g) Not Winslow's view (p. 293).
           (h) Not Hodge's view (pp. 293–294).
       2. Positive: Haldane's interpretation (pp. 294–295).
       3. Support (pp. 296–299).
           (a) Scripture parallels (pp. 296–298).
           (b) History and biography (pp. 298–299).
           (c) Revivals (p. 299).
       4. Conclusions (pp. 299–301).
           (a) This is a work of the Spirit (pp. 299–300).
           (b) Part of the baptism of the spirit (p. 300).
           (c) Same as the 'sealing' (pp. 300–301).
   D. The character of the witness of the Spirit (pp. 301–305).
       1. A direct assurance of sonship (pp. 301–302).
       2. An addition to the Spirit of adoption (p. 302).
       3. The highest form of assurance (pp. 302–304).
           (a) Not a deduction (p. 302).
           (b) Not a test arising from our lives (p. 303).
           (c) Beyond Romans 8:15.
       4. Its repercussions (pp. 304–305).
           (a) Illumines plan of salvation (p. 304).
           (b) Leads to love (p. 304).
           (c) Leads to desire to please (p. 304).
           (d) Leads to desire to witness (pp. 304–305).
           (e) May be accompanied by gifts (p. 305).

151

John 1:26, 33

The sermons of Lloyd-Jones on John 1:26 and 33 (preached in late 1964 and early 1965) were made available by the Martyn Lloyd-Jones Recordings Trust before they appeared in their printed form. The printed version appeared in two volumes entitled *Joy Unspeakable* and *Prove All Things* in 1984 and 1985.

The material in these two volumes constitutes the fullest statement of Lloyd-Jones's views on the baptism with the Spirit. They are worthy of detailed study and to assist in such study I present the following outline of the material in them. I outline the material following the tapes rather than the books. Thus the outline follows the order in which the sermons were originally preached, which corresponds to *Joy Unspeakable*, chapters 1–7, followed by *Prove All Things*, followed by *Joy Unspeakable*, chapters 8–16.

I. **Two dangers**
   The first sermon warns of over-interest in 'experiences' on the one hand and satisfaction with less than what is available to the Christian, on the other hand.

II. **Principles**
   Lloyd-Jones lays down some central principles concerning the baptism with the Spirit.
   A. It is possible to be a Christian without being baptized with the Spirit. The second sermon continues to argue the same point.
   B. The third sermon urges that the baptism with the Spirit is the direct activity of Christ.
   C. The fourth sermon defines what the baptism with the Spirit is and urges that it is not the Spirit's regular work in each Christian but something exceptional and direct.
   D. The baptism with the Spirit is a gift of direct assurance of salvation.
   E. The baptism with the Spirit is associated with witness, testimony and service.

III. **The results of the baptism with the Spirit**
   The fifth sermon and the following three develop a description of the characteristics or the results of the baptism with the Spirit. Lloyd-Jones divides these into subjective results (*i.e.* experiences within the believer) and objective (*i.e.* those which are evident to onlookers).
   A. Subjective.
      1. A sense of the glory of God.
      2. A sense of awe.
      3. Humbling.

    4. God's love experienced (Lloyd-Jones digressed to explain three types of assurance of which 'the baptism' is the highest).

    5. Sermon six continues: joy and gladness.

    6. Desire to glorify Christ.

    8. Increase in understanding of God's truth.

B. Objective (commenced in the seventh sermon).

    1. Transformation of appearance.

    2. Liberty of speech.

    3. Eighth sermon: possession of authority.

    4. Boldness and fearlessness.

IV. The gifts of the Spirit

Dealing with the results of the baptism of the Spirit leads Lloyd-Jones on to a detailed consideration of the gifts of the Spirit.

A. Three hostile approaches.

At the end of the eighth sermon Lloyd-Jones outlines three ways in which the gifts of the Spirit may be disparaged.

    1. By asserting they were only intended to convince the Jews.

    2. By asserting they were only intended for the foundation of the church.

    3. By asserting they were only intended before the formation of the canon.

B. Reply.

Lloyd-Jones seeks to reply to these ways of disparaging the present-day relevance of the gifts of the Spirit.

    1. He refutes what he considers to be an erroneous interpretation of 1 Corinthians 13.

    2. He points out (in the ninth sermon) that gifts of the Spirit were exercised among the Gentiles as well as among the Jews.

    3. He urges that to say the gifts of the Spirit were only for the church before the rise of the canon of Scripture would be to make large sections of Scripture quite irrelevant, notably 1 Corinthians 12 to 14.

C. Conclusions

Finally Lloyd-Jones asserts four conclusions:

    1. Gifts may be withheld as well as given.

2. One should never speak of 'claiming' a gift of the Spirit.
3. There is a variation as to how gifts are given.
4. The explanation in the decline of the gifts of the Spirit in the post-apostolic church is diminished spirituality.

V. **Testing the Spirits**
A. The dangers of the counterfeit.
Beginning with the tenth sermon, Lloyd-Jones warns of the need to test claims to charismatic manifestations. He presents evidence of this danger from Scripture, history, spiritualism and psychology.
B. Three negative warnings.
1. Don't rely on inward feelings.
2. Don't decide by a feeling of greater love for God.
3. Don't decide according to respect for the person seeking to persuade of the authenticity of the gifts.
C. Two positive principles (the eleventh sermon).
1. The use of reason.
2. The use of Scripture.
D. Some words of advice.
1. Be suspicious of claims to fresh revelation.
2. Reject what contradicts Scripture.
3. Beware what is merely spectacular.
4. Beware the prophesying of future events (the twelfth sermon commences at this point).
5. Beware excessive claims to direct guidance.
6. Beware anything that makes 'self' prominent.
7. Beware occasions when the physical element is prominent.
8. Beware of the power of suggestion.
E. Direct Scripture teaching.
In the thirteenth sermon Lloyd-Jones comes to the directly scriptural tests concerning the authentic work of the Spirit. This sermon has two principles:
1. The first concerns 1 Corinthians 12:13 and 1 John 4:1.
2. The second is the fact that this test is not sufficient in itself.

156

F. 1 Corinthians 12–14 (the fourteenth sermon).

Lloyd-Jones now picks out key principles from 1 Corinthians 12–14.

First he asks: what is the purpose of the gifts of the Spirit?

Seven negative and three positive answers are given.

Secondly, he elucidates the way to seek the gifts, focusing especially on 1 Corinthians 13.

G. The gift of tongues. The fifteenth sermon is wholly given over to the discussion of the gift of tongues. Lloyd-Jones argues that it is not an indispensable part of the baptism of the Spirit; it cannot be initiated by man at all but is a sovereign gift of God.

VI. **Difficulties and remaining questions**

The sixteenth and following three sermons take up various difficulties and remaining questions.

A. Spirit and baptism and sanctification. Lloyd-Jones argues there is an indirect but no direct connection between Spirit baptism and sanctification (sixteenth sermon).

B. The baptism of the Spirit and other terms.

In the seventeenth sermon he argues that the baptism of the spirit is the same as the sealing of the Spirit and the same as the direct witness of Romans 8:16.

C. Difficult texts (eighteenth sermon). Three texts are considered in detail, all of which have been thought to create difficulty in the way of his view of the Spirit: Luke 11:13; Acts 2:38–39; 1 Corinthians 12:13.

D. Does the New Testament not assume all were baptized in the Spirit? Lloyd-Jones seeks to reply to this difficulty (the nineteenth sermon).

VII. **Seeking and experiencing the baptism of the Spirit**

The discussion of the difficulties attending the subject gradually leads Lloyd-Jones in four sermons to discuss the question of whether the baptism of the Spirit is to be sought and, if so, how it should be sought.

A. Some instructions. The twentieth sermon commences some positive words of advice in seeking the baptism of the Spirit.

1. Realize the possibility.
2. Watch your motives.
3. Obey the Lord.
4. Make this a matter of prayer.
5. Be prepared for surprises (the twenty-first sermon starts here).
6. Let God lead you on.
7. Be persistent.
8. Be patient.
B. Encouragements.
C. A digression: tarrying meetings (Lloyd-Jones cannot forbid them but has words of warning about their dangers).
D. How is it given?
   In the twenty-second sermon he discusses five circumstances in which the gift may be given.
   1. While praying.
   2. While reading Scripture.
   3. During preaching.
   4. While meditating.
   5. Apart from Scripture altogether.
E. When is it given?
   Lloyd-Jones now discusses the epochs of life in which this blessing might be expected.
   1. After mourning for sin.
   2. When led to acts of self-denial.
   3. After seasons of conflict with Satan.
   4. In connection with trying circumstances.
   5. Before a special task.
   6. As preparation for dying.
F. Its durability. He argues the blessing may be lost and may be regained.

VIII. **Ascension and Pentecost** (the twenty-third sermon).
   Lloyd-Jones returns to difficult texts and discussed John 20:22–23 and John 7:37–39.

IX. **Two approaches to the baptism of the Spirit**
   Lloyd-Jones's final sermon in this series, the twenty-fourth, preached on Pentecost Sunday 1965, summarized two approaches to the spirit, and argues that Pentecost was

the first of the great spiritual revivals of history, that it was the first 'baptism of power' the church experienced and that it is to be sought again in the twentieth century.

This chapter has consisted of analysis and nothing but analysis. I have made no comments on Lloyd-Jones's teachings because it is preferable that objective consideration precede assessment. Yet anyone who works through Lloyd-Jones's material with the aid of the skeleton outlines I have provided will find that despite the initial impression of wordiness, and the obvious fact that Lloyd-Jones was a preacher not a lecturer, he knew exactly where he was going from the start and has presented the fullest and most detailed study of his particular view of the baptism with Spirit.

Notes

[1] The printed version is found in D. M. Lloyd-Jones, *Joy Unspeakable: The Baptism with the Holy Spirit*, edited by C. Catherwood (Eastbourne: Kingsway, 1984); and *Prove All Things: The Sovereign Work of the Holy Spirit*, edited by C. Catherwood (Eastbourne: Kingsway, 1985). The order of the original sermons will be followed if the first seven chapters of *Joy Unspeakable* are read, followed by the whole of *Prove All Things* and then chapters 8–16 of *Joy Unspeakable*. It is this order that I follow – but from the recordings themselves.

[2] D. M. Lloyd-Jones, *God's Ultimate Purpose*, chs. 21–25.

[3] D. M. Lloyd-Jones, *Sons of God*, chs. 16–31. The dates of the individual sermons are available to me through personal contacts with Westminster Chapel. My copy of *Sons of God* is annotated with the dates of each sermon and the Scripture reading at the church meeting concerned. Sometimes a sermon reflects upon the Scripture reading, although the readings are not mentioned in the published expositions. Chapter 15 of *Sons of God*, for example, reflects upon Galatians 5:16–26 and James 4:1–16. These two passages of Scripture were read at the meeting at Westminster Bible-exposition on 28 September 1960.

The Preface of *Sons of God* is slightly inaccurate, I believe, in mentioning April 1961. The last sermon in that volume was preached, according to my records, on 24 March 1961.

[4] D. M. Lloyd-Jones, *Sons of God*, p. 150.

[5] Lloyd-Jones is alluding here to the theology of the 'Keswick Convention' which, in its early years, regarded Romans 7 as concerned with the unsanctified Christian. See J. M. E. Cruvellier, *L'Exégèse de Romains 7 et le Mouvement de Keswick*, (Den Haag: Pasmans, 1961), esp. ch. 2.

[6] D. M. Lloyd-Jones, *Sons of God*, p. 152.

[7] Lloyd-Jones was troubled at one stage, with the contention of Edwin Hatch in the Hibbert lectures of 1888 that the earliest Christian preaching was entirely prophetic with little structure of pre-arrangement. See E. Hatch, *The Influence of Greek Ideas on Christianity*, edited by F. C. Grant (New York: Harper, 1959), ch. 4, Greek and Christian Rhetoric, esp. pp. 105–107; the earlier edition was entitled *The Influence of Greek Ideas and Usages Upon the Christian Church*, edited by A. M.

Fairburn, 2nd ed. (London and Edinburgh: Williams and Newgate, 1891). However, he felt that despite some measure of truth in Hatch's contention, there was evidence of structure in (for example) the sermon on the day of Pentecost. Accordingly Lloyd-Jones did not believe, generally speaking, in *announcing* the structure of his sermons. On occasions he abandoned what he had planned and developed the material differently, in the inspiration of the moment. For these remarks, see D. M. Lloyd-Jones, *Preaching and Preachers* (London: Hodder and Stoughton, 1971), pp. 73–80, 83–84, 213–214.

9

The sealing of the Spirit

It is not my intention at this point to discuss the minutiae of Lloyd-Jones's approach to the baptism with the Spirit. Rather I plan to focus on certain key aspects of his teaching which are of interest in current charismatic debate. Nor is it yet my purpose to assess Lloyd-Jones's view; at this point I simply wish to state as clearly as I can some key matters, exegetical and theological, which characterize his teaching.

Interchangeable terms

An aspect of Lloyd-Jones's teaching which is rarely discussed but constantly assumed is the interchangeability of terms. In 1955 he simply assumed that the sealing and the baptism of the Spirit are identical . He spoke of 'the sealing with the Spirit, or the baptism with the Spirit'.[1] Then he again assumes, without discussion, that 'receiving the Spirit' refers to the same spiritual experience. Acts 19:2 is brought into the discussion; Lloyd-Jones without hesitation relates 'sealing' and 'receiving' as variant expressions for the same blessing. He can say of Paul in Acts 19: 'he saw at once that they had not had the seal of the Spirit, they had not received the Holy Ghost.'[2]

In a further sermon at that time he also relates Ephesians 1:13 to the promises of the Old Testament. The phrase 'that promise' (Lloyd-Jones's translation follows Goodwin) reminds us of the covenant-promise of the Old Testament. This means that the various 'promise-passages' of the Old Testament (Ezekiel 36, 37; Isaiah 40–66; Joel 2) are drawn into the discussion concerning the baptism of the Spirit.[3]

Lloyd-Jones occasionally relates the 'baptism' to the 'filling' of the Spirit. He is insistent that Ephesians 5:18 has no connection with the baptism with the Spirit,[4] yet the term 'filled' is used in Acts 2. Lloyd-Jones comments: 'The explanation seems to be that the baptism with the Spirit is the first experience of the fullness of the Spirit; it is the Spirit poured upon us in exceptional fullness. The first time something outstanding happens is always unique.'

Later in the same series of expositions Lloyd-Jones identifies the 'baptism with the Spirit, with the experience mentioned in Romans 8:16 and Galatians 4:6 and with the 'receiving' of the Spirit mentioned in Galatians 3:2.[5] Then in his exposition of Ephesians 1:4 the 'earnest' of the Spirit is said to be 'another aspect of the truth' concerning the 'sealing of the Spirit'.[6] Similarly in the study of Romans 8:15b–16, Lloyd-Jones identified Romans 5:5, Galatians 4:6 and 1 John 2:27 with the baptism with the Spirit.[7] Then, in expounding Romans 8:16, he finds parallels in John 7:37–39, Romans 5:5; Acts 2, 4 (where we are said to find 'the same thing . . . repeated') and Acts 8, 10, 19. Rather strikingly the baptism of the Spirit is also found in Revelation 2:17, 28, 3:12 and 1 Peter 1:8.[8] In a later sermon he identifies the baptism of the Spirit in the case of Saul's experience, recorded in Acts 9, and the reference to 'receiving the Spirit' in Galatians 3:2, 14. Comparatively little is said in these sermons about the promise of the Spirit as recorded in John 14 to 16, but it is also clear that Lloyd-Jones identified these promises with the baptism of the Spirit. He speaks of 'John 14, where our Lord makes the gracious promise which was afterwards fulfilled'.[9]

Lloyd-Jones rarely explicitly *discussed* the matter of interchangeable terms. Rather he simply assumed their virtual identity. On one occasion, however, he did explicitly take up the question of interchangeability. 'We have arrived at the point,' he said in April 1965, 'at which we are now considering the relationship of this term to certain other terms that are used in the New Testament with regard to the operations of the Holy Spirit . . . It is important that we should be clear in our minds even with

162

regard to terms and terminology . . . I am often asked to explain the relationship between the baptism with the Holy Ghost and sanctification or the sealing of the Spirit and the earnest of the Spirit, the unction of the Spirit and so on . . . These different terms are used in describing the operations of the Holy Spirit.'[10] This particular sermon goes on to argue: 'The sealing of the Spirit is the same thing as the baptism of the Spirit' and that 'What Paul says in Romans 8:16 is again the same thing.' It is not that the terms are *identical*. Each one focuses on different aspects, but they all refer to the same spiritual event. 'Thank God for the very multiplicity of terms', remarked Lloyd-Jones towards the close of this sermon in April 1965, 'for they all together, in showing us this great same truth from different aspects, help to enhance its glory and its wonder.'[11]

The participle in Ephesians 1:13

Although Lloyd-Jones's preaching was addressed to a popular audience and therefore lacked the visible apparatus of biblical scholarship, yet underlying his sermons was careful exegetical work. Implicit in his view of the baptism with the Holy Spirit were key exegetical decisions. For example, Lloyd-Jones's exposition of Ephesians 1:13 implies a particular interpretation of the aorist tense of the Greek word *pisteusantes* ('having believed' or 'upon believing'). The Authorized Version of the Bible (1611) translated this 'after ye believed'. Lloyd-Jones admitted that this was *technically* incorrect, yet he urged that the aorist tense of the participle could be understood in such a way that it implied the same teaching as the translation in the AV. He urged that 'the men who gave us the Authorised Version were interpreting Ephesians 1:13 correctly!'[12] In 1955 there was little argument concerning this; Lloyd-Jones simply quoted the occasions in Acts where faith and sealing were distinct, in order to urge that 'having believed' was the correct translation of the participle.[13]

The matter received attention again in 1965: He said 'the Authorised translation here is not literally accurate . . . I am not saying it is not accurate. I am saying it is not *literally* accurate . . . The better translation is "believing" or "having believed". You can take it in both ways.' He went on to argue that it does not

163

make any difference as to the meaning. 'It is presumed and taken for granted that they *have* believed, they were already believers, when they were sealed.' Lloyd-Jones quotes in support the words of Charles Hodge: 'This is more than a translation. It is an exposition of the original.' As in 1955 he went on to urge the correctness of his view in the light of the incidents in Acts.[14]

Baptism 'with' and 'by' the Spirit

Lloyd-Jones was aware of those expositors who put considerable emphasis on 1 Corinthians 12:13 as a refutation of any view of the baptism of the Spirit which regarded it as subsequent to regeneration. In London in the 1950s and 1960s the two most prominent evangelical churches were Westminster Chapel (of which Lloyd-Jones was the minister) and All Souls, Langham Place (where the Reverend John Stott was the rector). These two well-known evangelical preachers in London took altogether different attitudes to 1 Corinthians 12:13 and when in 1964 the first edition of Stott's *The Baptism and Fullness of the Holy Spirit* was published it, could only accentuate the difference between the two men.[15]

For Lloyd-Jones the difference between Jesus' baptizing with the Spirit and the Spirit's work of baptizing the believer into the body of Christ was crucial. It was entirely mistaken, in his judgment, simplistically to equate the two. Baptism with the Spirit is an act of the ascended Lord Jesus. It is vibrantly experiential, so much so that it will never be forgotten as a memorable experience in the Christian life. It does not have to be 'reckoned' as does our union with Christ (Romans 6:3, 11). It experientially 'seals' our salvation, gives us a foretaste of heaven, empowers for witness and results in great boldness and liberty of speech. It does not take place *automatically* at conversion.

To be 'baptized into the body of Christ' is, for Lloyd-Jones, something altogether different. This is not in itself experiential (although Lloyd-Jones would not have denied that it leads to wonderful experience). It is 'an action of the Holy Spirit, which is non-experimental'. Initially 'we must regard it objectively, and take it on the bare Word of God'.[16] He disagreed with Charles Hodge at one point. With regard to being baptized into Christ and into the church and our knowledge of it, he said, 'I am again surprised that the great Charles Hodge says that this is "experimental knowledge". My entire position asserts the exact opposite and says that it is not experimental.'[17] This distinction between two kinds of knowledge, one of which comes by direct experience and the other by sheer faith in God's Word, goes back to Calvin who said, 'There is a twofold knowledge, – the knowledge of faith, received from his word, – and the knowledge of experience, as we say, derived from actual enjoyment.'[18] He also referred to 'the knowledge of faith, and what they call experimental knowledge'.[19] In terms of this distinction baptism into Christ and into the body of Christ is a matter of 'the knowledge of faith'; the baptism with the Spirit is par excellence known 'experimentally'.

Lloyd-Jones complained of those who think 'that one verse is enough in and of itself'[20] and settles the matter of the intepretation of the baptism with the Spirit. This criticism may possibly have Stott in mind, for his *Baptism and Fullness* (which was originally an address to the Islington Clerical Conference)[21] bases virtually everything on the interpretation of 1 Corinthians 12:13 and Ephesians 5:18 neither of which, in Lloyd-Jones's judgment, had anything to do with the baptism with the Spirit. Again in 1955 he mentioned the difficulty: 'It is assumed that whenever the words "Spirit" and "baptism" are found in the same statement the meaning must always be the same, and so it is concluded that the baptism of the Spirit means our incorporation into Christ, which is an event entirely outside one's consciousness and the realm of experience.' Lloyd-Jones does not agree with this; he draws a distinction between baptism *with* and baptism *by* the Spirit. 'The fallacy here', he says 'is surely due to a failure to realize that the word "to baptize" is used in many different ways in the Scripture.'[22] Later he says:

'There are many different particular usages with regard to this word 'baptism', and the statement in 1 Corinthians 12:13 is but one of them. We are all placed into the realm of Christ by the Holy Spirit and into His body which is the Church. All Christians are in that way made members in particular of the body of Christ. But it does not follow that that is the only possible meaning of the expression 'baptized with the holy ghost'.[23]

165

A similar point was made in January 1961:

1 Corinthians 12:13 has nothing whatsoever to do with the 'baptism with the Holy Spirit'. The great theme of that chapter is the theme of the Church as the body of Christ, and the Apostle is simply saying in that verse that every Christian is a member in particular of the body of Christ.' Lloyd-Jones argues this is not the baptism *with* the Holy Spirit: 'It is the Lord Jesus Christ himself who baptized with the Holy Spirit – which is a very different thing.[24]

In April 1965 he gave fuller consideration to the matter. He complains that the argument based on 1 Corinthians 12:13 was 'being used a great deal at the present time as it has always been used by those who don't believe in the baptism with the Holy Spirit as a separate experience, and they emphasize this word "All".' He goes on to urge that this verse 'does not deal at all with the doctrine of the baptism with the Holy Spirit'. He is aware of the Greek and of those who urge that the word *en* is used, and that the text therefore speaks of being baptized *in* the Spirit. At this point the sermon focuses on the exegesis of the word *en*. He points out that virtually all translations do in fact translate the word 'by', with only the RSV having 'in'. He quotes the lexicon of Arndt and Gingrich and cites instances where an 'instrumental usage' or 'causal sense' is used: Matthew 26:52; Matthew 7:6; Luke 1:51; Romans 5:9. Then Lloyd-Jones quotes extensively from Dr Wuest's *Untranslatable Riches from the New Testament Greek*, in support of the same exegesis.

The word 'Spirit' is in the instrumental case in the Greek. Personal agency is expressed occasionally by the instrumental case. At such times the verb is always in the passive or middle voice. The Greek construction here follows this rule of Greek grammar. The personal agent in this case who does the baptizing is the Holy Spirit. He places or introduces the believing sinner into the body of which the Lord Jesus is the living head. We could translate therefore 'by means of the personal agency of one Spirit we all were placed in one body'. It is not the baptism *with* the Spirit or *of* the Spirit in the sense that the Holy Spirit is the element that is applied to us; it is the baptism *by* the Spirit. This baptism does not bring the Spirit to us in the sense that God places the Spirit upon us or in us. Rather this baptism brings the believer into vital union with Jesus Christ.

Wuest went on to contrast this with the different matter of baptism *by* the Spirit (as Wuest and Lloyd-Jones saw it) in Luke 3:16; John 1:31; Acts 1:5 and Acts 11:16. Wuest is again quoted: 'This kind of a verb is not found in the passages from Matthew to Acts but is found in 1 Corinthians 12:13. Therefore our rendering "baptized by means of the Spirit" is correct for the Corinthians passage but not correct for those others commented upon.'

Leaving aside Wuest, Lloyd-Jones goes on to urge: 'In every reference to baptism with the Spirit the baptizer is the Lord Jesus Christ, and what he does when he baptizes with the Spirit is what we have seen. It is a baptism to give power; it is a baptism to create witnesses, the enable us to testify.' But 'here the apostle is dealing with something entirely different'. It is the *Spirit* that baptizes and he does so by placing each believer into the body of Christ, and giving gifts. 'He is the agent who has given you them all', Lloyd-Jones paraphrases. 'By one Spirit' is correct in 1 Corinthians 12, for Paul is dealing with the activity of the Spirit. 'What he is talking about here is not power, it's not witness. . . . The Holy Spirit at the moment of regeneration also takes each person who is regenerated and puts him into the body of Christ.' This, in Lloyd-Jones's view, is an entirely different matter from the baptism *with* the Spirit *by* the Lord Jesus Christ.[25]

'Again' in Romans 8:15

Lloyd-Jones inherited from Sibbes and similar expositors a view concerning the 'spirit of bondage' which had two significant exegetical decisions built into it. As John Preston had said: 'If you have never been afrighted with the terror of God, if you have never been put into any feare by this spirit of bondage, be assured that you have not the Spirit of Adoption.'[26] In Lloyd-Jones's exposition this involved taking the word 'again' with the verb 'received' and interpreting the 'spirit of bondage' as referring to the Holy Spirit.

Thus Lloyd-Jones deliberately rejects the interpretation that sees in 'spirit of bondage . . . spirit of adoption' a reference to 'a disposition, a feeling',[27] and that which regards 'spirit of bondage' as a disposition, but 'Spirit of adoption' as an allusion to the Holy Spirit.[28] He consciously opts for taking 'Spirit of bondage . . . Spirit of adoption' as *both* referring to the Holy Spirit. Spirit of bondage refers, then, to the work of the Spirit producing conviction of sin, prior to the Spirit of adoption and the baptism with the Spirit.

This means that the 'Spirit of bondage' is actually 'received', and *palin* ('again') is attached to the verb. 'Received again' thus implies a prior receiving of the Spirit as a Spirit of bondage.

Lloyd-Jones shows no awareness of and does not discuss the possibility of attaching *palin* in Romans 8:15 to the phrase 'for fear'. The RSV had taken it this way ('to fall *back* into fear') and Lloyd-Jones normally refutes major interpretations that he disagrees with. The matter is of some importance and we shall return to it. At this point I merely note it as a significant exegetical decision.

Interpretation of key passages in Acts

Lloyd-Jones's view of the baptism with the Spirit involved a particular understanding of six passages in Acts chapters 2, 8, 9, 10–11, 18 and 19.[29] The main features of Lloyd-Jones's exegesis are as follows.

The event on the day of Pentecost is interpreted as a 'baptism of power' coming upon a fully constituted church. In Lloyd-Jones's opinion John 20 tells of the crucial gift of the Spirit given by the glorified head of the church.[30] The events of Pentecost had a 'vital transforming effect' upon men who were already regenerate.[31] To interpret the gift of the Spirit as identical to regeneration 'does great violence to what we read in the second chapter of Acts', thinks Lloyd-Jones.[32] 'Clearly they were believers and regenerate well before the day of Pentecost but it was only on the day of Pentecost that they were "baptized with the Holy Ghost" in fulfillment of the promise recorded in Acts 1:8.'[33]

Lloyd-Jones viewed Acts 8 as, 'another illustration' of the baptism with the Holy Spirit.[34] He dissents from the 'popular teaching' that 'the Holy Spirit was given once and for all at

Pentecost'.[35] Philip did not have to tell 'the believers in Samaria that the Holy Ghost had been given on the day of Pentecost'.[36] They came to salvation under Philip's preaching but they did not receive the Spirit until the occasion of the apostolic visit and the laying on of their hands.[37]

Acts 9 is referred to less frequently, for Lloyd-Jones did not regard it as so clear an example of the baptism with the Spirit. Yet it too comes in the same category. Paul was converted on the road to Damascus but received the sealing of the Spirit, three days later. Lloyd-Jones felt that, 'The apostle himself is as clear an illustration of this essential distinction between "believing" and "receiving the Spirit", or being "baptized with the Spirit", or being "sealed by the Spirit", as any.'[38]

Similarly the Cornelius incident (Acts 10 and 11) is another example of a post-conversion receiving of the Spirit.[39]

Acts 18 is not mentioned by Lloyd-Jones as frequently as Acts 19, but preaching upon that passage in 1965 he revealed that he regarded the cause of Apollos' deficiency to be that he lacked the baptism with the Spirit until taught more fully by Priscilla and Aquilla.[40]

Acts 19 is interpreted, then, along the lines already mentioned. The translation of the RSV is correct ('*when* ye believed') but the difference between that and the AV ('*after* ye believed') does not in any way affect the overall theology.[41] 'The very question Paul puts to them . . . shows clearly that it is possible to believe without receiving the Holy Ghost. These examples show clearly that we must not say that at the moment of belief, or regeneration, every Christian automatically, as it were, receives the baptism of the Holy Spirit.'[42]

'All these', said Lloyd-Jones on one occasion (having referred to Acts 2, 4, 8, 10 and 19), 'are examples of what we are dealing with here in Romans 8:16'.[43]

Baptism with the Spirit – an experiential blessing

Over against much modern exegesis Lloyd-Jones was insistent that the baptism with the Spirit was experiential or (to use old-fashioned terminology), experimental. 'Sealing', he said, 'is an experience, something that God does to us, and we know when it happens.'[44] He complained that 'most of the books which have been written on the Holy Spirit go out of their way to emphasize that the sealing of the Spirit is not experiential and has nothing to do with experience as such'. Lloyd-Jones rejected the equation of 'baptism by the Spirit' in 1 Corinthians 12:13 and 'baptism *with* the Spirit' because 1 Corinthians 12:13 referred, he believed, to 'an event entirely outside one's consciousness and the realm of experience'.[45] The baptism *with* the Holy Spirit was, he maintained, altogether different in this respect.

He could become quite scornful of the view he was rejecting. How could the baptism with the Spirit be non-experiential, he would ask. He would point to the authority and power the apostles received at Pentecost and similar events within Acts. He would remind his readers of their ecstatic joy.[46] 'Not experimental! Nothing can be more experimental; it is the height of Christian experience.'[47] Then he would point to the experiences of the various accounts in Acts and to the questions in Acts 19:2 and Galatians 3:2. 'How can anyone answer that question', he said of Galatians 3:2, 'if this is something outside the realm of experience? How can I know whether I have or have not received the Spirit if it is not something experimental?'[48]

Similar points were made when preaching on Romans 8:16. 'To say that this happening was "non-experimental" is simply to fly in the face of the facts . . . If the object and the purpose of this assurance which we receive when the Spirit bears witness with our spirits, or when the Spirit seals us, is that we might be made sure and certain that we are "children of God" and "heirs of God and joint heirs with Christ", how can it possibly do so if it is "non-experimental"?'[49] Then in 1964, during the expositions of John 1:26 and 33, the same point recurs.[50]

It is vital at this point to grasp hold of Lloyd-Jones's use of the term 'experimental' or its modern equivalent, 'experiential' (which I prefer). Various writers use the term 'experience' but not always in the same way as Lloyd-Jones. John Stott repeatedly calls the baptism with the Spirit an 'initiatory experience'.[51] However, he *also* says: 'there is no biblical warrant for the view that regeneration' (which he identifies with the baptism with the Spirit) 'is a conscious process'. So he can say, 'there is no reason to insist that it must be conscious, let alone dramatic'.[52] The difference in usage must be noted. When Lloyd-Jones uses the term 'experience' in connection with the baptism with the Spirit he does *not* use the term of something that could be unconscious. For him an 'experience' of the baptism with the Spirit is conscious and sufficiently dramatic that it will never be forgotten, though its impact may subside.

There is no 'right' or 'wrong' way in which the word 'experience' must be used, yet when Stott says baptism with the Spirit is an initiatory 'event', his terminology reflects his position more clearly than when he uses the term 'initiatory experience'. In Lloyd-Jones's terminology Stott does *not* believe in the baptism with the Spirit as necessarily experiential. (However, thinking of initiation into Christ as a totality he would want to add that we know what we are doing when we repent and believe, and he does believe in the possibility of 'joy unspeakable and full of glory'.)

Similarly Donald Macleod insists that his view of the baptism with the Spirit is 'experiential' but immediately says it may not be 'vivid and unforgetable'; it may not be 'conscious and memorable'.[53] Again it must be noted that an 'unconscious experience' is a contradiction in terms in Lloyd-Jones's terminology. Using the terminology of Lloyd-Jones, Macleod's view is certainly non-experiential. What Macleod calls 'unconscious' Lloyd-Jones calls 'non-experiential' or 'non-experimental', following a long-standing usage in the Christian church.

Lloyd-Jones would have agreed that regeneration is unconscious or non-experiential. However, he would have said that all descriptions of the baptism with the Spirit are vibrantly experiential, so much so that 'experience' in his sense of the term is a *sine qua non* of the baptism with the Spirit. It is not my task at this point to agree with either side. But we are implictly invited to look at the New Testament to enquire whether or not 'experience' is the inevitable characteristic of the baptism with the Spirit, and whether it is the inevitable characteristic of regeneration, and whether the two could be distinct.

Baptism with the Spirit as assurance of salvation

For Lloyd-Jones the central characteristic of the baptism with the Spirit was that it was an experience of directly given assurance, bestowed by Christ, surpassing any other form of assurance of salvation, and unmediated by any kind of syllogistic argumentation. It was thus identical with having one's salvation 'sealed'. In his thinking it is this central characteristic of the baptism with the Spirit that leads into other subsidiary characteristics or by-products of the experience. I have several proposition to make which may help to unfold this paragraph.

Firstly, baptism of the Spirit is primarily (for Dr Lloyd-Jones) an experience of assurance. The imagery of 'sealing' in Ephesians 1:13 focuses mainly on authentication.[54] The authentication operates in two ways. It authenticates *to others* the salvation of the Christian. The Spirit 'bears witness' to others of the salvation and sonship of God's people,[55] or (in the case of Jesus) the Spirit witnesses to the authentic divine sonship and Messiahship of Jesus.[56] Also (and this is where Lloyd-Jones's expositions put the emphasis) the Spirit witnesses to the person *himself* concerning his sonship and salvation. 'It is God's authentication of the fact that we really belong to him.'[57]

In developing this point while expounding Ephesians 1:13 Lloyd-Jones uses Romans 8:16 and Galatians 4:6.[58] He believes these verses of Scripture give the essential *content* of what happens at the sealing. What takes place in the baptism with the Spirit is that the Christian has his salvation confirmed to him. It is not that he becomes a Christian at that point; that has happened already. Rather, he says, 'You now begin to "experience" what you were before, in fact without realizing it.'[59] What this last phrase means is that it is possible to believe one is a Christian by *sheer* faith, but that in the baptism with the Spirit what before was a matter of *sheer* faith now becomes a matter of *conscious* experience. The gift is 'not the fact that we are sons, but our realization of it'.[60] Lloyd-Jones calls this the *first* result of the Spirit's baptism.[61] Everything else which characterizes the baptism with the Spirit flows from this primary point.

When expounding Romans 8:16 Lloyd-Jones says this baptism takes place when 'the Spirit by a direct operation on our minds and hearts and spirits gives us an absolute certainty and assurance of our sonship'. 'It is the Spirit telling us in this unusual way that we are the children of God. He lets us know in a way we have never known before that God loves us.[62] It is 'the highest form of assurance possible; there is nothing beyond it. It is the acme, the zenith of assurance and certainty of salvation!'[63]

Secondly, the assurance given in the baptism with the Spirit is immediate. That is to say, it is not mediated by any syllogistic argumentation. Lloyd-Jones calls it 'direct assurance' or 'direct and immediate testimony'. 'It is', he says, 'no longer something which I reason out of the Scripture; it is not the result of spiritual logic or deduction; it is direct and immediate.'[64] He quotes Wesley to the effect that, 'It is something immediate and direct, not the result of reflection or argumentation.'[65] Compared to other forms of assurance it is 'exceptional assurance'.[66]

In other words, unlike Sibbes and Goodwin, Lloyd-Jones maintains that a revelation is given to the Christian in the baptism with the Spirit which is over and above Scripture. It does not mean that an audible voice is heard or a vision seen,[67] although even that is not ruled out.[68] It may well be connected with a promise of Scripture.[69] Yet in the final analysis the assurance given in the baptism of the Spirit is a direct revelation from the Spirit of God to the Christian.

In addressing students in Canada in 1957 he said, 'This is not a form of assurance that I may deduce from the Scriptures, or from evidences which I find in myself. Here is a direct witness of the Spirit; the Spirit Himself beareth witness with my spirit.'[70]

One way Lloyd-Jones had of elucidating this point was to compare and contrast several forms of assurance of salvation. Again, this is concisely expressed in the lecture given in Canada in 1957. 'There are', he says, 'three main ways in which assurance comes to us. . . . The first is that to be obtained by believing and applying to ourselves the bare word of the Scriptures as the authoritative word of God. It tells us that "he that believeth on him is not condemned". There is God's Word, we believe it and rest upon it.'[71]

Yet Lloyd-Jones does not like to over-use this mode of assurance. He calls it 'the lowest form of assurance'.[72] He thought that, used alone, it could be quite delusive. This led him to a second form of assurance. 'We need something further, which is the second ground of assurance. The First Epistle of John provides us with certain criteria. John says that there are certain tests of spiritual life.' Lloyd-Jones goes on to list them: love of the brethren, finding the commands of the Lord no longer grievous, knowing one's faith in Jesus, awareness of the Spirit's working within us, awareness of the fruit of the Spirit within ourselves. 'If we find these things', he says, 'we can be assured that we are born again.'

It is in this context that Lloyd-Jones describes the witness of the Spirit as 'a further form of assurance ... the highest and most certain of all'. He goes on to say, 'It is possible for us to have the first two grounds of assurance without having this third. Here is something that the Spirit Himself alone can give us.'[73]

Although a variety of terms are, for Lloyd-Jones, closely related, several expressions used in the New Testament focus on the assuring aspect of the Spirit's work. The terms 'beareth witness' in Romans 8:16 speaks of the Spirit's work in assurance;[74] that in turn is 'just another way of stating the doctrine of the "sealing of the Spirit".'[75] The term 'baptism' is used to express the profusion of the gift: 'it is called a baptism because the Spirit was poured out upon men and women'.[76] 'Sealing' is the more appropriate term when authentication of God's promise is the point being emphasized.[77]

Subjective accompaniments of assurance

Although for Lloyd-Jones the *primary* characteristic of the direct witness of the Spirit was the assurance of salvation that it brought, that assurance had many repercussions. Thus in the expositions of Romans 8:16 and John 1:33 he spent some time describing the results or the characteristics of the baptism of the Spirit.[78] In the exposition of John 1:33 he divided his material concerning this matter into 'subjective' and 'objective' accompaniments. I shall make use of his division, although I shall also draw on statements he made while expounding Romans 8:16. I refer to eight subjective results of the baptism with the Spirit that Lloyd-Jones mentions.

'First and foremost,' says Lloyd-Jones, 'we have got to put this, a sense of the glory of God, an unusual sense of the presence of God.' This, he thinks, stands out both in the New Testament accounts in Acts and in the subsequent history of the church. He illustrates this from the story of Jonathan Edwards that has been mentioned above,[79] and also from an incident in the life of Thomas Charles Edwards, the principal of a theological college in Wales, who had an experience in which he was 'more certain of God than he was of even the things he could see with his naked eyes. He had met with God, he had felt the presence of God, he knew that God *is*. The glory of God had appeared to him.'

Secondly, Lloyd-Jones mentions a sense of awe. He refers to the experiences of Isaiah, of Moses before the burning bush, of John in the book of Revelation, of Paul on the Damascus road. 'Isn't this our trouble ... we talk about God and we believe in God but do we know God? The glory of God!' 'When we are baptized in this way with the Spirit, he makes all this thing vital and real to us. There is a kind of luminosity, an immediacy.'

Thirdly, he mentions that the baptism with the Spirit always humbles. This, he argues, is something that distinguishes true and false experience. He refers to an incident in the life of Whitefield in which Whitefield says he 'wept before the Lord under a deep sense of my own vileness'.[80]

A fourth subjective mark of the baptism with the Spirit which Lloyd-Jones mentioned in 1965 was 'an assurance of the love of God to us in Jesus Christ'. 'On the one hand, you see, you have such a conception of the glory and the greatness and the majesty of God, your own vileness and filthiness and foulness and unworthiness. "Well," you say, "it must be a most depressing experience." It isn't, for at the same time you have an over-whelming knowledge given to you of God's love to you in our Lord and Saviour Jesus Christ. . . . This is the greatest and most essential characteristic of the baptism with the Spirit.'[81]

In a further sermon in 1965 he continued his list of the 'marks' of the baptism with the Spirit. The next to be mentioned is, he believes, 'the element of joy and of gladness'. This is something to be found running through the New Testament, and he cites Acts 2:46–47, 1 Thessalonians 1:5–6.; Romans 5:1–5; 1 Peter 1:8. 'These people when they became Christians were subjected to the most terrible persecution ... yet we are told that though they were thus afflicted there was accompanying the affliction this joy in the Holy Ghost.' 'The inevitable result of a knowledge and an assurance of the love of God toward us is to fill us with this great joy.'[82] He says the same thing when expounding Romans 8:16: 'It is an experience ... which leads to great joy and love to God. There is no instance of it in the Bible which lacks this feature. How obvious it is in the second chapter of Acts! One can almost feel the exuberant joy that was in Peter and the others, lifting them up above their circumstances and giving them holy boldness.' 'This witness or sealing of the Spirit always leads to great joy and to a great love to God.'[83]

Another 'mark' of this experience is, in Lloyd-Jones's view, 'love to God', citing 1 John 4:18–19. 'You cannot know the love of God to you without loving God in return. . . . Our love to God rises as a response to his love to us. . . . It is a love which, as John puts it, casteth out fear.' 'It does not get rid of the awe, it increases that, but it removes fear. We realise we are no longer under law but under grace; we realise that we are the children of God and therefore we cry "Abba Father".' 'How do we approach God? How do we pray to God? . . . Do we know anything of a love rising up within us, a desire to know Him more and more and a desire even to be within Him. These are the things that are testified to in the Scriptures and by the saints throughout the centuries.'[84]

'The desire to glorify him' is yet another mark. Jesus, in promising the Spirit said, 'He shall glorify me'. 'One of the greatest results of the work of the Spirit and especially in the baptism is the desire to glorify the Lord Jesus Christ.' In the accounts in Acts, 'the first thing that happened when these apostles were baptized with the Holy Spirit was this: they began to speak and to tell forth the wonderful works of God.' 'A recent writer[85] on the fullness of the Spirit tries to say that the first sign of being filled with the Spirit is that we speak to one another. He is there countering the tendency to speak and pray in tongues to God, and he thinks he disposes of that by saying that in Ephesians 5:18 and following you find "speaking to one another" . . . Actually that isn't so. The first thing a man who is filled with the Spirit does is to speak to God! He praises God! And his first desire is to glorify the Lord Jesus Christ.'[86]

In preaching on Romans 8:16, Lloyd-Jones spoke of a desire to please God. The baptism with the Spirit 'leads to a great desire to please Him in everything, to keep His commandments, never to offend Him in anything, to honour His law'.[87]

Finally, Lloyd-Jones mentions 'light and understanding'. 'When a man is baptized with the Spirit he knows the truth as he has never known it before.' 'The test of the baptism of the Spirit is that it leads a man to the truth and to an understanding of the truth. It gives him light and understanding.' 'Would you know the Christian truth? Would you know Christian doctrine? Would you have a firm grasp and understanding of God's great and glorious purpose? The highway to that is the baptism of the Holy Ghost. It gives greater light and knowledge and instruction than anything else, and it does so in order that we may be witnesses.'[88]

Objective accompaniments of assurance

It was only in the series of sermons on John 1:26 and 33 that Lloyd-Jones made a clear distinction between the subjective and the objective results of the baptism with the Spirit. It must be mainly from these sermons that I draw out his 'objective' marks of the Spirit's seal. In two sermons preached on 24 and 31 January 1965, he presented four such objective results of the Spirit's work.

The events recorded in Acts 2 and 10 both contain the thought that what happened when the Spirit 'fell upon' the hearers was immediately apparent. On both occasions the visibility of the event to others is mentioned. Peter, according to the Acts account, speaks of 'this which you see and hear' (Acts 2:33) and of being immediately aware of the Spirit's coming upon the Gentiles (Acts 10:46). It is these visible objective characteristics which Lloyd-Jones wishes to list.

The first that he mentions is the transformation of facial appearance. He is aware that it might surprise the congregation that he puts this first but he deliberately does so. He cites the incident of the shining face of Moses. 'Moses did not know it but his face was shining. And his face was shining because he had been in the presence of God and something of the glory of God was being reflected back from the face of Moses.' Lloyd-Jones finds something similar in the transfiguration narrative in the gospels. 'What seems so clear is that because the baptism with the Holy Spirit does bring one into the presence of God and into a living and an active realisation of God and his glory it is not at all surprising that one of the inevitable concomitants is that something happens even to the physical facial appearance of people

177

who receive this baptism.' In connection with this Lloyd-Jones quotes the way in which 'it was evident at once to the populace of Jerusalem that something had happened to these men ... not only because they spake with other tongues, with other languages but everything about them, their very appearance, their conduct and various other things.' They *saw* something as well as *heard* something, he says, citing again Acts 2:33.

He points also to the incident in which Stephen's face is said to have shone (Acts 6:15), and urges that something similar occurs in the baptism with the Spirit. 'If you read the accounts of the great revivals in the history of the church you will find that this is something that has been frequently noted', he says and goes on to tell of the experience of a woman who had become a Christian in a 'visitation of the Spirit' in the Scottish island of Lewis in 1949:

> She was not very interested in these things but a friend of hers became interested and at last she was persuaded to go to one of these meetings of prayer ... The thing that led to her conversion was the sight of the face of a little child in that house ... This woman suddenly saw the child's face shining and that was the means of her conviction of sin, her need of a saviour and of her salvation ...

He also says this took place in the revival in Wales in 1904.

> I have often heard it from people whom I have known well and intimately who experienced something of the revival in Wales of 1904 and 1905 and it was frequently said about Mr Evan Roberts who was so signally used in that revival. People were amazed when they just saw his face and this shining quality.

Robert Murray McCheyne was known for the same thing.[89]

A second objective characteristic of the baptism with the Spirit is the effect it has upon men's speech. Lloyd-Jones is not referring at this point to the gift of tongues but to preaching and personal conversation. 'When people are baptised with the Spirit they discover certain things happen in this matter of testimony and of speaking to others whether in private conversation or, as

I say, in a more public manner.' This is why the disciples were to wait until they were endued with power which would enable them to speak. There are anticipations of this in the Old Testament, in Lloyd-Jones's opinion, in the stories of the prophets. They receive a 'divine afflatus' to enable bold speech. Lloyd-Jones ended this particular sermon by telling the story of something that had happened in his own experience. In a prayer meeting one Monday evening during his ministry at Aberavon, a man began to pray. He was not a man who was in any way gifted or of exceptional ability. But, says Lloyd-Jones, on this occasion:

. . . this man had not uttered more than two or three sentences before I was aware and everybody else became aware of something most extraordinary. He was halting normally, fumbling, pedestrian, ordinary, let me even use the word boring, but suddenly this man was entirely transformed. His voice deepened, a power came into it, even in his speech, and he prayed in the freest, most powerful manner I think I've ever heard in my life. . . . The prayer continued without any intermission and the freedom that had accompanied this man's prayer was given to all the others and that went on until ten to ten. I hadn't said a word, there was no hymn-singing, there was nothing. It was just this tremendous freedom, power in prayer. Once felt that one was outside time. One felt that one was in heaven. One was really lifted up to the spiritual realm. And here I was listening to people whom I knew so well with freedom and power and assurance, people taking part who had never prayed in public in their lives before and who had been terrified at the very thought of it found themselves praying.

A similar point is made in the stories of Tauler, Savonarola, John Livingstone, Howell Harris, David Morgan, D. L. Moody, R. A. Torrey and A. B. Simpson.[90]

The following week, 31 January 1965, Lloyd-Jones went on to list two further objective characteristics of the baptism with the Holy Spirit.

A third characteristic is the note of authority given to one baptized in such a way. This was what struck people about Jesus.

179

Although only a carpenter, the note of authority was conspicuous, and was the result of his having been baptized with the Spirit at his baptism with water. Lloyd-Jones quotes also Jesus' reading from Isaiah in the synagogue at Nazareth ('He has anointed me to preach . . .'). Similarly with Peter the contrast before and after Pentecost is striking. Other instances are found in Acts 3 and Acts 4 which may be described as 'another baptism of power and authority'. 'All these men always *knew* they had this authority in speech, they had this authority in performing miracles. It's always a characteristic. And as you read again the subsequent history of the church you will find that this is the thing that always characterizes these people, this authority. You get it in every revival. . . . It's characterized, I say, all men always who have received the baptism of the Spirit.'

Closely allied to the previous point are the boldness and fearlessness that accompany the baptism with the Spirit. Lloyd-Jones regards Peter the apostle, again, as a classic example of this boldness. 'This is obviously one of the great characteristics of the baptism with the Spirit, it gives this boldness and fearlessness.'[91]

It is in connection with the matter of the 'objective' marks of the baptism with the Spirit that Lloyd-Jones proceeded, in 1965, to deal with the gifts of the Spirit.[92] I have outlined above the gist of Lloyd-Jones's arguments in 1965. Here I simply emphasize that in his view the gifts of the Spirit were a possible manifestation of the baptism with the Spirit. This matter was given its most detailed consideration in 1965, but Lloyd-Jones had said much the same thing before: 'the Spirit's witness may, or may not, be accompanied by gifts and phenomena. . . . A man may receive this witness, this sealing, with no such phenomena.'[93]

Baptism with the Spirit and power for witness

It is helpful to explore the relationship, as Lloyd-Jones saw it, between the baptism with the Spirit and power for testimony. As we have already seen there was a school of thought represented particularly by D. L. Moody and R. A. Torrey that especially linked the baptism with the Spirit and power for service. Torrey had written that 'the baptism with the Holy Spirit is a work of the Holy Spirit always connected with and primarily for the purpose of testimony and service.'[94] Lloyd-Jones agreed, but the particular way in which he viewed the matter is significant. The *primary* purpose of the sealing of the Spirit was to give an intensified and unmediated assurance of salvation. However, such an added assurance immediately enabled the Christian to function as a witness. The power for testimony comes *via* the assurance of salvation.

In the sermons on Ephesians 1:13 it is mainly the assurance of salvation that receives mention. Lloyd-Jones speaks of 'joy of salvation',[95] and refers to Romans 8:16 and Galatians 4:6 for further elucidation.[96] He mentions that *lack* of the sealing with the Spirit will hinder witness: 'if we feel that we are ineffective as Christians and that our usefulness is not very evident, then I suggest that it is again due to this selfsame thing, namely, our failure to realize what is meant by God's sealing of His children by "that Holy Spirit of Promise".'[97] If the sealing is neglected or misunderstood the church will be 'lacking in vital power in her capacity of witness'.[98]

In expounding Romans 8:16 he goes slightly further. The 'witness' is 'the highest form of assurance',[99] but Lloyd-Jones mentions more clearly the consequences it will have in giving power to witness. It will lead, he says, to 'a desire to witness to Him, accompanied by the power and ability to do so'.[100] He emphasizes that it is the assurance that leads to the enabling power behind Christians' testimony. The apostles 'had great boldness and power.... They could not witness until they were absolutely certain of their position, until they were given this tremendous certainty. That is what happened on the day of Pentecost. That is what happens always when one receives "the baptism of the Spirit".'[101]

It is during the sermons on John 1:33 that Lloyd-Jones mentions most emphatically that this is of crucial importance in the baptism with the Spirit. Once again he stresses that 'one of the main effects and results of the baptism with the Holy Ghost is to give us an unusual assurance of our salvation'. Yet now he emphasizes even more than before that the assurance given in the baptism with the Spirit is primarily designed to enable testimony. Even Jesus needed such an experience to seal *his* sonship. Though he was 'more than regenerate' he 'needed to receive the Spirit in his fulness.... Our lord himself could not act as witness

181

and as preacher and as testifier to the gospel of salvation without receiving this enduement of the Spirit, and that . . . is the purpose of the baptism with the Holy Ghost.'[102]

It is this point that is frequently mentioned and developed in the sermons on John 1:33. 'Without this baptism of the Spirit, this baptism with power, no one can witness to him, neither a preacher in a pulpit nor an individual living life day by day or talking to men and women about the world and its state and condition and all its affairs.'[103] In a later sermon he lays it down as an explicit proposition: 'The baptism with the Spirit is always associated primarily and specifically with witness and testimony and service. . . . Go through your book of the Acts of the Apostles and you will find in every instance when we are told that the Spirit either came upon these men or that they were filled with the Spirit it was in order to bear a witness and a testimony.'[104] The next sermon makes the same point: 'Beyond any question the primary purpose and function of the baptism with the Spirit is to enable us to be witnesses to the Lord Jesus Christ and to his great salvation.' We must . . . hold in our minds, I say, this great vital central principle that the baptism with the Holy Ghost is essentially concerned with our witness, to make us witnesses, to make us powerful witnesses.' Later he connects the themes of assurance and witness. An overwhelming experience of God's love to us 'is *the* greatest and most essential characteristic of the baptism of the Spirit. He makes us witnesses because of our assurance. That's his way of making us witnesses.'[105]

Baptism with the Holy Spirit and sanctification

Lloyd-Jones was repeatedly at pains to distinguish the baptism with the Spirit from sanctification. Several reasons for his concern are apparent. One was that in popular evangelicalism the term 'filled with the Spirit' was widely used. This was not altogether a mistake, in Lloyd-Jones's view, because the terms 'filled' and 'baptized' are implicitly interchangeable in Acts 2 where it is said that the disciples were 'filled with the Holy Spirit' (Acts 2:4).[106] Yet because this was associated with Ephesians 5:18 which clearly deals with the responsibility of the Christian to live by the power of the Spirit, many Christians in the 1950s and 1960s used the text in Ephesians 5:18 to urge Christians to seek the baptism with the Spirit. It was this that led J. R. W. Stott to address himself to that particular text when he wrote *The Baptism and Fullness of the Holy Spirit.* Lloyd-Jones felt that the baptism with the Spirit and Ephesians 5:18 had no direct connection.

Another reason for his concern was the historical association of the baptism with the Spirit with sanctification in the Wesleyan-Methodist tradition. Wesley was guilty of confusion in his teaching, Lloyd-Jones believed, because he linked the sealing of the Spirit with 'perfect love' or what he called 'scriptural holiness'.[107] In his address to the Westminster Conference in 1974 he surveyed the history of this line of thinking, illustrating it particularly from the origins of the Primitive Methodist Church. 'These men', said Lloyd-Jones, 'passed through a great experience which they interpreted as being "a baptism of the Spirit". They called it a "spirit of burning", a burning away of the dross.'[108] He admired these men and recommended the reading of their history, yet he also believed they added to the confusion concerning the baptism with the Spirit. 'I believe these men confused in their thinking a baptism of power with sanctification. There is no doubt about their power – the historical records prove this – but they clearly got confused in their doctrine as between power to witness and to preach and sanctification.'[109]

Three points worth considering are: the way in which Lloyd-Jones tried to clarify the usage of the term 'filled with the Spirit'; the lack of direct connection between the baptism with the Spirit and sanctification; and the indirect links between the two themes which Lloyd-Jones asserts.

It was when preaching on Ephesians 5:18 that he gave his most detailed consideration of the way in which terms like 'full' or 'filled' are used in the New Testament.[110] He maintained that there were two distinct usages of the term, one of which had no connection with the baptism with the Spirit. He pointed to a series of texts (Exodus 31:3; Luke 1:41,[111] 67; Acts 2:4; 4:8, 31; 13:9) in which an abrupt and sudden enabling came upon a believer to enable him to fulfil a particular task. This is a 'special enduement, a special filling with the Spirit, in order that he might fulfill that task'.[112]

Then Lloyd-Jones maintains there is a distinct usage of the

term where men are said to be 'full' of the spirit. Acts 6:3; 7:55; 11:24; 13:52 are quoted (although he is doubtful about the interpretation of Acts 7:55 and thinks that could come in either category). These verses are 'an account of a state or condition'.[113] It is this that is being referred to in Ephesians 5:18 when the mood is imperative and the tense is a present tense with continuous force. In Ephesians 5:18 Christians are being urged that they should let the Spirit control them and that this should be the regular state of their life. It is an ethical injunction. For Lloyd-Jones this is an entirely different matter from the baptism with the Spirit which can never be the subject of a command ('Be baptized with the Spirit') and which is a 'definite concrete experience'.[114] One may distinguish therefore between what we may call a 'continuous' and an 'aoristic' filling with the Spirit. (Lloyd-Jones does not use these precise terms but I employ them for the purposes of discussion.)

Lloyd-Jones is not always very clear in his discussion of the precise relationships between the 'baptism' and the two kinds of 'filling'. He maintains that there is no *direct* connection between the *continuous* filling of the Spirit (which concerns sanctification) and the baptism with the Spirit (which concerns assurance and power for witness). The relationship between the baptism with the Spirit and the *aoristic* (to use my term) filling of the Spirit is more subtle. Lloyd-Jones wrestles with Acts 2:4 and his comments on it are not always consistent. On one occasion he said 'the word "baptized" is not used in Acts 2; the word used is "filled". Clearly the terms are used interchangeably.' At this point then, Lloyd-Jones maintained that 'filled' *could* be interchangeable with 'baptized' but that it did not *have* to be. 'The explanation seems to be', he says, 'that the baptism with the Spirit is the first experience of the fullness of the Spirit; it is the Spirit poured upon us in this exceptional fullness. The first time something outstanding happens is always unique.'[115] This means that Lloyd-Jones can occasionally describe what happened in Acts 4:31 ('they were all filled with the Holy Spirit') as 'another baptism'.[116] In addition he interprets Acts 9:17 (where the term 'filled' is used) as the occasion when the apostle Paul was baptized with the Spirit.[117]

On another occasion, however, Lloyd-Jones can say that what is happening at the point recorded in Acts 2:4 is that two things are coming together. The disciples are being baptized with the Spirit *and* they are being specially filled so as to be able to speak in tongues. 'That is a unique statement because the two things happened together. There is the baptism plus, or including, the filling; and it is this that enables them to speak with other tongues.'[118]

To summarize Lloyd-Jones's view of the terminology then: the idea of being 'filled' with the Spirit is used in two ways. When it refers to a continual state, Christian obedience is being dealt with. This may be the subject of ethical exhortation; this is the significance of Ephesians 5:18. When 'filled' is used in an aorist tense or speaks of a particular event on a particular occasion, it *may* refer to the 'baptism with the Spirit'. When a person is 'baptized with the Spirit' it is always an enduement of power and therefore the word 'filled with the Spirit' in an aorist tense is appropriate. The baptism of the Spirit may be repeated. When it is repeated the New Testament may use the word 'filled' (as was the case in Acts 4:31). The terminology of the New Testament confines being 'baptized with the Spirit' to the first occasion when such an enduement is experienced. However, Lloyd-Jones is quite happy to use the term 'baptized again' when further enduements of power are experienced. This *aoristic* use of the term 'filling' has no direct connection with sanctification and to refer Ephesians 5:18 to the 'baptism with the Spirit' is disastrously confusing.

On several occasions[119] Lloyd-Jones explains that the baptism with the Spirit has no direct connection with sanctification. Lloyd-Jones puts forward a series of arguments to refute the idea that the two are identical or inseparable.[120] Acts 15:9 and 26:18 refer not to *progressive* sanctification but to definitive sanctification at conversion. The state of the church of Corinth clearly indicates the distinctness of the baptism with the Spirit and sanctification, for that congregation was clearly endowed with the gifts of the Spirit that follow the baptism with the Spirit, yet was in a state of serious moral compromise.[121] The exhortations of Scripture imply that sanctification is a matter of human conflict, not of receiving an 'experience' of sanctification.[122] The 'baptism with the Spirit *is* a tremendous experience, sanctification is not'.[123]

On the other hand, Lloyd-Jones believes that there is an

indirect connection with the baptism with the Spirit. 'Those who have had this experience say that, when the Spirit bore witness with their spirit that they were children of God, they were aware that they were in the presence of the holy God ... they hated sin, and never wanted to sin again.... It can easily be understood how people feel at the moment of the experience that they are entirely cleansed from sin.' 'The baptism of the Spirit does stimulate and promote sanctification, indeed it is the greatest possible help to it.'[124] 'It is the greatest stimulus to sanctification but it is not sanctification itself.'[125]

Baptism with the Spirit and the gifts of the Spirit

Lloyd-Jones was sympathetic to Pentecostalism, as indeed he was sympathetic to any evangelical group which emphasized the need of the working of the Holy Spirit. Shortly after his death a Pentecostal minister, Wesley Richards wrote of him: 'The breadth of vision and immense spiritual stature of Dr Martyn Lloyd-Jones have long been appreciated by many of us in "classical Pentecostal" circles.'[126]

Unlike many who were known as 'Reformed' ministers, Lloyd-Jones firmly believed in the possible continuation in the church of gifts of the Spirit. He was, however, exceedingly cautious about accepting the validity of particular claims. His address to the Christian Medical Fellowship which was published under the title *The Supernatural in the Practice of Medicine* expressed words of caution about Kathryn Kuhlman's work which he said contained an 'obviously powerful psychological element'.[127] His most detailed exposition of the subject is summarized, in outline analysis form, above. Five highlights of his doctrine at this point may be summarized here.

Firstly, Lloyd-Jones was not impressed by 'phenomena' in and of themselves. This receives full treatment in the lecture mentioned above. He felt that 'those who are over impressed by the occurrence of certain phenomena' were making a mistake. He called this 'capitulation to phenomena'.[128] His conviction was that since there were a number of agencies other than the Holy Spirit that could give rise to impressive phenomena, unusual occurrences were not in and of themselves particularly significant. He accepted the *facts* that were reported concerning not only evangelical Christians such as Kathryn Kuhlman but also concerning Harry Edwards the spiritualist, and concerning the inexplicable healing at Lourdes. 'I cannot say that they are liars', he said of such people, 'neither can I believe they are deluded. Everything that one knows about these people, or can discover about them, suggests that they are reliable witnesses.'[129] Yet he believed that both the mysterious psychological element in man and even demonic forces could so counterfeit miracles that the phenomena did not prove anything in themselves.

Secondly, Lloyd-Jones accepted that miracles and gifts had at certain times been known in the post-apostolic church. He accepted the claim to the miraculous that had been reported in the Indonesian revival.[130] He would cite approvingly the miracles reported in connection with the ministry of the Chinese Christian known as Pastor Hsi.[131] He recommended and wrote a foreword to H. W. Frost's book *Miraculous Healing*,[132] in which several incidents of miraculous healing are related. He accepted as authentic the accounts of a resurrection from the dead in the ministry of John Welch, the son-in-law of John Knox, and he accepted the stories of accurate predictions made by the Scottish covenanter, Alexander Peden.[133]

Thirdly, he also warned of the danger of credulity. Just as some are too fearful of extremism, he thought that others were too fearful of unbelief and so open to easy acceptance of anything that claims to be miraculous. 'There are credulous people,' he said. 'There are some men, they are always anxious for the unusual, it's their danger. . . . This is often the result of a spirit of fear.' Some are not afraid of quenching the Spirit, others are terrified of quenching the Spirit. 'They are so afraid of standing against a work of God that they pass things that they should not pass'; there may be 'an uncritical attitude resulting from a spirit of fear. This is what leads always to fanaticism.' It was a constant danger, says Lloyd-Jones, in revival as it had been earlier in the church of Corinth.[134]

For Lloyd-Jones, the key to this matter was the phrase 'as He wills' in 1 Corinthians 12:11. He pointed out that in the vast majority of the accounts of spiritual awakening in the story of the church and in the vast majority of accounts of men who have been baptized with the Spirit, claims to gifts of the Spirit are not included. The heroes whom Lloyd-Jones admired, George Whitefield, D. L. Moody, Jonathan Edwards and many others, had never made any claim to speak in tongues or to have any other gift. It was just as big a mistake to make the gifts of the Spirit indispensable to the baptism with the Spirit as it was to dismiss the gifts of the Spirit altogether. His conclusion was, 'that this question of the gifts is entirely in the sovereignty of the Holy Spirit. He "giveth severally to each one *as He wills*". We must never use this word claim. We must realise that the Spirit may give or not give.... Because these matters are in the sovereignty of the Spirit they are always possible ... but we mustn't say that we should expect them always.' He thought they might be expected in times of declension in the story of the church where a new revival was needed.

The history of revivals, however, has many lessons. 'There are always certain phenomena.... Sometimes there is a kind of prophetic gift given.... Yet this is a point that I want to note and to emphasize.... In the great revivals in the church throughout the centuries there has not been very much by way of the manifestation of some of these particular gifts such as tongues.... I am not saying that it is absent altogether but I am saying that it is uncommon, unusual, and likewise the evidence of miracles.' Lloyd-Jones believes that 'This establishes ... quite clearly ... that the baptism of the Spirit is not always accompanied by particular gifts.' Later he said, 'You may have a baptism of the Spirit and a mighty baptism of the Spirit with none of the gift of tongues, none of the gift of miracles, and various other gifts.' There is an all-important principle: 'You must draw a distinction between the baptism of the Spirit itself and its occasional or possible concomitants. We must keep these things distinct in our minds.' The dominant factor is the sovereignty of the Spirit.[135]

Another significant element in Lloyd-Jones's doctrine was his teaching concerning the Spirit's commissioning before any gift of the Spirit could be exercised. For him a gift of the Spirit could not be exercised at will. He believed that the gift of tongues could not be initiated by the Christian and that the person who was enabled to speak in tongues could not do so at will. He argues this point from 1 Corinthians 14:18. When Paul said 'I thank my God I speak with tongues more than ye all', he was

188

claiming to speak *more frequently* than the Corinthians. Lloyd-Jones goes on to argue:

> If it is true to say that a man can speak in tongues whenever he likes what is the point of the apostle's statement? If it is true of all who have the gift of speaking in tongues that they can do so whenever they like, at will, well what is the point of the apostle saying that he speaks in tongues more frequently than they all do? It would simply mean this that he *decides* to do so more frequently than they do. But there's no purpose in saying that and indeed in the next verse he makes that explanation impossible for this reason. He says 'Yet in the church I had rather speak five words with my understanding that by my voice I might teach others also than ten thousand words in an unknown tongue.' No, it seems to me there is only one explanation of this statement. . . . The apostle says 'I think I know more than any of you do what it is to be taken up by the Spirit. . . . The Spirit comes more frequently upon me than any of you. . . . You are making me boast'.

1 Corinthians 14:30 implies the same point. A message is *given* to a prophet; he cannot speak at will in a prophetic manner. 'Now the whole of these gifts are *given*,' says Lloyd-Jones. A man cannot work a miracle whenever he likes even if he has the gift of miracles. 'I am here to suggest', he says, 'that if a man tells me that he can speak in tongues whenever he likes it is probably something psychological and not spiritual. These are always controlled by the Holy Spirit. They are given and one does not know when it is going to be given.' He goes on to point to the miracles of the book of Acts. The apostles never *tried* to heal someone and then failed; they never made an announcement that they would work a miracle. In Acts 3 the apostles passed the beggar at the gate regularly but on one day were given a commission to heal. The same thing is true in Acts 14 and Acts 16 where we are told that a demon-possessed woman troubled the apostles for 'many days' before a miraculous exorcism took place.[136]

Lloyd-Jones links this with the 'prayer of faith' in James 5:15. It is a 'given' faith. 'All true divinely wrought miracle is "given";

189

and "the prayer of faith" is given. No one can work it up; he either has it or he does not have such faith. It partly depends upon a man's general spirituality and his general faith in God, and still more upon His sovereign will.'[137]

It was this that made Lloyd-Jones cautious about accepting claims concerning the gift of tongues. He tells the story of one man who had found himself being given such a gift but being very distressed that he could not ever exercise the gift again. 'I know a man', said Lloyd-Jones, 'a missionary for years in China, who tells me that on one occasion when alone in his room he was baptized with the Holy Ghost and found himself speaking in tongues. He has never done so since. Now this man was often worried about this and had spoken to me about it. . . . I said "My dear friend the fact that you tell me that it's only happened to you once makes me say that it was genuine and authentic. If you told me that you could do it whenever you liked I'd be really troubled".'

This means that Lloyd-Jones was sceptical of those who thought they could 'switch on' tongues at will. Also he disagreed with those who taught that the gift of tongues is the initial evidence of the baptism with the Spirit.

Such was Lloyd-Jones's approach then to the gifts of the Spirit. They could be given with the baptism with the Spirit but were not indispensible to it. Other agencies, psychological and demonic, could produce phenomena and so phenomena in themselves were non-significant. Gifts could only be exercised when a commission was given.

Seeking the baptism with the Spirit

Lloyd-Jones taught that every believer should seek the baptism with the Spirit. The fact that exhortations to seek the Spirit are not found in the New Testament did not overthrow this. In New Testament times most Christians had received the baptism with the Spirit, so the apostles had to assume a kind of norm when writing to the churches, and thus take it for granted that every Christian has received the baptism with the Spirit. Our danger, however, is to estimate the possibilities of spiritual experience in terms of what we are familiar with. The New Testament era started with a tremendous outpouring of the Spirit. 1 Peter 1:8

could be written to Christians that had never been directly known by the apostle Peter. The modern Christian should therefore seek what was the norm of New Testament times.[138]

Seeking the baptism of the Spirit is therefore very much a matter of prayer and living in such a way that God is likely to hear our prayer. The Christian must realise the possibility of altogether greater and richer experience than he perhaps knows at present. He watches his motive, which is to glorify the Lord Jesus Christ, not merely to have an 'experience'. He obeys his Lord and makes the baptism of the Spirit a matter of prayer. In doing this he may find anything happening to him. Trials and discouragements may come his way. But he allows God to lead him on. He is persistent and patient.

At this point in the argument Lloyd-Jones considers 'tarrying meetings'. He cannot forbid them altogether but feels the Christian should be wary of the psychological pressures that come in such gatherings.[139] Lloyd-Jones was very fond of quoting in this connection some words of Thomas Goodwin: 'Seek it', said Lloyd-Jones. 'Be satisfied with nothing less. Has God ever told you that you are His child? If not, seek it, cry out to Him, saying, "Speak, I pray Thee, gentle Jesus", and "Sue Him for it", and keep on until He speaks to you.'[140]

Notes

[1]D. M. Lloyd-Jones, *God's Ultimate Purpose*, p. 249; see also p. 264 ('I am suggesting therefore that the "baptism with the Spirit" is the same as the "sealing with the Spirit".') and p. 269.

[2]*Ibid.*, p. 253.

[3]*Ibid.*, p. 256.

[4]*Ibid.*, p. 265.

[5]*Ibid.*, pp. 271–274.

[6]*Ibid.*, p. 301.

[7]D. M. Lloyd-Jones, *Sons of God*, pp. 267–268.

[8]*Ibid.*, pp. 296–298.

[9]*Ibid.*, p. 391.

[10]D. M. Lloyd-Jones, *The Gospel of John* (sound recording [Barcombe Mills, East Sussex: Martyn Lloyd-Jones Recording Trust]), sermon 1098.

[11]*Ibid.*, sermon 1098.

[12]D. M. Lloyd-Jones, *God's Ultimate Purpose*, p. 253.

[13]*Ibid.*, pp. 249–253.

[14]D. M. Lloyd-Jones, *John* (sound recording), sermon 1098; the citation is from C. Hodge, *A Commentary on the Epistle to the Ephesians* (London: Banner of Truth, 1964), p. 62.

[15]This is currently available as *Baptism and Fullness: The work of the Holy Spirit*

today, J. R. W. Stott (London: IVP, 1964; 2nd ed., Leicester: IVP, 1975).

[16]D. M. Lloyd-Jones, *The New Man*, pp. 66–67.

[17]*Ibid.*, p. 61.

[18]J. Calvin, *A Commentary on the Twelve Minor Prophets* (reprinted Edinburgh: Banner of Truth, 1986), vol. 2, p. 136.

[19]*Ibid.*, vol. 5, p. 73. See also p. 117.

[20]D. M. Lloyd-Jones, *John* (sound recording), sermon 1099.

[21]This observation stems from first-hand knowledge, for I was present at the Islington Clerical Conference which (as I recall) was in 1962 or 1963. Despite the title of the conference it was not held at Islington in north London but at Westminster less than a kilometre away from Westminster Chapel.

[22]D. M. Lloyd-Jones, *God's Ultimate Purpose*, p. 267.

[23]*Ibid.*, p. 268.

[24]D. M. Lloyd-Jones, *Sons of God*, p. 314.

[25]D. M. Lloyd-Jones, *John* (sound recording), sermon 1099. See K. S. Wuest, *Untranslatable Riches from the Greek New Testament* (Grand Rapids: Eerdmans, 1942, reprinted 1983), pp. 83–90. I have punctuated the citation in the way that Lloyd-Jones read it.

I have been asked, 'If one work is ascribed to Jesus and the other to the Spirit, does not this affect one's doctrine of the Trinity and introduce a division into the Trinity?' I do not know that Lloyd-Jones ever addressed this question – and it is *his* doctrine that I am expounding – but he might have replied: The doctrine of the atonement has faced the same objection but the objection is not valid. The works of the trinity *ad extra* (outside the Godhead) are undivided. Yet it was Jesus who died, not the Father. It was the Father who sent the Son. It was the Spirit sent by the Father who empowered Jesus.

The New Testament *does* ascribe (Lloyd-Jones might have said) the work of shedding forth the Spirit to Jesus; and it does ascribe the work of placing the believer in Christ to the Spirit.

Yet both ministries are trinitarian. In the one case baptism *by the Spirit* into *Christ* (Romans 6:3) and into the body of Christ (1 Corinthians 12:13) is also ascribed to *God's* sovereignty over his church (1 Corinthians 12:18). There are different gifts but 'the same Lord . . . the same God . . . the Spirit' (1 Corinthians 12:5, 6, 11). In the other case *Jesus* prays to *the Father* and the result is an experiential outpouring of *the Spirit* (John 14:16); the *Father* exalts *Jesus* who pours forth *the Spirit* (Acts 2:33).

[26]Quoted from John Preston, *New Covenant* (1692), p. 202. in I. Morgan, *Puritan Spirituality* (London: Epworth Press, 1973), p. 59.

[27]D. M. Lloyd-Jones, *Sons of God*, p. 197. For this view, see R. C. H. Lenski, *The Interpretation of St Paul's Epistle to the Romans* (Minneapolis: Augsberg, 1961), p. 522; W. Sanday and A. C. Headlam, *A Critical and Exegetical Commentary on the Epistle to the Romans* (Edinburgh: T. & T. Clark, 5th ed., 1902), p. 202.

[28]D. M. Lloyd-Jones, *Sons of God*, pp. 197–198. For this view, see R. Haldane, *Exposition of the Epistle to the Romans* with Foreword by D. M. Lloyd-Jones (London: Banner of Truth, 1958), p. 353. Lloyd-Jones is here disagreeing with his favourite commentator on Romans.

John Murray and C. E. B. Cranfield take both occurrences of *pneuma* as alluding to the Holy Spirit but point out that the first occurrence comes in a negative statement. The point is, in their view, that the Spirit is *not* received as a 'Spirit of bondage' (J. Murray, *The Epistle to the Romans* [Grand Rapids: Eerdmans, 1968]), p. 296. C. E. B. Cranfield, *A Critical and Exegetical Commentary on the Epistle to the Romans* (Edinburgh: T. & T. Clark, 6th ed., 1975), p. 396.

[29]Occasionally Acts 4 is also mentioned as 'the same thing . . . repeated' (D. M. Lloyd-Jones, *Sons of God*, p. 297).

[30]D. M. Lloyd-Jones, *John* (sound recording), sermon 1104.

[31]D. M. Lloyd-Jones, *Sons of God*, p. 297.

[32]*Ibid.*, p. 310.

[33]*Ibid.*, p. 311; see also D. M. Lloyd-Jones, *God's Ultimate Purpose*, pp. 250–251, 259.

[34]D. M. Lloyd-Jones, *Sons of God*, p. 297.

[35]*Ibid.*, p. 264.

[36]*Ibid.*, p. 264.

[37]*Ibid.*, p. 311; D. M. Lloyd-Jones, *God's Ultimate Purpose*, pp. 251, 259.

[38]D. M. Lloyd-Jones, *Sons of God*, p. 358; see also D. M. Lloyd-Jones, *God's Ultimate Purpose*, p. 251.

[39]D. M. Lloyd-Jones, *Sons of God*, pp. 265–266, 311. Lloyd-Jones seeks to refute the suggestion that Acts 11:15 ('when we believed') is opposed to his view. He quotes A. T. Robertson and makes the point that 'the statement about "believing" may apply equally well to the apostles themselves or to Cornelius', and urges that the participial phrase only means 'having believed'. The situation is similar, he believes, to that in Ephesians 1:13 (D. M. Lloyd-Jones, *Sons of God*, pp. 312–314).

[40]D. M. Lloyd-Jones, *John* (sound recording), sermon 1080.

[41]D. M. Lloyd-Jones, *Sons of God*, p. 267.

[42]*Ibid.*, p. 311. See also *God's Ultimate Purpose*, pp. 252–254. I comment on this below, [pp. 234–235.]

[43]D. M. Lloyd-Jones, *Sons of God*, p. 297.

[44]D. M. Lloyd-Jones, *God's Ultimate Purpose*, p. 262.

[45]*Ibid.*, p. 267.

[46]*Ibid.*, p. 269.

[47]*Ibid.*, pp. 269–270.

[48]*Ibid.*, p. 271.

[49]D. M. Lloyd-Jones, *Sons of God*, p. 327; also pp. 309–310.

[50]D. M. Lloyd-Jones, *John* (sound recording), sermon 1085.

[51]John R. W. Stott, *Baptism and Fullness* (Leicester: IVP, 2nd ed., 1975), pp. 36–37, 43.

[52]*Ibid.*, pp. 64–65.

[53]Donald McLeod, *The Spirit of Promise* (Fearn: Christian Focus, 1986), p. v.

[54]D. M. Lloyd-Jones, *God's Ultimate Purpose*, pp. 245–248.

[55]*Ibid.*, p. 265.

[56]*Ibid.*, pp. 346–347, 266.

[57]*Ibid.*, p. 265.

[58]*Ibid.*, p. 271.

[59]*Ibid.*, p. 272.

[60]*Ibid.*, p. 274.

[61]*Ibid.*, p. 279.

[62]D. M. Lloyd-Jones, *Sons of God*, p. 301.

[63]*Ibid.*, p. 301.

[64]D. M. Lloyd-Jones, *God's Ultimate Purpose*, p. 274.

[65]*Ibid.*, p. 275.

[66]*Ibid.*, p. 301.

[67]*Ibid.*, p. 274.

[68]In a sermon preached in 1968, shortly before his retirement, Lloyd-Jones spoke of the experience of a certain Colonel Gardiner whose experience did involve a vision of Christ; see D. M. Lloyd-Jones, *John* (sound recording), sermon 1178.

193

[69]D. M. Lloyd-Jones, *God's Ultimate Purpose*, p. 274.

[70]D. M. Lloyd-Jones, *Authority* (London: IVF, 1958), p. 77.

[71]*Ibid.*, pp. 76–77.

[72]D. M. Lloyd-Jones, *John* (sound recording), sermon 1086.

[73]D. M. Lloyd-Jones, *Authority*, pp. 76–78.

[74]D. M. Lloyd-Jones, *Sons of God*, pp. 287–288.

[75]*Ibid.*, p. 301.

[76]D. M. Lloyd-Jones, *God's Ultimate Purpose*, p. 264.

[77]*Ibid.*, pp. 264–265.

[78]Lloyd-Jones varies in the precise term he uses. In one sermon he speaks of the 'marks and signs or, if you prefer it, the results of this baptism with the Holy Spirit'; D. M. Lloyd-Jones, *John* (sound recording), sermon 1086.

[79]See pp. 115ff.

[80]*George Whitefield's Journals*, edited by I. Murray (London: Banner of Truth, 1960), p. 487.

[81]D. M. Lloyd-Jones, *John* (sound recording), sermon 1086.

[82]*Ibid.*, sermon 1087.

[83]D. M. Lloyd-Jones, *Sons of God*, p. 328.

[84]D. M. Lloyd-Jones, *John* (sound recording), sermon 1087; see also D. M. Lloyd-Jones, *Sons of God*, p. 304.

[85]Lloyd-Jones refers here to John Stott's *Baptism and Fullness*. See the second edition, 1975, p. 57.

[86]D. M. Lloyd-Jones, *John* (sound recording), sermon 1087.

[87]D. M. Lloyd-Jones, *Sons of God*, p. 304.

[88]D. M. Lloyd-Jones, *John* (sound recording), sermon 1087.

[89]*Ibid.*, sermon 1088. McCheyne's story is told in A. A. Bonar, *Robert Murray McCheyne: Memoirs and Remains* (London: Banner of Truth, 1966 [reprinted from 1892 edition]). See especially ch. 5, 'Days of Revival'.

[90]D. M. Lloyd-Jones, *John* (sound recording), sermon 1088.

[91]*Ibid.*, sermon 1089.

[92]*Ibid.*, sermons 1089–1090.

[93]D. M. Lloyd-Jones, *Sons of God*, p. 328.

[94]R. A. Torrey, *The Holy Spirit* (London: Revell, 1927), p. 117.

[95]D. M. Lloyd-Jones, *God's Ultimate Purpose*, p. 244; see also p. 274.

[96]*Ibid.*, p. 271.

[97]*Ibid.*, p. 244.

[98]*Ibid.*, p. 255.

[99]D. M. Lloyd-Jones, *Sons of God*, p. 302.

[100]*Ibid.*, pp. 304–305.

[101]*Ibid.*, p. 305.

[102]D. M. Lloyd-Jones, *John* (sound recording), sermon 1083.

[103]*Ibid.*, sermon 1084.

[104]*Ibid.*, sermon 1085.

[105]*Ibid.*, sermon 1086.

[106]See his remarks concerning this confusion in D. M. Lloyd-Jones, *Life in the Spirit in Marriage, Home and Work: An Exposition of Ephesians 5:18 to 6:9* (Edinburgh: Banner of Truth, 1974), p. 41; D. M. Lloyd-Jones, *John* (sound recording), sermon 1085.

[107]See, for example, Lloyd-Jones's remarks in *God's Ultimate Purpose*, p. 284.

[108]'Living the Christian Life', 5. 'New Developments in the 18th and 19th Century Teaching', in *Living the Christian Life* (Huntingdon: Westminster Conference, 1975), p. 89.

[109]*Ibid.*, pp. 89–90.

[110]D. M. Lloyd-Jones, *Life in the Spirit*, ch. 3, pp. 40–54.

[111]Luke 1:4 is actually quoted in *Life in the Spirit*, p. 42, but this is a mistake. The text is Luke 1:41.

[112]*Ibid.*, p. 42.

[113]*Ibid.*, p. 46.

[114]*Ibid.*, p. 41.

[115]D. M. Lloyd-Jones, *God's Ultimate Purpose*, p. 264.

[116]D. M. Lloyd-Jones, *John* (sound recording), sermon 1089.

[117]D. M. Lloyd-Jones, *Sons of God*, p. 358.

[118]D. M. Lloyd-Jones, *Life in the Spirit*, p. 43.

[119]D. M. Lloyd-Jones, *God's Ultimate Purpose*, pp. 261, 284–286; D. M. Lloyd-Jones, *Sons of God*, pp. 370–374; D. M. Lloyd-Jones, *John* (sound recording), sermon 1097.

[120]D. M. Lloyd-Jones, *Sons of God*, pp. 371–380.

[121]*Ibid.*, p. 380; D. M. Lloyd-Jones, *John* (sound recording), sermon 1097.

[122]D. M. Lloyd-Jones, *Sons of God*, pp. 380–381; D. M. Lloyd-Jones, *John* (sound recording), sermon 1097.

[123]*Ibid.*, sermon 1097.

[124]D. M. Lloyd-Jones, *Sons of God*, pp. 381–382.

[125]*Ibid.*, p. 383.

[126]A. Wesley Richards, 'Dr Lloyd-Jones and the Pentecostals', in *Evangelical Times* (April 1981), p. 16.

[127]D. M. Lloyd-Jones, *The Supernatural in the Practice of Medicine* (London: Christian Medical Fellowship, 1977), p. 21.

[128]*Ibid.*, p. 4.

[129]*Ibid.*, p. 7.

[130]*Ibid.*, p. 3; see K. Koch, *The Revival in Indonesia* (Baden, Germany: Evangelisation Publishers, n. d.), pp. 121–153; *Wine of God* (Laval, Canada: Christian Evangelism Publications, 1974), pp. 19–76.

[131]D. M. Lloyd-Jones, *The Supernatural in . . . Medicine*, p. 12. See Mrs Howard Taylor, *Pastor Hsi (of North China): One of China's Christians* (Toronto: China Inland Mission, 1904), pp. 18–21.

[132]H. W. Frost, *Miraculous Healing* (London: Evangelical Press, 1972 [reprint of 1952 edition with foreword by D. M. Lloyd-Jones]).

[133]D. M. Lloyd-Jones, *John* (sound recording), sermon 1090. See *Miscellany of Sermons Preached by Sundry Divines* (Edinburgh: Drummond, 1744), pp. xvii–xviii. Welch was reported to have prayed over a young man who had lain dead in a coffin for 48 hours. Then abruptly the young man 'awoke'.

[134]D. M. Lloyd-Jones, *John* (sound recording), sermon 1091.

[135]*Ibid.*, sermon 1091.

[136]*Ibid.*, sermon 1096.

[137]D. M. Lloyd-Jones, *The Supernatural in . . . Medicine*, p. 22.

[138]D. M. Lloyd-Jones, *John* (sound recording), sermon 1100.

[139]*Ibid.*, sermons 1101 and 1102.

[140]D. M. Lloyd-Jones, *God's Ultimate Purpose*, p. 300.

10

Wider concerns

My exposition of Lloyd-Jones's doctrine of the witness of the Spirit would be deficient if mention were not made of the impact his doctrine had on his overall theology. Lloyd-Jones's doctrine was strongly experiential. Indeed it was his practice to divide his preaching ministry into roughly three kinds of sermon. On Sunday evenings he addressed himself mainly to non-Christians and those who did not generally attend a Christian church. On Friday evenings he dealt with more directly instructional material. On Sunday mornings he explicitly focused on the *experiential* aspect of the Christian life.[1]

This is noticeable when one listens to the final series of sermons that Lloyd-Jones preached at Westminster Chapel on Sunday mornings during 1962–1968, on John's Gospel, chapters 1 to 4. There were more than twenty sermons on John 1:12–13.[2] Each of them was strongly experiential, dealing with the marks of being truly Christian,[3] being led by the Spirit,[4] assurance of salvation[5] and love of the brethren.[6] Then when preaching on John 1:16 (and there were more than thirty sermons on this verse)[7] he again preaches on predominantly inward-looking themes including again the marks of being truly Christian[8] and the peace of God.[9] The sermons on the new birth follow similar themes,[10] as do the sermons on the woman at the well.[11]

The view that Lloyd-Jones held concerning the direct witness of the Spirit, and the tradition of 'experimental religion' that he inherited from Puritanism and the Welsh Methodists, may be seen in four matters that are worthy of further attention: the connection between Lloyd-Jones's view of the baptism with the Spirit and revival; the preparationism that he taught concerning salvation and the receiving of the Spirit; his view of preaching and the need of the power of the Spirit in preaching; and his intense dislike of a view of the Spirit, associated with a Scot by the name of Robert Sandeman, which was virtually the opposite of the view held by Lloyd-Jones and which therefore incurred his opposition.

Baptism with the Spirit and revival

When D. M. Lloyd-Jones spoke of revival he did not always use the term 'baptism with the Spirit'. This was probably a matter of tact for the subject of revival was more acceptable in the 1950s and 1960s than was Lloyd-Jones's interpretation of the baptism with the Spirit.[12] Despite the occasional avoidance of the term 'baptism with the Spirit' in Lloyd-Jones's preaching on revival, there can be no doubt that for him they were virtually the same thing. Revival views the matter corporately; the 'baptism with the Spirit' is his term for the experience viewed more individually.

Thus, when preaching on John 1:33, Lloyd-Jones repeatedly makes this point. He spoke of revivals as 'nothing but further baptisms with the Holy Spirit in large numbers of people at the same time'.[13] Some weeks later he emphasized this point: 'A revival is nothing but a large number of people being baptized with the Holy Ghost at the same time. It can happen to one man, you don't call it revival then. If it happens to a number you call it a revival of religion.'[14]

An illustration of the relationship of the baptism with the Spirit and the *corporate* outpouring of the Spirit in revival is conspicuous in two stimulating and interesting sermons preached on the Sunday after Ascension Day and on Whit Sunday in 1965. On the week prior to Whit Sunday 1965 Lloyd-Jones took up the question of the relationship of John 20:22–23 and Acts 2, and the relationship of the baptism with the Spirit to the ascension of Jesus. He argues as follows. The common teaching of the twentieth century has asserted that the day of Pentecost is the constitution of the Christian church. The baptism of the Spirit formed the church as a body and as an organism. Then the modern view has gone on to urge that at the moment of regeneration Christians are placed into the body which has already been constituted. The baptism with the Holy Ghost simply means that we are placed in the body of Christ, the church. 1 Corinthians 12:13 is cited in this connection. The baptism with the Holy Spirit is thus 'non-experimental'. The baptism of the Holy Spirit is the constitution of the church as a body, an organism. On this view John 20:22–23 is purely a *prophetic* act. The disciples did not actually receive the Spirit until later.[15]

However, Lloyd-Jones disagrees with this view altogether. He wishes to argue that John 20 records the occasion when the church as an organism was formed and that Acts 2 records a baptism of power given to a constituted church.[16]

His reasons for this view are presented as follows. He first protests that:

> . . . in connection with Acts 2 there is not a single word said in the Scripture about the constitution of the church or about the formation of a body or of an organism. Not a single word! It is just not mentioned at all and therefore, you see, this is something that is imported into the Scripture . . . I just defy you to find any suggestion, any statement there in any way suggesting that what was happening there was the formation or the constitution of the Christian church as a body and as an organism.

Secondly, he urges that John 20:22 contrasts with Luke 24:49. 'There is nothing in the text which suggests that this was a prophetic enactment.' If it had been a prediction it surely would have resembled Luke 24:49. There is a clear announcement of something future.

Thirdly, Lloyd-Jones points out that grammarians are unanimous that an aorist imperative never has a future meaning. 'I defy you to find a single exception,' he says. 'When our Lord said to them "Receive ye the Holy Ghost" they did receive the Holy Ghost . . . The very word that he used makes it impossible that he was here uttering a prophetic utterance and preparing them for something that was going to happen to them.'

Then Lloyd-Jones points to the identical verb in the

Septuagint of Genesis 2:7. He argues from this verse and from Ezekiel 37:5 that just as man was fully made man by the inbreathing of the breath of life, so the church was formed by Jesus' breathing-out the Spirit on the resurrection.

A further indication that the church is being formed and constituted by the event of John 20:22 is to be found in the next verse which in Lloyd-Jones's view describes the commissioning of the church.

> Our Lord here now is giving the commission to the church that has thus been constituted and formed into a body and into an organism. He is sending them out now to do the work. He gives them the authority, he has given them the life, the body is now constituted and here he immediately gives them this commission.

The commissioning of the church at this point thus follows from the fact that the church comes into being with the disciples reception of the Spirit (v. 22). Having been constituted as a spiritual organism, the church may now be commissioned to go into the world with the gospel.

> What is abundantly clear in chapter 20 of John's Gospel surely is that the church was constituted as a body and as an organism there and then. Our blessed Lord having finished his work had presented himself and his blood in heaven and he is now the head of the church. And here he comes to these chosen disciples and apostles and makes it clear to them that they are already the body and he breathes this Spirit of life into the body, this extraordinary parallel with what happened in man's creation at the very beginning.

Lloyd-Jones acknowledges that he has not always held this view of the relationship of our Lord's act of breathing upon the disciples (v. 22) and the words of verse 23: 'I confess that for years I was troubled by this. I could not understand it, as to why it came at that particular point.' But now he has no difficulty with it: 'the church did not come into being on the day of Pentecost in Jerusalem; the church was already in being.' John 20:22–23 is thus parallel to Matthew 28:19–20.

The view Lloyd-Jones is refuting assumes that on the occasion recorded in Acts 2 the disciples were a company of units separated from the Lord and from each other and were fused together on that occasion. But, Lloyd-Jones objects, in Acts 1 and 2 they are as much 'of one accord' (*homothymados*) before Pentecost (Acts 1:14) as they are after Pentecost. What they were in Acts 2:46 they were already in Acts 1:14.[17] They were a united body before Pentecost because of what had happened according to John 20:22. 'It is utter confusion to say that the day of Pentecost is the beginning of the Christian church and to bring 1 Corinthians 12:13 into this discussion as to the meaning of the baptism of the Holy Ghost.'

A final proof is the nature of the feast of Pentecost. It did not celebrate the beginning of anything; the celebration of the harvest was fifty days before. Rather the Pentecost festival joyfully celebrates the end of the harvest.

So it was on the day of Pentecost. 'The Spirit fell upon them and they were all filled with the Spirit and they began to praise God and to tell forth the wonderful works of God. This great harvest as it were that had been completed by the perfect work of Christ. Here the enjoyment of it all comes, the certainty and the enthusiasm and the boldness that led to the subsequent witness.'

Then Lloyd-Jones relates all of this to John 7:37–39. Does it not say that the Spirit would not come till Jesus was glorified? Surely this would imply that the coming of the Spirit would be beyond the ascension? The church could not have been constituted on the night of the resurrection because Jesus had not yet been glorified.

Lloyd-Jones's reply is that 'glorification' in John's Gospel does not exclusively refer to what has traditionally been called the ascension. 'Glorification' took place according to John 12 even before the cross. Then the cross was further 'glorification' and the resurrection was further glorification still. Then he argues that by John 20:22 the glorification had already taken place. He points to the difference between John 20:17 and John 20:27, and argues that Jesus' ascending was taking place on that very day. He presented his blood in the heavenly tabernacle (to use the language of Hebrews 9) on the resurrection day. John 7:37–39 cannot be used to refute the notion that the church was constituted on the resurrection evening.

Lloyd-Jones's conclusion concerning Acts 2 is this: 'What happened on the day of Pentecost is what our Lord had promised should happen and he never promised that the church should be constituted on the day of Pentecost . . .'. What he did promise is that they should receive power. The baptism of the Holy Spirit is a baptism of power. It gave power to the church that was already constituted. That is what had been promised. 'There is not a single suggestion anywhere that the church was constituted or formed as a body or as an organism on the day of Pentecost at Jerusalem. All we are told is this, that that was the day when they received the power. Already in existence but lacking the power.' Jesus 'did not say "Stay where you are until you are fused into one body . . ." All he keeps on saying . . . is that the one great function of the baptism of the Holy Spirit is not to form the body of Christ, is not to baptize anybody into the body of Christ . . . This is something that applies only to power, power to witness.'[18]

The following Sunday, 6 June 1956, was Whit Sunday. Lloyd-Jones brought his series of sermons on the baptism of the Spirit to an end in a sermon that contrasted two differing views of the way in which Whit Sunday was significant.[19] He begins by emphasizing the historicity of the event. 'We on these occasions always remind ourselves of the historicity of that which we are considering.' Then he explains that on the first day of Pentecost '. . . the early church was baptized with the Holy Ghost.' Thus the predictions made in Old Covenant and by John the Baptist were fulfilled at Pentecost.

Then he faces the question of the relevance of that event. 'What is the relevance of all this to us? . . . Is this merely a commemoration of something that once happened? Are we just looking back at a great fact in history? Is it just that or is there more than that to it? . . . Is this – what we are doing – a *purely* commemorative act or is there another factor, something that goes beyond that?' The answer, says Lloyd-Jones, is determined entirely by our attitude to the doctrine concerning the baptism with the Holy Spirit.

This leads Lloyd-Jones on to outline two different approaches to the interpretation of the day of Pentecost. Though evangelicals are agreed about much of their doctrine there is a major cleavage over the interpretation of the day of Pentecost. He plans to outline the 'modern' evangelical view and to describe the 'older' evangelical view which he believes is the correct one.

The first view (with which Lloyd-Jones does not agree) is that on the day of Pentecost the church was constituted. The disciples were already regenerate but owing to special circumstances they could not be baptized with the Spirit until the day of Pentecost. The time-gap was solely due to the historical circumstances. Then on the day of Pentecost the church was formed. In the disciples' case only there was a time-gap, 'a unity came into being that was not there before and so the church as an organism, as a body, comes into being and is given the power to do the work to which she has been sent.' The event is therefore a once-and-for-all event. All we can do is to look back and commemorate this once-and-for-all event. Since then, and especially since the events of Acts 10, baptism with the Holy Ghost takes place synchronously with regeneration. Such is Lloyd-Jones's summary of the view he rejects. Commenting on that view he says the Christian has only to yield to what he already has. 'Such a teaching rarely, if ever, speaks about revival. It's not interested in revival.' This is only natural, thinks Lloyd-Jones. 'There is no room left for revival in that teaching. Every Christian has been baptized with the Spirit at the point of regeneration, has had the fulness of the Spirit. Well, there's nothing more that he can receive. His future now and the future of the church depends entirely upon his obedience, his yielding to the Spirit who remains in him in spite of his rebellion and disobedience. There is no room left whatsoever for revival, and it's very interesting to notice that the people who teach this view of the Holy Spirit never mention it.'[20]

Over against this view Lloyd-Jones goes on to summarize what he calls 'the old evangelical view'. 'I call it that', he says in 1965, 'because I am speaking strictly historically. The view I have been dealing with is still not fully a hundred years old. But prior to that and even continuing since there is this other view, the view that has obtained in the church throughout the centuries.'

He goes on to outline this 'older view', building on what he had said the previous week. He had argued on the previous Sunday morning that the formation of the church took place as recorded in John 20:22–23. 'On the day of Pentecost what happens is that the Lord sends upon the church this power to witness that he had promised. "You shall receive power".' 'On the day of Pentecost in the baptism of the Holy Ghost the church received the power.' It was not a secret operation in the depth of the personality, but the Spirit's falling upon the gathered church. So the church found herself filled with power, authority, certainty and joy.

Now the question is asked: is this repeatable or is it a once-and-for-all matter? It is unique 'in one sense only and that is that it was the first time it ever happened, but it is not once and for all in any other sense'. Lloyd-Jones now argues the possibility of Pentecost being repeated in revival. It was repeated, he argues, even within Acts itself. Acts 4 and 10 record repetitions of Pentecost. As one studies the history of the church one finds again occasions when the Spirit 'falls upon' the church. This, believes Lloyd-Jones, is the point of celebrating the day of Pentecost. In every great revival there is a communal baptism of the Spirit; Pentecost is repeated. The church becomes herself again. He hurriedly mentions the famous occasions of revival in the church: Montanism, Donatism, southern France in the middle ages, the Waldensians in Italy, the Brethren of the Common Life in Germany and Holland, what happened through Reformation preachers such as Hugh Latimer, the revivals of seventeenth-century Puritanism, what happened at Kirk O' Shotts in the 1630s,[21] the Great Awakening under the Wesleys, under Jonathan Edwards and under Daniel Rowlands,[22] the movement of the Spirit in 1857 to 1859 in America, in 1859 in Ulster[23] and Wales,[24] the Welsh revival of 1904,[25] the Korean revival of 1906,[26] the twentieth-century revival in Lewis[27] and in Congo (now Zaire).[28]

Lloyd-Jones sweeps through a survey urging upon his listeners that every revival is a repetition of Pentecost, a communal baptism with the Holy Spirit. 'If you read the history of the church you can come to only one conclusion. This has been God's way of keeping the church alive.' 'This is the true meaning of the word revival, it is God pouring out His Spirit on an assembled church or company or many churches or countries even, at a time. This has been God's way of preserving the church. What he did at the beginning he has done again.' 'If you say the baptism was once and for all on Pentecost and all who are regenerated are just made partakers of that there's no room left for this objective coming, this repetition, this falling of the Holy Ghost in power and authority upon a church.' 'What are you trusting? Are you trusting in the organising power of the church? Or are you trusting in the power of God to pour out His most blessed Holy Spirit. The church needs another Pentecost. Every revival is a repetition of Pentecost and it is the greatest need of the Christian church at the present hour.'

On another occasion Lloyd-Jones preached a single sermon on revival while interpreting Ephesians 4:4–6. He makes the same points that we have seen above and defines revival as 'a repetition in some degree, or in some measure, of that which happened on the Day of Pentecost'.[29] Here he also hurriedly summarizes the characteristics of revival. He speaks of its suddenness: 'We cannot tell when the Holy Spirit is going to visit us.'[30] Then he recalls occasions when the Spirit has suddenly worked in answer to a few folk who have been praying.[31] Again, as when preaching on the phrase 'baptism with the Spirit', he mentioned the awareness of God's presence. 'Christians suddenly become aware of a presence, of a power, of a glory, and are filled with a sense of marvel.' Then, 'Its effect upon believers is to give them a new clarity of understanding of truths they have previously believed.'[32] There follows a desire to tell others of salvation and to tell forth the wonderful works of God. Another characteristic is a new oneness found by the church. 'This sense of unity is inevitable when the Spirit is present in power.'[33] Lastly, revival is noticeable for the effects it has on others. On the day of Pentecost the crowds rush to see what is happening, Peter preaches, unbelievers cry out. Thus it has happened, says Lloyd-Jones, in all revivals in the church throughout the centuries; 'often it happens that "fools who came to scoff remain to pray".'[34]

Lloyd-Jones's preparationism

We have already considered a teaching concerning conviction of sin that began in English Puritanism with William Perkins, and continued in the teaching of Richard Sibbes. As Puritan theology developed, this teaching was decreasingly mentioned. Goodwin mentions it less than Sibbes; Owen mentions it rarely, if at all. Lloyd-Jones was much influenced by this strand of Puritan theology and gave it considerable emphasis in his ministry, especially in his later years. In one respect, however, Lloyd-Jones developed his viewpoint in a way that diverged from Puritanism. He related the 'Spirit of bondage' to the description in Romans 7:14–25 of a person delighting in the Law but failing to keep it and so crying out, 'O wretched man that I am!' In this respect Lloyd-Jones was departing from the common Puritan exegesis of Romans 7:14–25 which followed Calvin and Luther in understanding this section of Romans to be a description of the Christian's struggle against sin, a struggle which continues even in the most mature Christian.[35]

In an appendix to *The Law: Its Functions and Its Limits*, Lloyd-Jones added a short note concerning William Perkins who, he says, gives the 'clearest account' of the Spirit of bondage.[36] He adds: 'What is surprising to me is that Perkins and other Puritans, in spite of this, when they actually comment on Romans 7 regard it as a description of the regenerate man. Their pastoral theology often seems to be superior to their actual exegesis of Scripture.'[37] We shall consider Lloyd-Jones's exegesis of Romans 7, his relating it to Romans 8:15, and the consequent preparationism in this theology, seen in an *ordo salutis* in his teaching.

Lloyd-Jones did not regard the controversial verses in 7:14–25 as the most important part of the chapter. Indeed he felt 'the greatest cause of trouble' in understanding the chapter was 'to become obsessed by the so-called "man of Romans 7", and to approach the entire chapter, as a consequence, from the standpoint of experience'.[38] Although experience is touched upon in the section that runs from Romans 7:7 to Romans 7:25, he thought that the more important point in the chapter dealt not so much with the Christian's experience as with his position. In his view Romans 7:5–6 were the crucial verses. The Christian, he believed, was in a new position in Christ. The law of God could not condemn him; the believer has an altogether new relationship with Christ. He is 'married' to his saviour.

The simplest way to lay out Lloyd-Jones's teaching at this point (to which he devoted virtually a whole book) is to list his analysis of Romans 7:14–25 and then to summarize the teaching which he deduced from it. The analysis of the section, as found in *The Law: Its Functions and Limits*, is as follows:[39]

1. General statement about the man (verse 14).
2. His position in daily experience (verse 15).
3. Two deductions (verses 16 and 17).
   a) The law is good (verse 16).
   b) The man is indwelt by sin (verse 17).
4. Fuller statement of what is said in verse 17 (verses 18–20).
5. A further general statement at a deeper level (verse 21).
6. Development of verse 21 (verses 22–23).
7. Cry of despair (verse 24).
8. Ejaculation of relief (verse 25a).
9. Summary of the entire section (verse 25b).

It is worth noticing that there is a slight ambiguity in Lloyd-Jones's analysis of the section in that at one point he seems to have considered dividing the section not at verse 14 but at verse 13. At the beginning of the exposition of the chapter he divided Romans 7 into three sections: verses 1–6, 7–12 and 13–25. By the time he got to his exposition of 7:14–25 he had fallen back into the more customary division and bracketed verse 13 with what preceded instead of with what follows. This is more important than one might think; I shall return to it in the assessment of Lloyd-Jones's doctrine.[40]

For Lloyd-Jones, the purpose of the chapter is 'to show what the Law is in and of itself, what it was meant to do, and especially what it was not meant to do'.[41] That is to say, the chapter does not discuss experience as such. Rather Paul brings in this argument merely to show that we must be dead to the law before we can bring fruit to God. The change of tense in verse 14 is not significant and cannot settle the interpretation. It is only a 'dramatic present' similar to the habit of a preacher who dramatizes his argument.[42] The term 'carnal' differs from its use in Romans 8 and 1 Corinthians 3. It cannot mean that the apostle is unregenerate (*cf.* Romans 8) or that he is a 'babe in Christ' (*cf.* 1 Corinthians 3). [43] The statement applies to the whole man not simply to a part of the man.[44]

At this point Lloyd-Jones makes the startling statement that the man of Romans 7:14–25 is neither regenerate or unregenerate! He says 'no unregenerate person can make, or even has made, such a statement about himself.'[45] The unregenerate man

206

neither recognizes the law's spirituality nor his own sinfulness.[46] Lloyd-Jones goes on to ask, 'Is this, then, a description of the regenerate man? Here again I have no hesitation in asserting equally strongly that it is not, and that it cannot be so. I assert that it is neither the unregenerate nor the regenerate.[47] This is a startling assertion and Lloyd-Jones gives little help in his expositions at this point to enable us to understand him.' The explanation is that for Lloyd-Jones, conversion is a *process*, however short a time it may take. It is therefore possible for someone to be neither regenerate or unregenerate, because he is being dealt with by the Spirit of God but has not yet come to full regeneration.

The reason why the man of Romans 7:14–25 cannot be regenerate, in Lloyd-Jones's view, is the note of despair in these verses: the fact that he is asking a question ('Who . . . shall deliver me . . .?') indicates that the man concerned has not yet come to faith. He has not been brought to the point of having died to sin and law, and being under a reign of grace. He is still asking a *question* concerning deliverance. The regenerate will know this 'in a measure'[48] but Romans 7:14–25 is not describing the regenerate man. Lloyd-Jones continues to insist that this man is neither regenerate or unregenerate. We need not follow every detail of his exposition. It is sufficient to quote his conclusion. For Lloyd-Jones this passage describes the necessary conviction of sin that precedes conversion and the receiving of the sealing of the Spirit. It is a description of those who:

> . . . are brought under conviction of sin by the Holy Spirit. They see that the whole of their past is wrong, that it is loss. They see the meaning of the Law for the first time. They have lost their self-righteousness, they are 'dead', they are 'killed' by the Law; and they then try to put themselves right, but they cannot do so. They may remain like that for days and for weeks, even for years. Then the truth about Christ and His full salvation is revealed to them, and they find peace and joy and happiness and power. They glory in Christ and His Cross and offer up their praise. But for a time they are in this position, as it were, of being neither the one nor the other, *neither unregenerate nor regenerate*. All we can say for certain is that they are under deep conviction of

sin. But they have not seen the truth clearly even about justification, leave alone about sanctification. This man is under the condemnation of the Law, and feeling his utter hopelessness, and helplessness, and spiritual death. He is 'under' what the Apostle calls 'the law of sin and death'.[49]

Having expounded Romans 7:14–25 in the way outlined above, Lloyd-Jones returns to this topic when expounding Romans 8:15. For he regards the expression 'Spirit of bondage' as another reference to this 'preliminary stage under conviction as the result of the Spirit's work'.[50] Again Lloyd-Jones makes the point that a person in such a stage of spiritual experience is neither regenerate or unregenerate, neither Christian or unchristian. The phrase 'Spirit of bondage' cannot possibly refer to the unconverted, he says.[51] Nor does it refer to the Christian. Yet every Christian must have known this 'conviction of sin': 'a Christian is a man who *once* received a "spirit of bondage to fear". How did he receive it? As a result of the operation of the Holy Spirit upon him!'[52] Lloyd-Jones views the long agony of John Bunyan as described in 'Grace Abounding', as being typical of the Spirit of bondage. Bunyan was at that point neither complacent, nor had he come to full assurance of salvation. Such a person 'is not undisturbed spiritually, but he is not regenerate; he is a man in this preliminary stage.'[53]

What is important in our study of Lloyd-Jones's doctrine of the sealing of the Spirit is that there is a clear *ordo salutis* here. The 'Spirit of bondage' *must* be experienced if a man is to come to assurance of salvation. A man who has not known the Spirit of bondage must positively seek it. Unless a man can say 'I know something of the Spirit of bondage' he is not a Christian at all.[54] Lloyd-Jones put this clearly in a sermon on 'the Spirit of bondage' which he preached in the late 1960s, when working through his exposition of John 3:8. A man, says Lloyd-Jones, may be a Christian without assurance. One proof of being 'born again' is that one has been *through* the Spirit of bondage and has come to assurance. 'Assurance . . . is a deliverance from and an absence of the Spirit of bondage and the spirit of fear.' Lloyd-Jones quotes Romans 8:15 again. Before a man can come to assurance the Spirit must come upon him and open his eyes to the law. Again Lloyd-Jones quotes Romans 7:7–25.[55]

The subject is raised explicitly in Lloyd-Jones's lecture on 'Sandemanianism' given to the Puritan and Reformed Studies Conference in 1967. Here he discusses 'the relationship between repentance and faith' and urges that repentance must be prior to faith *in time*, urging the priority of the coming of John the Baptist in respect to the coming of Jesus and the priority of repentance over faith in the texts that mention both concepts (Mark 1:15; Acts 2:38–39; 3:19; 5:31; 20:21; 26:18; Luke 18:9–14).[56]

Then shortly before his retirement in 1968, preaching on John 4:29, he again spoke of the priority of repentance over spiritual blessing. One cannot 'receive of this fullness' (John 1:16) without repentance. Repentance is prior. 'What I want to show you, this morning', said Lloyd-Jones, 'is the primacy of this. . . . There are certain rules in this spiritual life and they are rules that have got to be observed. . . . There are certain things that are absolutes. . . . The first thing is conviction of sin.' This is what Lloyd-Jones feels to be most lacking in the Christian church. 'It is our failure to put this in the first position that accounts for so many of our troubles and certainly accounts for the poverty of our Christian lives.' He again summarises his argument for positing the chronological priority of repentance. 'This is the thing that always comes first in the New Testament itself and its teaching; . . . What is the first teaching of the New Testament? It is this. It is always a message of repentance. . . . Who is the first preacher in the New Testament? The answer is John the Baptist. . . . What did he preach about? He preached a baptism of repentance for the remission of sins.' Jesus again is said to put repentance first (Mark 1:14–15). 'Water and the Spirit' (John 3:5) is said to put the 'water' (the baptism of repentance) first. Matthew 21:28–32 and Luke 18:9–14 are quoted to the same effect. Repentance is implicit in the Sermon on the Mount, which is 'nothing but an exposition of the law'. It was designed 'to convict men who thought they could keep the law of God but could never do so'. The same thing is true, according to Lloyd-Jones, in the Acts of the Apostles. Again he cites Acts 2:38–39, 17:30 and 20:21.[57]

Thus there was a definite sequence of events that were necessary in Christian experience according to Lloyd-Jones's thinking. Repentance, including conviction of sin and the beginnings of turning from sin, is prior to every other spiritual blessing. It is possible that God's 'life' is at work in a man before he has come to faith. This inevitably produces grief and the struggle to turn from sin. Faith in Jesus brings release from this. Peace of conscience is found. Then the Spirit of adoption is given. This Spirit of adoption may be subsequent to coming to faith and therefore to peace with God. The final stage is the 'sealing' of the Spirit which ratifies and doubly reaffirms the assurance which has already come to the believer by his faith in the promise of the gospel and the imparting to him of the Spirit of adoption. In all of this the 'preparationism' of the Perkins tradition is clearly visible.

Lloyd-Jones and Sandemanianism

Another aspect of Lloyd-Jones's view of the Spirit was his intense dislike of what has come to be called Sandemanianism. He rarely mentioned it in public preaching, no doubt because of the obscurity of the subject. Occasionally, however, he would allude to it, and sometimes do so even by name. In October 1957 when preaching one Friday evening on Romans 4:18 he said: 'You may have heard of the heresy called Sandemanianism that troubled the church in the eighteenth century ... It is a teaching that declares that as long as you say "Jesus is Lord", that as long as you say you believe, you are saved. It excludes all feeling and all assurance.'[58] Sandemanianism was the opposite of everything that Lloyd-Jones stood for. If Lloyd-Jones's theology was intensely experiential and perhaps even introspective, Sandemanianism stood for a rationalistic approach towards faith and discouraged any reliance on 'feelings' as a subtle form of justification by works. Not surprisingly Lloyd-Jones intensely disliked it.

On one occasion in 1967 he devoted an address to the subject of Sandemanianism, when he put to the Puritan and Reformed Studies Conference a definitive statement of his view. We may consider the matter in four stages: the history of the Sandemanians, the views upheld, the relevance of the subject and the reply that Lloyd-Jones and earlier writers gave to it.

Lloyd-Jones outlined briefly the salient facts concerning Robert Sandeman and what became known as Sandemanianism.

It started with three Scotsmen, John Glas, Robert Sandeman and Archibald Maclean. Glas seceded from the Church of Scotland in the 1720s because of his change of view concerning the church and the state. His daughter married Robert Sandeman who took up his father-in-law's opinions. These two men developed a particular view of faith which stood in contrast to the experiential emphasis of an earlier generation of Calvinists in Britain. Sandeman especially attacked James Hervey, a Methodist with a strongly experiential note in his works.[59] Alongside these men was Archibald Maclean who developed an immersionist approach to baptism and became the father of Baptist churches in Scotland.[60] From these three men a particular view of faith spread into the whole of Britain, being propagated in Wales by J. R. Jones and a man named Popkins. Sandemanianism was criticized by Daniel Rowlands and William Williams, two men whom Lloyd-Jones greatly admired. But Sandemanian's teaching affected many people including, for a while, the famous preacher Christmas Evans.

The essence of Sandeman's teaching was that there was no element of *feeling* in saving faith. Faith, according to Sandeman was believing the apostolic report concerning Jesus and it was no more than that. Those who feel burdened by sin are relieved not by finding any favourable symptoms in their hearts but by simply accepting that the apostolic report about Jesus is true. Faith is the acceptance of the propositions concerning the gospel. Thus the faith that saves is 'naked faith' ('notional faith').

Lloyd-Jones does not quote from Sandeman's major work, the *Letters Of Theron And Aspasio*,[61] which sparked off the controversy. Rather he refers extensively to the reply to Sandemanianism given by Andrew Fuller in *The Gospel Worthy of All Acceptation*.[62] A glance at the work which was the source of the controversy will help us get our bearings.

Sandeman presented a number of criticisms of James Hervey. He complained that although there was much that he found admirable in Hervey's work, Hervey had obscured justification by faith. He had 'so embarrassed, or rather shut up our access to the divine righteousness, as to hold forth a *preliminary* human one, as something expedient, or rather necessary, to our enjoying the comfort and benefit of it!'[63] Sandeman disagrees with Hervey's definition of faith as 'a real persuasion, that the blessed Jesus has shed his blood *for me*, fulfilled all righteousness in *my stead*' or that 'an *appropriation* of Christ is essential to faith'.[64] He protests when Theron (*i.e.* Hervey) puts to Aspasio (*i.e.* the would-be convert) that faith involves a *feeling* of the heart. In Aspasio's doctrine, faith involves effort and feeling on man's part: 'You must endeavour, diligently endeavour, to believe; and wait and pray for the divine Spirit.'[65] For Sandeman this is a kind of 'work' prior to faith.

> Every doctrine, then, which teaches us to do or endeavour any thing towards our acceptance with God, stands opposed to the doctrine of the apostles; which instead of directing us what to do, sets before us all that the most disquieted conscience can require. . . . What Christ has done, is that which pleases God; what he hath done is that which quiets the guilty conscience of man as soon as he knows it: so that whenever he hears of it he has no occasion for any other question but this; Is it true or not? If he finds it true, he is happy; if not, he can reap no comfort by it.[66]

Sandeman was an admirer of John Owen and accepted Owen's doctrine of 'limited atonement'. He therefore believed that Hervey's doctrine concerning faith as a real persuasion that Christ died 'for me' resembled 'a bridge . . . having the one end settled on a rock, and the other on sand or mud'.[67] 'That Christ died *for me* is a point not so easily settled,' he said.[68]

It would take us too far afield to review all the aspects of Sandeman's doctrine. It must suffice to say that Lloyd-Jones saw Sandeman's view of faith as disastrously opposed to 'experiential' religion.

Lloyd-Jones believed that the topic of Sandemanianism was relevant for the 1960s. He felt that the church during the previous fifty years had fallen into a coldly propositional view of faith. No doubt what Lloyd-Jones had in mind at this point was the lack of emphasis on the baptism with the Spirit in twentieth-century evangelicalism. In the 1960s British evangelicals were putting increasing stress on academic training. Crusade evangelism as practised in the campaigns in London held by Billy Graham, Tom Rees and others, often played down the 'conviction of sin' aspect of faith that Lloyd-Jones made much of. It was no doubt these aspects of contemporary evangelicalism that made Lloyd-Jones feel that the subject of Sandemanianism, though obscure, was of relevance. He thought it to be 'our major problem today – Calvinists as well as Arminians'.[69]

Lloyd-Jones cited the replies of the critics of Sandemanianism. In doing so he was virtually putting his own objections to the coldness and lack of emphasis upon experience that characterized the evangelicalism of the 1960s. He put forward, mainly from the writings of Andrew Fuller, the following points. Firstly, he stressed (contrary to Sandeman's exegesis of Romans 4:5) that when Scripture speaks of God's justifying the ungodly, it is referring to men like Abraham and David who could not be called enemies of God at the time being referred to by Paul. All men are ungodly. Paul does not mean that Abraham and David had not experienced conviction of sin. Secondly, he urged (again contrary to Sandeman's exegesis) that 'heart' in Romans 10:9–10 means more than the mind but includes the feelings. Thirdly, he argued from 1 Corinthians 13, Romans 4:20, John 5, 2 Thessalonians 2:10, Hebrews 3, Ephesians 4:17 and Romans 8 that faith is considerably more than 'notional'. Fourthly, he felt that in Scripture, repentance is prior to faith, and lastly, that regeneration is also prior to faith.

It can be seen that Lloyd-Jones's goal in seeking to refute this old error, as he saw it, was to counter what he felt to be insufficient emphasis on Christian experience in the evangelicalism of his day.[70]

Sandeman's doctrine started a new minor denomination in British evangelicalism. Yet most eighteenth and nineteenth-century evangelicals were critical of Sandeman.[71] In the 1830s reviewers found it 'antiquated and obnoxious doctrine'; yet a sympathizer said its critics found it 'an antagonist they have learned to fear'.[72] A few took a more balanced view and admitted 'the many great things he has said'.[73]

By the twentieth century Sandeman had been largely forgotten. However, such was Lloyd-Jones's historical knowledge and sympathy with the Calvinism of the period from the sixteenth to the nineteenth century, that he identified himself with the opposition Sandeman received from the protagonists of 'experimental religion' and saw the spectre of Sandemanianism in the intellectualism of the 1950s and 1960s.

Lloyd-Jones was possibly not altogether fair to Sandeman, for Sandeman held a doctrine of *assurance* given by the Spirit. Sandeman drew a distinction between the assurance of faith and the assurance of hope.[74] The former was *saving* faith; the latter was concerned with an *experiential confirmation* of salvation. Saving faith or the assurance of faith has, according to Sandeman, no experiential note in it; the assurance of hope *is* experiential. Lloyd-Jones says nothing about this experiential aspect of Sandeman's teaching. One wonders how much access Lloyd-Jones had to Sandemanian works, for he cites only Sandeman's critics. (The Evangelical Library, of which Lloyd-Jones was the president, holds scarcely any Sandemanian works. There is no reason to think that Lloyd-Jones made much use of the British Library and Sandemanian works may therefore not have been easily available to him.)

Sandeman views assurance of hope as 'an enjoyment proposed to them who believed and had begun the Christian race'; it 'holds pace, first and last, with the work and labour of love'.[75] Sandeman taught that 'no professor of faith can form a judgment of his state, merely by "poring on his own heart", and examining whether his religious concepts be of the right kind or not'.[76] 'The greatest saints on earth, when disquieted with the sense of guilt, or fear of condemnation, can no otherwise find relief, but by the same truth that relieved them at first when sitting in darkness.'[77]

Sandeman speaks of a 'bare persuasion'.[78] By 'bare' he means without feelings. Yet he does use the term 'persuasion'. Faith is being *gripped* by the truth. In Sandeman's thought assurance of hope of the sealing of the Spirit is *subsequent* to conversion. 'He already dwelleth with you as the Spirit of truth, and shall hereafter be in you as the Comforter ... the promise of the Comforter is only to Christ's friends.'[79] 'The Holy Spirit then acts a twofold part. . . . He reconciles enemies, and he comforts friends.' Thus Sandeman *was* concerned about *experiential* assurance. He thought that the 'assurance' in Calvinist orthodoxy of his day was, 'a doubtful, fearful, and diffident assurance'.[80] Like Lloyd-Jones, Sandeman takes Galatians 4:6 to refer to a post-conversion gift of the Spirit.[81] He teaches that to have the Holy Spirit, as the Comforter, and earnest of the heavenly inheritance, is an attainment 'beyond the regenerating work of the

Spirit by which men are at first brought to the knowledge of the truth.'[82]

A distinctive and crucial point is found in that Sandeman views the witness of the Spirit as attached to Christian love.[83] He summarizes his doctrine as follows: 'Faith, then, respects the truth of the testimony ... Faith comes by evidence of testimony, and the assurance of hope through faith working by love, to which the Holy Spirit never fails to bear witness as the Comforter.'[84] This has certain resemblances to Lloyd-Jones's doctrine. However, the lack of an experiential note in Sandemanian evangelism coupled with its 'coldness' in practice rendered it offensive to Lloyd-Jones.

Sandeman saw a strongly introspective note in eighteenth-century methodism, but was mistaken in holding to limited atonement. He attacked preparationism (but not under that name) because he saw that it undermined assurance. Yet he did not see that limited atonement *also* undermines assurance. His followers ended up with a cold religion lacking enthusiasm or joy. Preaching became argumentative debating. Faith became *cold* assent to propositions. Not surprisingly, his view was rejected by mainstream evangelicalism. If Sandeman had criticized preparationism, pointed to an objective source of assurance in a universal atonement, and held to a direct sealing of the Spirit, his theology might have had a different impact. In practice, while criticizing preparationism, he continued to hold the Owenian view of limited atonement, and he so attached the direct witness of the Spirit to Christian love that a coldly intellectualist moralism emerged. Men like Christmas Evans were drawn to it for a while, for it seemed a counter to introspection, but after its 'coldness' had become apparent Evans and others like him withdrew back to introspective and preparationist Calvinist orthodoxy.[85]

Baptism with the Spirit, preaching and the future of the church

In addition to his interest in the baptism with the Spirit, Lloyd-Jones had a lifelong interest in preaching. The two subjects were not unconnected. He rarely lectured on preaching, believing that the power of the Spirit upon the preacher was the most important aspect of preaching and that it was vastly more important than the technicalities of sermonic method. Only after his retirement did he give a series of lectures on preaching to the students of Westminster Theological Seminary, a series of lectures in which he drew upon a lifetime's experience.

A crucial aspect of Lloyd-Jones's view of preaching was his conviction that, in his words to the students of Westminster Seminary, 'We have to draw a distinction between two elements in preaching.' 'There is first of all the sermon or the message – the content of that which is being delivered. But secondly, there is the act of preaching, the delivery if you like, of what is commonly called "preaching".'[86] In Lloyd-Jones's thinking you could have a bad sermon but good preaching.[87] The 'sermon' was that which had form and structure. The 'preaching' was when the sermon was 'set on fire' by the power of the Spirit. For Lloyd-Jones it was the latter aspect that was supremely important. Indeed at one time he wondered whether the 'form' of the sermon really mattered at all. When reading Edwin Hatch's Hibbert Lectures of 1888, he was struck by Hatch's assertion that the earliest Christian preaching was entirely 'prophetic' with no pre-planned structure at all. Hatch maintained that it was the influence of Greek rhetoricians that led to the emphasis on 'form' in a sermon. Referring to Hatch, Lloyd-Jones comments, 'He says that Christian men received messages through the Holy Spirit and got up and delivered them without premeditation, thought, or preparation. ... There are indications of this in 1 Corinthians 14 and in other places.'[88] Lloyd-Jones was impressed by this assertion and thought that there was an element of truth in it. 'One can see this pneumatic, this prophetic element clearly in the New Testament,' he said. Yet he did not wholly agree with Hatch and maintained that it was possible to see some element of 'form' in New Testament sermons as found for example in Acts 2, 7 and 13.

Vastly more important than the form was the 'fire'. He defines twelve characteristics of true preaching in his chapter on 'The Act of Preaching'. The first is 'that the whole personality must be involved'.[89] Another is that the preacher has a sense of authority and control when preaching.[90] The third is 'freedom'. Lloyd-Jones maintained that the preacher should always be free in the act of preaching. He must be able to derive something from the 'inspiration of the moment'. He must be able to be taken up by the Holy Spirit and to be given something over and above what he had been prepared to say.[91] True preaching derives something from the congregation; there is a sense of rapport with the hearers.[92] The next element mentioned was seriousness.[93] Another was liveliness,[94] another was zeal.[95] Warmth, urgency,[96] persuasiveness and pathos[97] were further necessary characteristics. The last in Lloyd-Jones's list was the need of power. It was this element that was so important to him. 'True preaching . . . is God acting. It is not just a man uttering words; it is God using him. He is being used of God. He is under the influence of the Holy Spirit; it is what Paul calls in 1 Corinthians 2 "preaching in demonstration of the Spirit of power"' (sic). This power is 'an essential element in true preaching.'[98]

Preaching for Lloyd-Jones consists in both of these elements. 'What is preaching?' he asks. 'Logic on fire! Eloquent reason! . . . It is theology on fire. Preaching is theology coming through a man who is on fire . . . What is the chief end of preaching? . . . It is to give men and women a sense of God and His presence.'[99]

A favourite text of Lloyd-Jones was 1 Thessalonians 1:5. Preaching on that text in Toronto, he brought out his convictions concerning the two elements of preaching. 'There are the two things, the message and the power of the Spirit upon it', there must be 'word' but 'not word only'. 'A church can be perfectly orthodox and at the same time perfectly dead and perfectly useless.' He paraphrases Paul: 'He says "You know when I preached to you I knew that it was not merely I, Paul, that was speaking. I knew that the Spirit was using me. I knew that I had got the power of the Holy Ghost, I knew that he had clothed himself upon me. I knew that I was nothing but the vehicle, the channel, the instrument, I knew that I was being used . . .".' 'It is not enough that we be certain of our message, we must be equally certain of our method, and the apostle's method was trusting the Holy Spirit.'[100]

The same emphasis is visible in Lloyd-Jones's words to the Westminster Conference in 1977 towards the end of his life at about the time of his 78th birthday. Revival, he urged, turns men into great preachers. It was the filling of the Spirit that made the pre-Reformation John Tauler the man that he became.[101] The Puritans were different from the Anglicans in that they sought

217

the liveliness and the energy of true preaching. Most of them did not read their sermons and quite often would not even have notes, because they believed in the freedom of the Spirit.[102] Some of the more radical non-conformists of the seventeenth century, he says, deliberately sought to be prophetic in their manner: 'when they come to the preaching they seem to leave that (*i.e.* biblical exposition) on one side and turn to some kind of prophetic utterance ... they seem to have been carrying the prophetic element in preaching to bounds that some of us might question. At any rate it is surely something that should make us consider again as to whether our preaching should not contain more of this prophetic element.'[103]

In Lloyd-Jones's thinking, what made the 'second element' in preaching all that it ought to be, was the baptism with the Spirit coming upon preachers of the gospel. Again he did not overuse the words 'baptism with the Spirit' in making this point. Many agreed with him in general, but disliked his use of this particular phrase. Yet there was no doubt that this is what he had in mind when he urged preachers to look for an enduement of power upon their preaching.

It is interesting to note that the vast majority of illustrations that come in his sermons on the baptism with the Spirit are stories taken from the lives of preachers. He constantly makes the point that the baptism with the Spirit is not only for special Christians or for preachers but is for every Christian. Yet when he comes to illustrate his teaching concerning the baptism with the Holy Spirit he is almost invariably drawn to tell of incidents from the lives of great preachers. In one sermon on Romans 8:16, for example, he relates incidents from Robert Bruce, John Preston, Thomas Horton, William Guthrie, Richard Sibbes, Edward Elton, Thomas Goodwin, George Whitefield, Gilbert Tennant, Jonathan Edwards, Mrs Jonathan Edwards, John Wesley, Howell Harris, Hugh Bourne, Christmas Evans, Edward Payson, Merle D'Aubigné, John McKenzie, Charles Finney, D. L. Moody and Charles Spurgeon. Of these twenty-one names, one was a preacher's wife, one was primarily a historian (D'Aubigné), the other nineteen were preachers.[104]

Lloyd-Jones's statement of this point was left to the last of the lectures given to the students of Westminster Theological Seminary. He begins by asking the preachers before him: 'Do you always look for this "unction" or "anointing" of the Spirit?' He then goes on to define what he means. 'What is this? It is the Holy Spirit falling upon a preacher in a special manner. It is an access of power. It is God giving power and enabling, through the Spirit, to the preacher in order that he may do this work in a manner that lifts it beyond the efforts and endeavours of man to a position in which the preacher is being used by the Spirit and becomes the channel through whom the Spirit works.'[105]

Lloyd-Jones then proceeds to survey hurriedly the scriptural support for his point. The experience of John the Baptist and the prophets is mentioned.[106] Then the example of Jesus himself is elucidated: 'the Holy Ghost descended upon Him as He was coming up out of the river Jordan after John the Baptist had baptized Him . . . He was anointed by the Spirit to preach . . .'.[107] 'Even our Lord Himself, the Son of God, could not have exercised his ministry as a man on earth if He had not received this special, peculiar "anointing" of the Holy Spirit to perform His task.'

Then he surveys the instances of enduement with power in the book of Acts, citing chapters 1, 2, 4, 6, 7 and 13.

> This 'accession of power', or if you prefer it, this 'effusion of power' upon Christian preachers is not something 'once for all'; it can be repeated, and repeated many times . . . the real object of 'the baptism with the Spirit' is to enable men to witness to Christ and His salvation with power. The Baptism with the Holy Spirit is not regeneration – the apostles were already regenerate – and it is not primarily to promote sanctification; it is a baptism of power, or a baptism of fire, a baptism to enable one to witness. The old preachers used to make a great deal of this. They would ask about a man, 'Has he received his baptism of fire?' That was the great question.'[108]

Similar points are made from 1 Corinthians 2:1–5 and 4:18–20, then from 2 Corinthians 4; 10:3–5; 12, then from Colossians 1; 1 Thessalonians 1:5; 1 Peter 1 and Revelation 1:10. Lloyd-Jones alludes briefly to instances of enduements of power upon the preachers of church history.[109]

How does one know when this has happened? Both the

preacher himself and the people, know it, Lloyd-Jones replies.[110] 'This is what the preacher must seek. This makes true preaching.'[111]

Lloyd-Jones's conviction that preaching must of necessity be with the power of the Holy Spirit, led him to develop a somewhat negative stance towards theological training. He pointed to the fact that interest in revival and the baptism with the Spirit began to go out of mainstream evangelicalism at the time when interest in increased academic training was gaining ground. He admitted he was not very certain about the matter but said, 'I cannot but feel that theological seminaries have been an important factor in the change [concerning revival].' He admitted that there was no *a priori* reason why spirituality and learning should be incompatible yet felt that 'as men become more and more learned they tend to pay less and less attention to the spiritual side of things.' Also he felt 'the theological thinker tends to be distrustful of emotion.'[112]

Later Lloyd-Jones played a major part in the formation of the London Theological Seminary and gave the inaugural address at the opening on 6 October 1977. In the address he gave a bird's-eye view of the history of theological training, as he saw it, and again he put forward his distinctive view of preaching and of the Spirit. 'What is preaching? Preaching is proclamation. . . . The preacher should be an evangelist, and should know how to bring people to conviction of sin. . . . We need men who are able to do this with great power. . . . We are hoping to encourage men who will be able to put everything in order on the altar so that the fire of God the Holy Spirit may descend upon it.'[113]

For Lloyd-Jones there was something more important than theological training. 'The greatest need of the hour as I see it is a mighty outpouring of the Spirit of God to authenticate, to prove the truth of this one and only message. . . . Let us . . . pray unto God to open the windows of heaven and to baptize us anew and afresh with the power of the Holy Ghost.'[114]

Notes

[1]For Lloyd-Jones's deliberate policy in this respect, see D. M. Lloyd-Jones, *Preaching and Preachers*, pp. 61–63. He taught that 'every preacher should be, as it were, at least three types or kinds of preacher'. There should be included

preaching which is 'primarily experimental' (p. 63).

[2]D. M. Lloyd-Jones, *The Gospel of John* (sound recordings [Barcombe Mills, East Sussex: Martyn Lloyd-Jones Recordings Trust, 1983]), sermons 1005–1028.

[3]*Ibid.*, sermon 1005.

[4]*Ibid.*, sermons 1008, 1011.

[5]*Ibid.*, sermon 1017.

[6]*Ibid.*, sermon 1019.

[7]*Ibid.*, sermons 1029–1065.

[8]*Ibid.*, sermon 1053.

[9]*Ibid.*, sermon 1064.

[10]*Ibid.*, sermon 1123–1135.

[11]*Ibid.*, sermon 1148–1184.

[12]One may illustrate this as follows: J. I. Packer and D. M. Lloyd-Jones were both founders of the Puritan and Reformed Studies Conference. Both of them regularly contributed a paper each year until the demise of the conference in 1969. However, whereas Packer held a similar view to Lloyd-Jones concerning revival (see J. I. Packer, 'Jonathan Edwards and the Theology of Revival', in *Increasing in the Knowledge of God* [London: Puritan and Reformed Studies Conference, 1961], pp. 13–28), his view of the baptism with the Spirit departed from that of Lloyd-Jones (see J. I. Packer, *Keep in Step with the Spirit* [Leicester: IVP, 1984], pp. 90–91, 167, 177, 197, 202–203, 225–228).

[13]D. M. Lloyd-Jones, *John* (sound recording), sermon 1087.

[14]*Ibid.*, sermon 1100. An almost identical statement is found in sermon 1102.

[15]For this view, see A. M. Stibbs and J. I. Packer, *The Spirit Within You* (London: Hodder and Stoughton, 1967), pp. 29–30, where John 20:22 is said to be 'an acted sign and pledge that the gift was now as good as theirs'.

[16]A third approach is that a real gift was given at the point recorded by John 20 but one which was not so great as that of Acts 2. Calvin maintained that 'the Spirit was given to the apostles now in such a way that they were only sprinkled with His grace and not saturated with full power'; *Calvin's Commentaries: The Gospel According to St John (part 2) and the First Epistle of John*, edited by D. W. Torrance and T. F. Torrance (Grand Rapids: Eerdmans, 1959), p. 205. This is not so different from Lloyd-Jones's view. It is held also by M. M. B. Turner, 'The Concept of Receiving the Spirit in John's Gospel', *Vox Evangelica*, vol. 10, 1977, pp. 32–35, 42; and by J. Dunn, *Baptism in the Holy Spirit* (London: SCM, 1970), pp. 178–182.

M. M. B. Turner describes the view that John 20:19–23 depicts the full giving of the Spirit as 'the most popular view' and lists seventeen scholars who hold to this approach (including C. K. Barrett, R. Bultmann, R. E. Brown, C. H. Dodd), 'The Concept of Receiving the Spirit . . .', pp. 28–29, 38–39.

[17]Lloyd-Jones is aware of *homothymados* in Acts 2:1 but since the manuscripts that have it are inferior he makes nothing of it.

[18]D. M. Lloyd-Jones, *John* (sound recording), sermon 1104.

[19]*Ibid.*, sermon 1105.

[20]J. I. Packer's *Keep In Step With the Spirit* urges a concern for revival (pp. 255–258) in the context of a view of the baptism with the Spirit that Lloyd-Jones repudiated. Lloyd-Jones would have said that the one view militates against the other.

[21]See Iain Murray, *The Puritan Hope: A Study in Revival and the Interpretation of Prophecy* (London: Banner of Truth, 1971), pp. 28–29.

[22]See Joseph Tracy, *The Great Awakening: A History of the Revival of Religion in the time of Edwards and Whitefield* (Edinburgh: Banner of Truth, 1976; reprint of work first published in 1842); A. Skevington Wood, *The Inextinguishable Blaze* (London: Paternoster, 1960).

221

[23] See Iain Paisley, *The "Fifty Nine" Revival* (Belfast: Free Presbyterian Church of Ulster, 1958).

[24] See Eifion Evans, *When He Is Come: An Account of the 1858–60 Revival in Wales* (Bala: Evangelical Movement of Wales, 1959).

[25] See Vyrnwy Morgan, *The Welsh Revival 1904–5: A Retrospect and a Criticism* (London: Chapman and Hall, 1909).

[26] See William Blair and Bruce Hunt, *The Korean Pentecost* (Edinburgh, Banner of Truth, 1977).

[27] See A. Woolsley, *Duncan Campbell, A Biography* (London: Hodder and Stoughton, 1974), esp. ch. 13, pp. 112–120.

[28] See the anonymous work, *This is That* (London: Christian Literature Crusade, 1954).

[29] D. M. Lloyd-Jones, *Christian Unity: An Exposition of Ephesians 4:1 to 16* (Edinburgh: Banner of Truth, 1980), p. 71.

[30] *Ibid.*, p. 77.

[31] *Ibid.*, pp. 77–78.

[32] *Ibid.*, p. 78.

[33] *Ibid.*, p. 79.

[34] *Ibid.*, p. 80.

[35] There seems to be no good survey of the interpretation of Romans 7 in the English language. Different interpretations (in English) may be seen in B. L. Martin, 'Some Reflections on the Identity of *ego* in Romans 7:14–25' (*Scottish Journal of Theology*, vol. 34, 1981), pp. 39–47. The classic Reformed view is still maintained by J. I. Packer (*Keep in Step Within the Spirit*, pp. 263–270). However, Packer does not refer to any of the discussion in scholarly literature since the early 1960s.

[36] D. M. Lloyd-Jones, *Romans: An Exposition of Chapters 7:1 – 8:4, The Law: Its Functions and Limits* (Edinburgh: Banner of Truth, 1973), pp. 357–359.

[37] *Ibid.*, p. 357.

[38] *Ibid.*, p. xi; see also p. 1.

[39] *Ibid.*, pp. 179–180.

[40] *Ibid.*, pp. 169–170.

[41] *Ibid.*, pp. 182–183.

[42] *Ibid.*, pp. 183–184.

[43] *Ibid.*, pp. 186–187.

[44] *Ibid.*, pp. 190–191.

[45] *Ibid.*, p. 191.

[46] *Ibid.*, pp. 191–192.

[47] *Ibid.*, p. 192.

[48] *Ibid.*, p. 199.

[49] *Ibid.*, p. 256.

[50] D. M. Lloyd-Jones, *Romans: An Exposition of Chapter 8:5–17, Sons of God* (Edinburgh: Banner of Truth, 1974), p. 205.

[51] *Ibid.*, p. 200.

[52] *Ibid.*, p. 205.

[53] *Ibid.*, p. 205. In a difficult sentence on p. 206 Lloyd-Jones says, 'It is the first preliminary work of the Spirit in bringing us to salvation and is therefore an indication of sonship.' This probably does not mean as one reviewer thought (see *Westminster Theological Journal*, vol. 38, 1976, p. 411) that one is a son of God while in preliminary conviction. Rather it means that the fact that a Christian can look back on such an experience is a sign that one is *now* a son of God.

[54] *Ibid.*, p. 216.

[55] D. M. Lloyd-Jones, *John* (sound recording), sermon 1133.

[56]D. M. Lloyd-Jones, 'Sandemanianism', in *Profitable for Doctrine and Reproof*, (London: Puritan and Reformed Studies Conference, 1968), p. 63.

[57]D. M. Lloyd-Jones, *John* (sound recording), sermon 1174.

[58]D. M. Lloyd-Jones, *Romans: An Exposition of Chapters 3:20–4:25, Atonement and Justification* (Edinburgh: Banner of Truth, 1970), p. 213.

[59]See James Hervey, *Theron and Aspasio: or, A Series of Dialogues and Letters upon the Most Important and Interesting Subjects* (London: Thames Valley, 2 vols., 1813).

[60]Lloyd-Jones is generalizing. Some modern Scottish Baptist churches do not originate from Maclean.

[61]See Robert Sandeman, *Letters of Theron and Aspasio*, 4th edition (Edinburgh: J. Turnball, 1803). I have not had access to the first edition.

[62]See Andrew Fuller, *The Gospel Worthy of All Acceptation and The Gospel Its Own Witness* (Grand Rapids: Sovereign Grace, 1961), pp. 73–96. Fuller deals mainly with Archibald Maclean.

[63]Sandeman, *Letters of Theron and Aspasio*, p. 4.

[64]*Ibid.*, p. 5.

[65]*Ibid.*, p. 6.

[66]*Ibid.*, p. 11.

[67]*Ibid.*, p. 13.

[68]*Ibid.*, p. 13.

[69]D. M. Lloyd-Jones, 'Sandemanianism', see n. 61 above.

[70]*Ibid.*, esp. pp. 60–66.

[71]See, for example, Isaac Backus, *True Faith Will Produce Good Works ... To Which Are Perfixed* (sic) ... *Some Remarks On the Writings of Robert Sandeman* (Boston [England]: Freeman, 1767); William Cudworth, *A Defence of Theron and Aspasio: Against the Objections Contained in a late Treatise, entitled, Letters of Theron and Aspasio* (London: G. Keith, 1760).

[72]David Robert Ross, *A Reply to An Author of an Article Entitled 'Sandemanian Theology', 'John Walker'* [J. A. Haldane] *Which Appeared in the Eclectic Review of November 1738* (Dublin: E. Madden, 1839?), p. 1.

[73]Samuel Ecking, *Three Essays on Grace, Faith and Experience ... And a Few Observations on Sandeman and Cudworth*, 3rd edition (Liverpool: W. Jones, 1806), p. 244.

[74]R. Sandeman, *Letters of Theron and Aspasio ...*, p. 393.

[75]*Ibid.*, p. 394.

[76]*Ibid.*, p. 395.

[77]*Ibid.*, p. 418.

[78]*Ibid.*, p. 402.

[79]*Ibid.*, p. 396.

[80]*Ibid.*, p. 403.

[81]*Ibid.*, p. 397.

[82]*Ibid.*, p. 420.

[83]*Ibid.*, p. 417.

[84]*Ibid.*, pp. 420–421. Similar points are made in Sandeman's *An Essay on Preaching* (Edinburgh: William Coke, 1763).

[85]For a brief outline of Christmas Evans' life and contact with Sandemanianism, see R. Oliver's article, 'Christmas Evans', in *Reformation Today*, no. 29, January–February 1976, pp. 24–33.

[86]D. M. Lloyd-Jones, *Preaching and Preachers*, p. 56.

[87]*Ibid.*, p. 58.

[88]*Ibid.*, pp. 73–75. The reference is to Edwin Hatch, *The Influence of Greek Ideas and Usages Upon the Christian Church*, edited by A. M. Fairburn (London: Williams and Norgate, 1890 [The Hibbert Lectures for 1888]).

[89]D. M. Lloyd-Jones, *Preaching and Preachers*, pp. 81–83.
[90]*Ibid.*, p. 83.
[91]*Ibid.*, pp. 83–84.
[92]*Ibid.*, pp. 84–85.
[93]*Ibid.*, pp. 85–87.
[94]*Ibid.*, p. 87.
[95]*Ibid.*, pp. 87–89.
[96]*Ibid.*, pp. 89–91.
[97]*Ibid.*, pp. 91–95.
[98]*Ibid.*, p. 95.
[99]*Ibid.*, p. 97.
[100]D. M. Lloyd-Jones, *Not in Word Only* (sound recording [Bromley, Kent: Send the Light Trust]), Message Cassette no. 159, date unknown.
[101]D. M. Lloyd-Jones, 'Preaching', in *Anglican and Puritan Thinking* (Huntingdon: Westminster Conference, 1978), p. 90.
[102]*Ibid.*, pp. 97–100.
[103]*Ibid.*, p. 100.
[104]D. M. Lloyd-Jones, *Sons of God*, ch. 25.
[105]D. M. Lloyd-Jones, *Preaching and Preachers*, p. 305.
[106]*Ibid.*, pp. 305–306.
[107]*Ibid.*, pp. 306–307.
[108]*Ibid.*, pp. 307–311, esp. p. 308.
[109]*Ibid.*, pp. 311–324.
[110]*Ibid.*, pp. 324–325.
[111]*Ibid.*, pp. 325.
[112]D. M. Lloyd-Jones, 'Revival: An Historical and Theological Survey', in *How Shall They Hear?* (London: Puritan and Reformed Studies Conference, 1960), pp. 42, 45.
[113]D. M. Lloyd-Jones, *Inaugural Address by D. M. Lloyd-Jones* (London: London Theological Seminary, 1978), pp. 6, 16.
[114]D. M. Lloyd-Jones, *Not in Word Only* (see note 100).

Part Four

Assessment

11

Strengths and weaknesses

The previous chapters have been largely descriptive and now it is appropriate to attempt some degree of assessment of Lloyd-Jones's teaching concerning the Spirit. The simplest way of doing this is to present a series of propositions concerning his doctrine, most of them appreciative, a few of them cautionary.

Lloyd-Jones's awareness of the interchangeable terms used to refer to the baptism with the Spirit is a significant observation of the New Testament data and is of importance in theological exposition.

The actual phrase 'to baptize with the Spirit' comes certainly six times in the New Testament (Matthew 3:11; Mark 1:8; Luke 3:16; John 1:33; Acts 1:5; 11:16) and possibly (if 1 Corinthians 12:13 is included) seven times. Reading the New Testament it soon becomes evident that this phrasing is by no means the only one that is used and that a number of other terms are used to describe the same spiritual blessing.[1]

Let us consider Acts 1 and 2. In Acts 1:4 Jesus refers to the 'promise of the Father' and immediately goes on to describe the promise as being 'baptized with the Spirit' (1:5). Three verses later – and there is no reason to think there is any change of subject – Jesus speaks of the Spirit's 'coming upon' the disciples and of their 'receiving power' (Acts 1:8). The four terms all refer to what is about to happen. The next chapter describes the event that is awaited, but now several other terms are introduced. The event is called 'being filled' with the Spirit (2:4); it

227

is the Spirit's being 'poured forth' (2:18, 33). It is identified with a term already used, the 'promise of the Father' (2:33). When at the end of Peter's sermon an offer is made to the responsive crowd, 'you shall receive the gift of the Holy Spirit', there is no reason to think anything different is being referred to. Therefore, we are left with the idea that the Spirit's being 'given' and the phrase 'you shall receive' still indicates the same spiritual blessing. This means that within two chapters eight expressions are used to refer to the one spiritual blessing: the promise of the Father, the baptism with the Spirit (if we make a noun out of the verb 'to baptize'), the Spirit's coming upon people, receiving power, being filled with the Spirit, the Spirit's being poured out or shed abroad, the gift of the Spirit and receiving the Spirit. I do not suggest that all of these terms are *precisely* synonymous, yet they do all refer to the same event. They pinpoint different aspects of one and the same blessing.

Consider Acts 10 and 11. We read of some Gentile people who received the Spirit. As Cornelius and his friends listened to Peter, the Spirit 'fell on' them (10:44). To describe the same event the verb 'poured out' is also used (10:45). Another phrase is that they 'received' the Spirit. When Peter tells the story he uses again the term 'fell on', and identifies what had happened with the day of Pentecost ('even as on us at the beginning', 11:15). Further on he uses the term 'baptized with the Spirit' (11:16). Most of these terms have already been used in connection with the day of Pentecost but there is a new term introduced ('fell upon'), which makes a total of nine terms that are used of the same spiritual experience.

Consider also what happened to Jesus in the river Jordan. In Luke 3:22 it is apparently 'receiving power'. We may compare Luke 3:22 with 4:14 and 4:18 and then note the similarity of phrasing which the same author uses in Luke 24:49 and Acts 1:8. Evidently what happened to Jesus is comparable to what happened to the disciples on the day of Pentecost, and, therefore, the same terminology may be used. Yet one term for this same spiritual experience is 'anointed' (see Luke 14:18; Acts 10:38). Can we believe this is something distinct? I think not.

In Ephesians 1:13–14 the Ephesians were described as being 'sealed with the Holy Spirit'. The fact that Paul adds 'of the promise' immediately reminds us of the 'promise of the Father' that we have already been considering. When Paul goes on to say that this *'is* the earnest of our inheritance' he is quite explicitly identifying the sealing of the Spirit and the earnest of the Spirit.

Then in 2 Corinthians 1:21–22, Paul refers to God's work of 'establishing' the believer; God has 'anointed us . . . sealed us . . . and has given the earnest of the Spirit'. Are not these three aspects of the one gift of the Spirit? We have seen an identification of sealing and the earnest (Ephesians 1:13–14). I have suggested we see in the Lucan writings an identification of receiving power and the anointing. It would cause no surprise to see anointing, seal and earnest mutually identified and this is apparently what we have in 2 Corinthians 1:21–22.

All these terms are more or less explicitly identified. What about the others that Lloyd-Jones uses: the 'Spirit of adoption', the Spirit's crying 'Abba, Father', the 'witness' of the Spirit? What of the 'firstfruits' of the Spirit in Romans 8:23? What of the references to the Spirit in John 7:37–39; and John 14–16?

It is not possible to show irrefutably that these terms refer to the same matter. Yet a consideration of the content of each phrase suggests precisely that. Is there any conceptual difference between the 'earnest' and the 'firstfruits' of the Spirit? Do they not both refer to the fact that the Spirit gives a touch of the glories of heaven, a taste of the world of the resurrection (2 Corinthians 5:5)? If they are conceptually similar do they not refer to the same spiritual blessing? In Galatians 4:6–7 reference is made to the Spirit's giving us a sense of sonship. Surely this would be a 'seal' to us of our salvation and a foretaste of the fellowship of heaven. Limitations of space prevent further expansion of this survey. One can only say that a study of what is involved in these terms reinforces the conviction that they all refer to the same spiritual blessing. Romans 8:16 perhaps requires comment since it refers not to an 'aoristic' event (*i.e.* an event on a definite occasion) but has a present tense (*i.e.* refers to something that is going on at the point being considered). Lloyd-Jones's view was that this was focusing in detail on what happens as the event of the baptism with the Spirit is taking place. It certainly seems to belong in the same circle of ideas as 'sealing', 'foretaste' and the other terms.

The Johannine[2] vocabulary has distinctives of its own. It lacks some of the terms used by Luke and Paul and must be considered on its own terms without an over-hasty integration with the Lucan and Pauline teaching. My own view is that the Paraclete-promises refer to what John had earlier called the 'baptism' with the Spirit (John 1:33), the receiving of the Spirit at an *experiential* level, and that John has other expressions (notably 'new birth') for designating what later theology would call regeneration.

It is beyond my purpose to attempt an exposition of New Testament vocabulary. A start in doing so has been made in a number of articles by M. M. B. Turner.[3] I merely make the observation that Lloyd-Jones seems to be entirely justified in treating a large number of biblical expressions as referring to the same spiritual reality.

The matter of interchangeable terms is important. To miss this observation will affect the exposition of the New Testament accounts of the work of the Spirit. Comments made by Stibbs and Packer on Acts 8 serve to illustrate this point. They argue that:

> . . . the Samaritan converts spoken of in Acts 8 . . . were persons whom Christ had undoubtedly baptized with the Spirit. Their subsequent 'receiving' of the Holy Spirit (verses 15, 17, 19) would appear to have had to do only with the special manifestations. . . . Note that in Acts 8:16 the record says that the Spirit 'had not yet fallen on any of them'. The point of this phraseology apparently is . . . that no one had experienced any accompanying special manifestations.[4]

However, to read through Acts 10 and 11 is to discover immediately that to 'baptize with the Spirit', to 'receive the Spirit' and to have the Spirit 'fall on' believers are equivalent expressions (*cf.* Acts 10:44 and Acts 11:15–17). To introduce a distinction between the Spirit's 'falling on' believers and their being 'baptized' with the Spirit is to neglect Luke's terminological usage and to fail to note the interchangeability of terms. (It is also worth noting that to accept such a distinction is also to admit that 'receive' is used of a post-conversion 'experience'.)

Lloyd-Jones has good reason for maintaining the essential identity of a large range of New Testament scriptures as source material for his view of the baptism with the Spirit. A full doctrine of the baptism with the Spirit must not confine itself to the six or seven references where that terminology is used (in verbal but not in substantial form). The major scriptures that must be contextually studied in elucidating a biblical doctrine of the baptism with the Spirit are: Isaiah 32:15; 44:3–5; Ezekiel 39:29; Joel 2:28–29; Matthew 3:11, 16; Mark 1:8; Luke 3:16; 4:14, 18; 24:49; John 1:33; 7:37–39; John 14 – 16; Acts 1, 2, 8, 10, 11, 19; Romans 5:5; 8:15–16, 23; 2 Corinthians 1:21–22; 5:5; Galatians 3:2, 14; Ephesians 1:13–14; 4:30; Titus 3:6.[5]

Lloyd-Jones's treatment of the baptism with the Spirit as an experiential blessing seems to be entirely justified by the standards of the Bible.

If the *entire* range of biblical material is surveyed, the irresistible conclusion is reached that the baptism with the Spirit is an experiential event. It is possible to maintain that the baptism with the Spirit is non-experiential *only* if one confines one's attention to the six basic texts which are then viewed in the light of the seventh (1 Corinthians 12:13). It is agreed by virtually everyone[6] that 1 Corinthians 12:13 speaks of a placement into the organism of the church which is not necessarily 'experiential'. If the other six texts are assimilated to 1 Corinthians 12:13 there can be no doubt, in my opinion, that the baptism with the Spirit would have to be interpreted non-experientially. What makes this difficult, however, is the demonstrable variety of terms that are used with references to the gift of the Spirit. It is entirely unjustified, in my opinion, to dismiss the question by seeing the whole matter of the baptism with the Spirit through the framework of 1 Corinthians 12:13. This is virtually what writers such as John Stott do.[7]

To survey the wider range of material leads to an altogether different conclusion. In Old Testament prediction, the 'outpouring' of the Spirit is portrayed in experiential terms. It is the end of being thirsty; it is calling oneself by the name of Jacob and writing on one's hands 'the Lord's' (Isaiah 44:3–5); it is the end of God's hiding his face, *i.e.* coming to a consciousness of God's presence (Ezekiel 39:29); it is the occasion when prophetic endowment comes upon God's people (Joel 2:28 – 29).

Similarly New Testament descriptions are irresistibly experiential. Can one experience 'rivers of living water' non-experientially (John 7:37–39)? When the love of God is 'shed

231

abroad' in (*not* into) one's heart, surely one cannot but be aware of it. To receive the Spirit as the Spirit of adoption in whom one 'cries Abba, Father' is by definition experiential. In 2 Corinthians 1:21 – 22 the surrounding context speaks of one's being 'established' and of Paul's not vacillating because he has received the anointing-seal-foretaste of the Spirit. Can something entirely non-experiential have a stabilizing effect in one's life? In 2 Corinthians 5:5 it is the 'foretaste' of the Spirit that is the guarantee of the resurrection. If the 'foretaste' is non-experiential, how can it be a foretaste? If the foretaste is *non*-experiential would there not have to be something *else* to make one sure one had received the foretaste? In Galatians 3:1–5 Paul looks back on a *memorable* event, connected with the coming of miracles. How can he use the receiving of the Spirit to prove justification by faith if the receiving of the Spirit is not an experienced and remembered event? Surely Galatians 3:1–5 alludes to something analagous or identical to Acts 10 where a 'receiving of the Spirit' put a complete end to the question as to whether Gentiles could or could not experience salvation.[8]

In Ephesians 1:13–14 the 'sealing' is identified with a foretaste of final redemption. Surely this too must mean that final glory is partially *experienced* in the here-and-now. Then each of the key events in Acts 2, 8, 10–11, 19, were experiential. No one could have been present on any of those occasions without an *awareness* of the spiritual events taking place. In short, the experiential nature of the gift of the Spirit can only be denied if attention is focused exclusively on 1 Corinthians 12:13 and the interchangeability of terms is ignored.

It is interesting to notice a number of writers who deny the Pentecostal theology but are, nevertheless, sensitive to this point. James G. Dunn is widely regarded as a writer who refutes Pentecostalism, yet closer attention to his work would reveal that he is more Pentecostal than the Pentecostals! Far from denying the experiential nature of the gift of the Spirit he asserts it very strongly. However, Dunn views this as Christian conversion. Unless one has had a Pentecostal-type experience one is not a Christian at all, when judged by New Testament standards. For him the baptism with the Spirit is 'the chief element in conversion-initiation' (Dunn's phrase for the whole complex of elements in conversion, including baptism). He goes on to say it was 'a very definite and often dramatic *experience*'; 'the Pentecostal's belief in the dynamic and experiential nature of Spirit-baptism is well founded.' Although in Dunn's view the Pentecostal's separation of spirit-baptism from conversion is objectionable, the nature of it as a Pentecostal *experience* is not. It is 'only by receiving the Spirit [interpreted in a strongly Pentecostal fashion] that one becomes a Christian', according to Dunn's interpretation of the Lucan writings.[9] He says, 'That the Spirit and particularly the gift of the Spirit, was a *fact of experience* in the lives of the earliest Christians has been too obvious to require elaboration.'[10] That being so, one of three things follow: either *only* those who have had Pentecostal experience may be called Christians, or such 'experience' is not the *sine qua non* of Christian salvation but may develop subsequently to salvation, or, thirdly, we accept that the New Testament presents one picture of a Christian but (on one ground or another) we justify an altogether different picture and treat the New Testament as without authority. This later option will raise questions as to our doctrine of the authority of Scripture and whether it is normative in its description of what a Christian is. It is quite possible, of course, for a theologian to accept the third route, but if this route is adopted it ought to be adopted explicitly and openly. I have adopted the second option (with Lloyd-Jones) and believe that *subsequent to Christian conversion* one's *experience* may catch up with what one possesses objectively and in principle from conversion onwards. The term 'baptism with the Spirit' ought, in my judgment, to be used *not* of what is *in principle* given at Christian initiation-conversion but of what is *in experience* known, which may or may not take place at the time of coming to faith in Christ.

Another writer who accepts that this experiential note is to be found in the New Testament descriptions of the gift of the Spirit, is the Roman Catholic, Francis A. Sullivan. Sullivan points to the 'experiential aspect of New Testament "baptism in the Spirit"'.[11] He wishes to argue that two aspects are involved in the 'baptism with the Spirit', the theological and the experiential. I am happy with this but wish to ask whether there would be any essential difference in theology if 'baptism in the Spirit' *is* used in the New Testament *only* of the 'experiential' half? What if everything that there is to have by way of Christian blessing is given *objectively and in principle* at Christian conversion but that the New Testament name for coming to an experiential *realization* of sonship is called 'baptism with the Spirit'?

The relation of the baptism with the Spirit to assurance, power for service, sanctification and the gifts of the Spirit is rightly evaluated in Lloyd-Jones's teaching.

Granted that a large number of biblical terms relate to an experiential receiving of the Spirit, one is led on to survey those passages of Scripture asking what are the major Christian blessings associated with such a receiving of the Spirit. As one does this, Lloyd-Jones's major conclusions seem to be substantiated. As the total range of Scriptures are surveyed, the baptism with the Spirit is seen as the end of thirst (Isaiah 44:3). It gives assurance of sonship (Isaiah 44:5), ends the hiding of God's face (Ezekiel 39:29), leads to an enlargement of gifts of understanding and speech (John 2:28). It is a profuse blessing, a 'baptism', 'water on thirsty ground', 'rivers of living water' (Isaiah 44:3; Matthew 3:11; John 7:37–39). It is receiving power (Luke 4:14; 24:49; Acts 1:8); it is the opposite of being an 'orphan' (John 14:18). It is illumination (John 14:26), glimpsing the glory of Jesus (John 15:26). It is the love of God shed abroad in the heart (Romans 5:5), a consciousness of God's love which seals salvation, gives a foretaste of heaven, gives assurance concerning the resurrection body, stabilizes one's life and enables ministry (Ephesians 1:13–14; 2 Corinthians 1:21–22; 5:5). It may be recalled as a conscious event some years after it happened (Galatians 3:1–5). Its connection with saving faith is such that it is an experiential proof of justification by faith (Galatians 3:1–5).

Lloyd-Jones was an insightful expositor and a number of his interpretations of key passages are worthy of serious consideration.

There are good reasons for not dismissing his interpretation of 1 Corinthians 12:13 as lightly as has often been done, as I shall argue below.

Again Lloyd-Jones's arguments concerning Ephesians 1:13 seem to be more capable of support than is generally thought. The aorist tense is not a difficulty. There are clearly attested occasions when the aorist participle refers to something that is prior to the action of the main verb. E. de Witt Burton has a section in his work on moods and tenses in New Testament Greek entitled 'The Aorist Participle of Antecedent Action', in which he says that the aorist participle 'is most frequently used of an action antecedent in time to the action of the main verb'. He mentions Matthew 4:2 ('having fasted'), John 5:13 ('*he that had been healed* did not know who it was'), Acts 14:19 ('having persuaded the multitudes they stoned Paul'), Romans 5:1 ('having been justified by faith we have peace . . .'), and others. It is by no means *necessary* to take the aorist tense in Ephesians 1:13 as synchronous with the main verb.[12]

Lloyd-Jones is surely correct to say that there is a development in Ephesians 1:3–14. At verse 3 the blessings that are in Christ are viewed objectively, but by the time one has reached verse 8, more experiential blessings are being mentioned. Knowing God's will (verse 9) is surely a conscious matter. So is the conversion of the Ephesians. Hearing the truth (verse 13) is not wholly objective.

Then the equation in verse 14 of the sealing of the Spirit with a foretaste of glory indicates that a subjective matter is being referred to. Can there be an *un*conscious enjoyment of the blessings of glory before the full inheritance is received? Surely not. In which case the 'sealing of the Spirit' is dependent on believing (whether immediately subsequent or after a time-gap is not discernible from Ephesians 1:13); it is an experiential foretaste of what will be fully received in the eschatological future; receiving the Spirit in such a way authenticates, ratifies and marks out one's salvation.[13]

Similarly Lloyd-Jones's view of Romans 8:16 is at least worthy of consideration. It depends largely on taking *synmartyreō* to refer to a *second* witness over and above the witness of the human spirit. Admittedly not all take it this way. F. J. Leenhardt, for example, concedes that 'If the word is taken in its original meaning (to join one's witness to that of another), it means here that the Spirit of Christ confirms what our own spirit has spontaneously realised.' Nevertheless he sees a difficulty here in that Paul 'certainly does not attribute to the spirit of man the knowledge of our adoption'.[14] I cannot entirely agree with this last remark. It seems to neglect the point that faith is inherently assuring. Thus there is the possibility of

235

man's faith (admittedly, wrought by the Spirit) being doubly confirmed by the Spirit's witness. Paul's emphatic phrase 'the Spirit himself' (*auto to pneuma*) seems to point this way. While Romans 8:16, taken by itself, could be interpreted in more than one way, taken in conjunction with the seal terminology and the incidents in Acts it is likely that faith in Jesus is thought of as giving assurance but that 'the Spirit himself' gives an *added* confirmation of salvation. M. Black comments on this verse: 'Two witnesses according to the Old Testament injunction, establish the truth of any statement.'[15]

There is good reason to think that Lloyd-Jones's approach to Acts is largely correct. I concentrate especially on Acts 8 and 19.[16] In my opinion it cannot easily be denied that the disciples of Acts 8 are believers, acceptable to God, before the experiential receiving of the Spirit. A group of people who have 'believed' the message concerning Jesus (Acts 8:12), who upon so believing have been baptized in the name of Jesus, who are said to have received the Word of God (a standard phrase for conversion) must surely be thought of as Christians. The force of this can be evaded in only three ways, so far as I can see. Firstly, the receiving of the Spirit may be understood only as the receiving of the charismata.[17] Secondly, despite all that is said positively about the Samaritan conversion, they may be thought to become Christians only at the point described at verse 17.[18] Thirdly, the point may be accepted that there was a time-gap between conversion and the receiving of the Spirit, yet that time-gap may be thought of as non-normative for the modern Christian.[19]

The first option is not so different from my own view and in effect *is* teaching a post-conversion receiving of the Spirit. The second view is simply not credible to me. I grant that the Samaritans were not all that they ought to be until verse 17, but I cannot accept that they were not believers acceptable to God. The 'hearing with faith' was sufficient to save. The receiving of the Spirit I conceive as a 'seal' upon what had already happened. To the third view I reply: it only takes *one* case where conversion and the receiving of the Spirit are distinct (however normative or non-normative that case may be) to prove that the two are distinct. A work of the Spirit is needful for *any* acknowledgment of Christ's lordship (Paul's point in 1 Corinthians

12:3). If only one case exists (which I do not believe) the question still arises: what on that *one* occasion took place at the 'second' stage? Even one incident where conversion and the receiving of the Spirit are distinct, proves that at least in principle the two are distinct. Why may the two elements not be separated again, however anomalous such a separation may be? If it was an anomaly in Acts 8, may the anomaly never be repeated?[20]

Likewise the incident at Ephesus seems to me to imply the possibility of receiving the Spirit *after* conversion-faith. The term 'disciples' occurs thirty times in the book of Acts. On twenty-eight occasions it clearly refers to Christians. On the only occasion when it clearly does not refer to a Christian a genitive expression is added, 'his' (*i.e.* Paul's disciples). That leaves Acts 19:1. In the light of the consistent usage in Acts the phrase 'he found some disciples' must mean (in my opinion) 'he found some Christians'. The genitive expression 'some disciples of John the Baptist' is *not* found. Surely anyone coming to the phrase 'he found some disciples' without any theological predisposition would take it to mean that Paul met some Christians.[21]

The question of Acts 19:2 – even when the AV is left aside and the RSV is followed – implies that one can believe without receiving the Spirit. If I ask: 'Did you visit Paris when you went to France?' I imply that it is possible to go to France without visiting Paris. If I ask: 'Did you receive the Spirit when you believed?' I imply it is possible to believe without receiving the Spirit. If I say: 'Did you visit Paris when you went to France?' I imply that I realise you went to France; I do *not* know whether you visited Paris. Similarly Paul's question implies that he accepts that they have believed; he questions whether they have received the Spirit. Such seems to be the natural way of understanding Acts 19:2. In my judgment only theological preconceptions would make anyone take it another way.[22]

Other interpretations of the passage fall into three categories. Some urge that the Ephesians were not Christians and that Paul is, in effect, 'tongue in cheek' when he asks the questions in the form that he does. He is then effectively querying their salvation and their faith.[23] Others accept the view that I am proposing but urge that the delayed receiving of the

237

Spirit is non-normative.[24] A third view sees here the receiving of the charismata.[25]

Lloyd-Jones's interpretation of the 'baptism with the Spirit' provides a category of interpretation by which to understand Christian experience.

A critic of Lloyd-Jones could easily protest at some of the illustrations he gives of the baptism with the Spirit. Jonathan Edwards' experience of the 'glory of the son of God as mediator' was never interpreted by Edwards as a baptism with the Spirit and he explicitly denied the interpretation of Romans 8:16 taught by Lloyd-Jones.[26] Is it right, therefore, that the term 'baptism with the Spirit' should be applied to such experiences and is any theological gain achieved by doing so? I personally think that there is a good deal to be gained.

There are those who are sympathetic to charismatic experience and would assess such accounts as that related by Edwards with sympathy. Yet they feel that there is no 'doctrine' of the baptism with the Spirit and that such a phrase is misused if applied to charismatic experiences.[27] In that view, such experiences as those reported by Edwards, Moody and others are theologically *random* experiences corresponding to no particular category of interpretation put forward in the New Testament. Such a view must lead to a detached attitude towards these experiences of God – if that is what they are judged to be. They just 'happen' to have taken place in the lives of Edwards, Moody and others. Their stories are interesting but there is no reason why anything like their experiences should happen to anyone else. The New Testament does not hold forth any such experience. If the baptism with the Spirit comes when I first believe, and I have faith now, I must *deduce* that I have been baptized with the Spirit.

In Lloyd-Jones's view, however, the baptism with the Spirit is a distinct event. The phrase 'baptism with the Spirit' or 'sealing with the Spirit' provides a category of interpretation by which to understand the experience of a wide range of Christians. The striking events that took place in the ministry of a man like D. L. Moody[28] are an example of something held out to every Christian; it is the definitive *experience* of the New Covenant promise of the Spirit. If I, as a Christian, am not jubilantly rejoicing in an assured salvation, then I may know that a direct awareness of sonship and salvation is definitely held out to me. 'The promise is to you and to your children, every one whom the Lord our God shall call.' If this 'promise' is interpreted as indubitably experiential and I have come to faith in Jesus but am not enjoying such an enduement, it is there for me to enjoy. The promise is mine. Thus the existence of a clear category of interpretation by which to understand the experiences of the past and by which to define the nature of Christian experience for the future, is theological gain not theological improverishment.

Several further issues are raised upon this construction, such as the question of a 'theology of subsequence' and of division into categories of Christians, also the understanding of 1 Corinthians 12:13 and the nature of Christian 'experience'.

It may be asked: is not the position presented above a 'theology of subsequence', implying the inadequacy of the saving work of Christ? Is it a 'second work of grace' theology, implying the inadequacy of the 'first' work of grace and therefore the inadequacy of the work of Christ, and of the work of the Spirit? At least one reviewer used strong language in criticizing Lloyd-Jones's work along these lines. 'It is becoming common now', he complained, 'to speak of those who have had *the baptism* and *the fire* and to contrast these favoured beings with the rest of us.' He thought Lloyd-Jones was seriously in error in his teaching: 'in Lloyd-Jones's new emphasis we have a reversion to the theology of *plus*, which in its various forms has bedevilled the Christian church'.[29]

F. D. Brunner also makes what is, in effect, the same objection when he protests against what he calls a 'theology of subsequence'. Although Brunner writes primarily with Pentecostalism in mind, his criticisms apply to any view of the baptism with the Spirit that treats it as an experiential blessing which is distinctively subsequent to conversion. He is unhappy with what, in reference to Methodist theology, has been called a 'second work of grace'[30] or what he calls 'the Pentecostal understanding of a crisis and conscious experience of the baptism in the Holy Spirit subsequent to conversion'.[31]

If this were so it would be a serious criticism; certainly it is possible to present a view of the baptism of the Spirit that has this theological implication. However, I reply as follows. If there is *any* experiential element in one's theology of the Christian life it is impossible to avoid *some* kind of 'theology of subsequence'. (This term is not a useful one; I merely use it because others have done so and I am replying using their language). There are, however, different ways of presenting a 'subsequent' work of the Spirit in the Christian's life. If it is true (as I think it is) that every blessing of the Christian is received 'in Christ' at the moment of earliest faith, how is it possible for any 'experience' subsequent to conversion to have any significance? Surely the New Testament would not have it that everything there is to be had in Christ is *experienced* at the point of initial faith. Where would be the room for exhortation, for growth, for sanctification, for eschatology? Something must be 'subsequent' to initial faith if there is to be any development at all.

Much depends on how 'experience' of the Spirit is conceived. If the baptism of the Spirit were an 'experience' of holiness, such would divide Christians into the 'sanctified' and the 'not-yet-sanctified'. There would be a 'before' and an 'after' in the Christian life. This would imply that new *objective* 'works of grace' take place in the Christian life subsequent to initial faith. If the baptism of the Spirit were primarily associated with the gift of tongues as an indispensable *sine qua non* of Christian maturity it would divide Christians into the 'gifted' and the 'not yet gifted'. If the baptism of the Spirit were *primarily* a power for service it would divide Christians into the empowered and the not-yet-empowered.

Lloyd-Jones's approach points the way to a resolution of this difficulty, and to a less invidious 'theology of subsequence' (which I prefer to call a 'theology of Christian experience'). The baptism of the Spirit is conceived as sealing what is *already present objectively*. The Christian who is 'assured' of salvation is not more Christian, or more forgiven, or more justified, or more regenerated. He is not *necessarily* more sanctified either before or after such an experience. The baptism of the Spirit is that work of the Spirit in which is given the *experiential* awareness of what is already present in the Christian 'in Christ'. It is not objectively a 'second work of grace'. It is a 'release of the Spirit' (to use Cardinal Suenen's term).[32] The Spirit, secretly or hiddenly, is given at the earliest point of faith or even before. This does not mean, however, that at that point the *experience* of the Spirit is known. The biblical term 'baptism of the Spirit' is the expression which focuses on the moment when the hidden presence of the Spirit becomes a matter of conscious '*reception*'. Such, I believe, is the way the New Testament views the receiving of the Spirit. There is a 'receiving' of the Spirit which is firmly placed in the realm of experience and not in the realm of the hidden or the secret.

Jesus is reported as saying to the disciples concerning the Spirit that he would send the Paraclete to be with (*meta*) them. He added that already the Spirit was known by them because he was alongside (*para*) and was or would be[33] among (*en*) them.[34] Why did Jesus need to tell the disciples that the Spirit was already present with them? Surely it is because they would not have known adequately if he had not done so. There is a presence of the Spirit which is hidden and which is not immediately self-evidencing. The promised 'receiving' of the Paraclete is the receiving of the Spirit at an experiential level. It is the presence of the Spirit already given, objectively, secretly, in a way that one has to be informed of, *now* becoming a matter of conscious experience. There is objectively no 'second work of grace' because nothing is added objectively to the salvation already given 'in Christ'. In the baptism with the Spirit *nothing is added to one's salvation.* The baptism with the Spirit makes one subjectively aware of what was previously objectively present.

This does not mean, however, that a 'subsequent' baptism with the Spirit is of no significance. The mere awareness of what is objectively true is in itself a transforming event. This, to me, is the New Testament presentation. It is 'because you *are* sons' that 'God sent the Spirit of His Son *crying* (*i.e.* working into the realm of experience and even of emotion), Abba Father'. This is a kind of 'theology of subsequence' but it does not posit a 'stage two' in the objective work of grace that is given us 'in Christ'. Biblical terms for the 'baptism with the Spirit' pinpoint this aspect of salvation, its being 'received' into conscious experience.

A closely related issue is that of the *divisiveness* of a doctrine of the 'baptism with the Spirit'. What of the classic objection concerning two 'types' of Christian? Is it not making an invidious class-distinction to posit a 'baptism with the Spirit' that is subsequent to Christian faith.[35] The reply to this is twofold. Firstly, any theology that allows *any* experiential element in the gift of the Spirit must *either* deny the salvation of those who have not had the experience *or* must allow that experience may develop subsequent to salvation. Which is the more invidious position? If the New Testament gift of the Spirit *is* experiential but some Christians have not yet had such an experience, must one deny their salvation? Or must one say that an *experience* of *assured* sonship is there for the Christian to enter into. Secondly, denial of a baptism with the Spirit because it makes two types of Christian proves too much. Are there two types of Christian because some Christians have experienced answers to prayer more than others? Are there two types of Christian because there are 'weak' and 'strong' Christians (Romans 14; 1 Corinthians 8)? Are there two types of Christian because some are 'carnal' others are not (1 Corinthians 3)? The fact of the matter surely is that there *are* gradations and differences and variety of levels of experience among Christians. *Objectively and in principle* all Christians are 'in Christ' and have all that there is to have in Christ. *Practically and in experience* some Christians lag behind in one respect, other Christians lag behind in other respects. The *experiential* assurance of sonship, the 'witness of the Spirit', the 'baptism with the Spirit', may be *experienced* by one Christian sooner than it is experienced by another. This is just part of the variety that pertains to Christian experience. Writers like Thomas Smail who wish to deny a 'theology of subsequence' still address *Christians* with the words, 'By whatever name receive!'[36] But that implies that 'by whatever name' some have received and some have not. Has Smail solved his problem of the theology of subsequence? I think not. When Smail makes a distinction between 'believing' and 'receiving' is he not still falling into a 'theology of subsequence'?[37] For even in his view while all have 'believed' only some have 'received'. There is the possibility of some being on-the-way-to-receiving. Unless one denies the possibility of 'experience' altogether one has *only* the alternatives of denying the salvation of those without the 'experience' or of allowing that in one way or another faith may come first and 'experience' second. I adopt the second view and believe that it is indisputable that the Spirit is 'received' experientially subsequent to the beginning of Christian faith, but that the Spirit is possessed inwardly and secretly from the very beginning of Christian faith and even before.

242

The above argument brings me to the same conclusion to which Lloyd-Jones was evidently driven. It requires accepting the fact that 1 Corinthians 12:13 does not have the same denotation as the more or less identical phrase in the gospels and Acts. This may be linguistically untidy, but if one is driven by contextual exegesis to understand 1 Corinthians 12:13 as something which is not necessarily conscious and if one is driven by comparison of terms to see the same phrase in the gospels and Acts as referring to something experiential, the resulting conclusion must be accepted: the usage varies and 1 Corinthians 12:13 must not be used as a pair of coloured spectacles with which to approach the other six references.

This leads one to the most difficult question of all: what exactly is meant by 'experience'? This is not an easy question to answer. Perhaps the simplest way to approach it is to contrast certain aspects of the Christian life that one *knows* about but has not *experienced*. The resurrection-body is objectively provided in Christ but has not been 'experienced'. Romans 6 speaks of a 'having died' to sin which must be 'reckoned' as having happened, presumably because the Christian will not always *feel* that he has 'died to sin'. Romans 8:28 asserts an objective promise that God works all things together for good. Presumably the Christian has often to hold on to that as a statement without experiencing it as a conscious event. It is along such lines that one may point to a real distinction between what one believes without that belief immediately impinging on one's awareness, and other matters where one's awareness is quickened and we use the word 'experience' to express that awareness. However difficult it is to define that distinction (and the difficulty is great)[38] most Christians are conscious of the fact that there is such a distinction. The question is: judged by New Testament standards is the baptism of the Spirit 'taken' by faith without experiential awareness? Or, judged by New Testament standards, is it something that cannot but impinge in some way or another upon one's awareness of God and one's relationship to him. It is the latter that wins my vote.

Lloyd-Jones's view of the baptism with the Spirit gives rise to one major criticism concerning its setting in the context of soteriological preparationism.

The tradition inherited from Sibbes and Goodwin in which *palin* ('again') in Romans 8:15 is interpreted as implying a 'receiving' of the Spirit as a 'Spirit of bondage' prior to salvation and prior to the receiving of the 'Spirit of adoption', rests upon a major mistake in exegesis. It is mistaken in my judgment to link the *palin* with the verb *elabete* ('received') which occurs three words previously. It is altogether more likely that the *palin* is to be linked not with the verb three words prior to it but to the very next phrase adjacent to it *eis phobon* ('to fear'). The RSV of Romans 8:15 would then be correct: 'You did not receive a spirit of slavery to fall *back* into fear'. A spirit (or Spirit) of slavery has not been received again-for-fear. The thought of the phrase would then be that the Holy Spirit has been given only as the Spirit of adoption. He has not *at all* been given to encourage the Christian in any way to lapse back into the fears that characterized his pre-Christian life.[39] To encourage the Christian to *want* to experience a 'Spirit of bondage' because such is the pathway to blessing, is surely the highway to acute introspection. Lloyd-Jones once recommended a book entitled *More Than Notion* in connection with 'experiential religion'.[40] It is a very introspective work and portrays a group of Christians intensely preoccupied with the states and conditions of their soul.[41] I cannot help but feel that such introspection belongs inseparably to such a view of the 'Spirit of bondage'.

I also doubt whether Romans 7:13–25 should ever be used as a mandatory *ordo salutis*. Lloyd-Jones's exegesis of this section is, in my judgment, very perceptive.[42] My point is that while Romans 7:7–25 outlines the only thing the law can do (objectively, to pin-point sin; subjectively, to induce despair) this by no means implies that such an experience is a mandatory phrase in an *ordo salutis* or that it is the *sine qua non* of salvation let alone of the witness of the Spirit. The whole point of Galatians 3:15–18 is surely that Abraham was justified *without* coming 'under the law'; no codified 'law' existed. The point of the 430-year time-gap (according to Paul) is that it demonstrated that godliness may be wholly 'without the law'. Paul describes all that the law can do; he does not, as I see it, prescribe a phrase that must be experienced by the Christian before salvation or before the witness of the Spirit.

It may be asked: since Lloyd-Jones was an admirer of Edwards and thought Edwards, 'would have nothing to do with the teaching of preparationism', should he be called a preparationist? Most illuminating in this respect are Lloyd-Jones's comments on preparationism in connection with Jonathan Edwards (comments which allude to R. T. Kendall's paper on the so-called 'antinomianism' of John Cotton in contrast to the introspection of much Puritanism). Lloyd-Jones points out that for Edwards (i) 'gradual change' is not needed in conversion; (ii) conversion is 'not brought to pass by men themselves' and (iii) Edwards 'believed in a direct and immediate influence of the Spirit, and in sudden and dramatic conversion'.[43] In all of this Lloyd-Jones followed Edwards. But on the other hand, Lloyd-Jones's teaching concerning Romans 7, his insistence that repentance precedes faith even chronologically, his urging that the Law must be preached before the gospel and his support of the teaching of Perkins, all indicate a measure of preparationism. This means that there is a balance in Lloyd-Jones's teaching between (on the one hand) the direct influences of the Spirit and sudden conversion and (on the other hand) the interpretation he had imbibed from the Perkins' tradition in which he placed repentance before faith. This means that on the one hand he agreed with Perkins that there were steps and stages in conversion, yet on the other hand he was sympathetic to John Cotton rather than his critics. He was critical of the extreme introspection of Thomas Shepherd and said that Edwards would 'never leave us confused and despondent as Thomas Shepherd does in his study of the "Parable of the Ten Virgins"'.[44] His admiration of Edwards meant that his preparationism was offset by his belief in the direct and sudden workings of the Spirit. Nevertheless a preparationist strand was retained in Lloyd-Jones's teaching. To place the matter of the baptism with the Spirit in such a setting was, in my opinion, a mistake.

This leads to a further, minor, point of disagreement. Although I accept Lloyd-Jones's contention that there is an *experiential* receiving of the Spirit, and that such an experience *may* be subsequent to conversion, it is *also* true that the baptism with the Spirit is tightly integrated into Paul's understanding of justification by faith, and that a *lengthy* time-gap between justification and the sealing of the Spirit is not envisaged, and would seem to be most unnatural. Lloyd-Jones clearly thought that many years could go by in a Christian's life without his receiving the Spirit. I agree, yet cannot but feel that judged by the New Testament such a state-of-affairs is to be considered a grotesque anomaly. Galatians 3:1–5 thinks of the giving of the Spirit at an experiential level as the *immediate* sealing of the salvation of the Galatians such that they can look back on it. The preaching of Christ that (without the preaching of the law) led to the Galatians' conversion may be confirmed by their remembering the circumstances in which they received the Spirit. Why is it then that a long delay and much diligent seeking is assumed in Lloyd-Jones's view of the sealing of the Spirit? Is the preparationist strand in his teaching in fact a restraint of Christian joy and a hindrance in Christian experience?

Likewise, though I understand the 'sealing' of Ephesians 1:13 as an experiential blessing distinct from faith, yet it cannot be denied that for a seal to seal salvation twenty years after conversion for example, is hardly to be a seal! In Acts 10 one finds the gift of the Spirit functioning as a 'seal' (although the term is not used). What ratifies the Gentiles' salvation in the eyes of a doubting apostle is the experiential, visible, obvious receiving of the Spirit. The *experience* of the Spirit is the *immediate* authentication of true salvation.

The promise of John 7:37–39 points in the same direction. If any man thirst he must come and drink from Jesus. He will experience rivers of living water. Jesus is referring to the Spirit which those who believed would receive. Again a lengthy time-gap can scarcely be justified. Similarly the promise of Acts 2:38 holds out hope of an experiential receiving of the Spirit such as has taken place among the 120 disciples. The structure of the sentence puts a slight gap between forgiveness and the Spirit. It is not 'for the forgiveness of your sins and the gift of the Spirit' but 'for the forgiveness of your sins – and [new clause] you shall receive the gift of the Spirit. . .'. It is possible to see here a distinction between receiving forgiveness and receiving the Spirit. On the other hand, again it must be said that a *lengthy* time-gap before the *experience* of the Spirit is known is not envisaged.

There is thus a difference of emphasis between the view of Lloyd-Jones and the view that I am supporting. In Lloyd-Jones's teaching delay seems normal. As I understand the New Testament, delay in (experientially) receiving the Spirit is violently abnormal.

This in turn leads to a further point. Lloyd-Jones mentioned on several occasions that he did not wish to make too much of the *intensity* of the experience of the baptism with the Spirit. I am happy he made this point and believe that it is important in conjunction with my previous point. There may be such a thing as a *mild* 'baptism with the Spirit'. One may be baptized with the Spirit *without* being compelled to 'ask God to stay his hand' (to use D. L. Moody's phrase). The experience may *not* be physically overwhelming. It is interesting that in the revival of the 1740s Jonathan Edwards reported how *gentle* were the experiential workings of the Spirit. Lloyd-Jones would have agreed with this but because his illustrations are invariably taken from the highly dramatic incidents in the lives of famous preachers, he tended to give the impression that the baptism with the Spirit is always a matter of great intensity. (I have been inclined to think this way myself but have been forced by pastoral experience to reconsider the matter.) A Christian who has experienced a 'Damascus Road' conversion tends to think that there is no other way to become a Christian and that anything less dramatic is not true conversion. Similarly a Christian who has been through a D. L. Moody-type of baptism with the Spirit tends to think that anything less is not a true 'sealing with the Spirit'. Though I am in large measure in agreement with Lloyd-Jones, I would prefer that the matter of variation of intensity be given considerably greater emphasis.

Approached along such lines Galatians 3:1–14 begins to be more meaningful than ever. There is a receiving of the Spirit held out to all who believe in Jesus. It may or may not be dramatically intense but it is characterized by directness and immediacy. It is not known by the works of the law for it seals *simple* faith in Jesus. Any Christian who does not know such a blessing is an anomaly by New Testament standards. A legalistic approach to the gospel will only suppress joy, a fact which was the essence of the Galatians' problem. Such an experience of the Spirit may be remembered; it may be the subject of reflection after the event. Such is the point of Galatians 3:1–5.[45] It proves justification by faith. Preparationism is a detour; one cannot be happy with long delays in the matter of a Christian's receiving the Spirit.

I would not wish my negative assessment of Lloyd-Jones's preparationism to overthrow my appreciation of his thesis as a whole. I can only agree with him when he says: 'there is a Christ-mysticism which we must not exclude'.

Lloyd-Jones loved to quote Augustus Toplady's hymn:

> While I feel Thy love to me,
> Every object teems with joy,
> May I ever walk with Thee,
> For 'tis bliss without alloy.
> Let me but Thyself possess,
> Total sum of happiness:
> Real bliss I then shall prove,
> Heaven below and heaven above.

Such, I submit, is the baptism with the Spirit.

Notes

[1] The matter of interchangeable terminology is stressed by M. C. Harper, *Power for The Body of Christ* (London: Fountain Trust, 1964), p. 10.

[2] Without detailed consideration of questions of authorship I refer to the gospel and epistles traditionally ascribed to John the apostle.

[3] See M. M. B. Turner, 'Spirit Endowment in Luke–Acts: Some Linguistic Considerations', *Vox Evangelica*, 12 (1981), pp. 45–63; 'Jesus and the Spirit in Lucan Perspective', *Tyndale Bulletin*, 32 (1981), pp. 3–42; 'The Significance of Spirit Endowment for Paul', *Vox Evangelica*, 9 (1975), pp. 56–69; 'The Concept of Receiving the Spirit in John's Gospel', *Vox Evangelica*, 10 (1977), pp. 24–42.

[4] See A. Stibbs and J. I. Packer, *The Spirit Within You* (London: Hodder and Stoughton, 1967), p. 35.

[5] This is of course a minimal list. I include it merely to protest at basing too much on 1 Corinthians 12:13. A survey of the baptizing work of the Spirit in these passages will (in my opinion) bring one to conclude that 1 Corinthians 12:13 stands outside the description of the baptizing work of the Spirit as described in those passages of Scripture which are central in elucidating the other six occasions where the phrase is used. I return to this below.

[6] An exception is J. P. Baker, who wishes to interpret 1 Corinthians 12:13 as referring to an experiential 'baptism with the Spirit'. *Cf.* J. P. Baker, *Baptized in One Spirit* (London: Fountain Trust, 1967), pp. 18–20.

[7] J. R. W. Stott, *Baptism and Fullness: The work of the Holy Spirit today* (London: IVP, 2nd ed., 1975). It is the linch-pin too of Peter Pytches's 'Problems for Pentecostals', *The Churchman*, vol. 86, no. 4 (Winter 1972), pp. 278–289. For Stott's use of the word 'experience', see p. 36.

[8] Some commentators fail to see Galatians 3:1–5 as an appeal to *conscious*

experience. H. D. MacDonald does not see any striking experience even in verse 5 (*Freedom in Faith: A Commentary on Paul's Epistle to the Galatians* [London: Pickering and Inglis, 1973], p. 68). Thomas Aquinas was much closer to Paul's argument, surely, in seeing allusion to '*manifest* signs of the Holy Spirit' which 'took place in the hearers immediately after the apostles preached the faith'. They '*openly* received the Holy Spirit at Paul's preaching', he says. Aquinas here identifies the receiving of the Spirit of Galatians 3:1-5 with the receiving of the charismata. This is not necessary but at least it focuses attention on the nature of Paul's appeal to experience (*St Thomas Aquinas, Commentary on Saint Paul's Epistle to the Galatians*, Aquinas Scripture Series, vol. 1 [Albany USA: Magi, 1966], p. 71, translated by F. R. Larcher; introduction by R. T. A. Murphy. The italics are mine). The evangelical understanding of the receiving of the Spirit in Galatians 3:1-5 as 'the initial entrance of the Holy Spirit into the hearts when they [*i.e.* converts] put their trust in the Lord Jesus' (Kenneth S. Wuest, *Galatians in the Greek New Testament* [Grand Rapids: Eerdmans], p. 85) is in effect a non-experiential understanding of the passage. Yet Paul's appeal to conscious experience is of the essence of his argument. Fuller emphasis on the experiential aspect of the gift of the Spirit is found in C. B. Cousar, *Galatians – Interpretation; a Bible commentary for teaching and preaching* (Atlanta: John Knox, 1982), esp. p. 69. A. Viard also links the gift of the Spirit mentioned here with the Spirit's bestowal in Acts 10:44 and draws attention to the Spirit's effusion with exterior manifestations (A. Viard, *Saint Paul, Epitre aux Galates, Sources Bibliques* [Paris: Gabalda, 1964], p. 62).

[9]See J. Dunn, *Baptism in the Holy Spirit* (London: SCM, 1970), p. 4.

[10]*Ibid.*, p. 225.

[11]F. A. Sullivan, *Charisms and Charismatic Renewal* (Dublin: Gill and Macmillan, 1982), pp. 66–70.

[12]E. De Witt Burton, *Syntax of the Moods and Tenses in New Testament Greek* (Edinburgh: T. & T. Clark, 3rd ed. 1898, reprinted 1973), p. 63; C. L. Mitton, *Ephesians: New Century Bible* (London: Oliphants, 1976), p. 61, sees here not baptism but the gift of the Spirit which he describes as 'something that was recognisable, and its absence in a Christian was noticeable.' The experiential aspect of the seal he interprets as 'a new sense of freedom, peace, and joy, an awareness of a power for goodness that brought possibilities of victory over evil, and of new love towards all men' (*op. cit.*, p. 60).

F. W. Grosheide mentions that later writers used 'seal' to refer to baptism but thinks here the reference is to the Spirit himself (*cf. De Brief van Paulus aan de Efziers* [Kampen: Koch, 1960], p. 24; *cf.* also his *Tweede Brief aan Korinthe* [Kampen: Kok, 1959], pp. 59–63).

[13]I thus reject views that take the participle synchronously and views that think the seal refers to baptism. I doubt whether baptism can be viewed as an *experiential* foretaste of glory. I doubt also whether a non-experiential foretaste is really a foretaste.

G. B. Wilson's dogmatic statement that '"Having believed" is the coincident aorist participle . . . Paul's use of it here shows that they were not sealed *after*, but *when* they believed', simply fails to consider other possibilities. The aorist does not have to be coincident (*Ephesians* [Edinburgh: Banner of Truth, 1978], p. 30). A similar remark could be made about H. D. MacDonald's comments in *The Church and Its Glory: An Exposition of Paul's Letter to the Ephesians* (Worthing, UK: Walter, 1973), p. 21. Similarly J. A. Allen's blunt statement: 'These verses refer to baptism' (*The Epistle to the Ephesians* [London: SCM, 1959], p. 53) does not consider other possibilities.

It is *not* necessary to regard the aorist participle as a 'coincident aorist' participle which is 'doctrinally important' in Ephesians 1:13, *Pace* James Hope Moulton, *A Grammar of New Testament Greek*, vol. 1 (Edinburgh: T. & T. Clark, 3rd ed., 1908), p. 131.

[14]*The Epistle to the Romans: A Commentary* (London: Lutterworth, 1961), p. 215.

[15]*Romans: New Century Bible*, p. 119. The alternative interpretation is argued by H. Strathmann in *Theological Dictionary of the New Testament* (ed. G. Kittel) vol. 4 (Grand Rapids, Michigan: Eerdmans, 1967), pp. 508–509.

[16]Other passages are either understood with greater consensus (Acts 2, 10 and 11) or are of more doubtful interpretation and less used in debate (Acts 9). The crucial chapters are 8 and 19.

[17]See J. I. Packer, *Keep in Step with the Spirit* (Leicester: IVP, 1984), p. 89 (expressed with less certainty than in A. M. Stibbs and J. I. Packer, *The Spirit Within You* [London: Hodder and Stoughton, 1967]), p. 35).

E. Haenchen, *The Acts of the Apostles: A Commentary* (Oxford: Blackwell, 1971), pp. 304, 308. (Haenchen speaks of the Spirit as 'the seal on the conversion' p. 304); J. Rawson Lumby, *The Acts of the Apostles* (Cambridge: Cambridge University Press, 1885 [Cambridge Greek Testament]), p. 181; F. F. Bruce, *Commentary on the Book of the Acts: The English Text with Introduction, Exposition and Notes* (London: Marshall, Morgan and Scott, 1954 [New London Commentary]), p. 181; N. B. Stonehouse, 'The Gift of the Holy Spirit', *Westminster Theological Journal*, vol. 13 (1950–1951), pp. 10ff.

[18]So C. W. Parnell, *Understanding Tongues-Speaking* (Johannesburg: South African Baptist Press, n.d. [1970s]), p. 93. 'It is questionable whether there was real faith in Jesus'.

[19]So F. D. Bruner, *A Theology of the Holy Spirit* (London: Hodder and Stoughton, 1971), pp. 173–181. J. R. W. Stott, *Baptism and Fullness*, pp. 31–34.

[20]One cannot read too much into Acts 8:12 ('believed Philip') as though the dative case or the human personage implies that the faith was defective. John 5:44 uses the same construction and has a human agent (Moses) but defective faith is not in view. In two other instances Luke mentions the human agent. Acts 2:41 says the crowd listened to 'his' (Peter's) word but the faith of 2:41–42 is quite genuine. Similarly the disciples continued in the *apostles'* doctrine (Acts 2:42) but are not defective in so doing. Even more decisive is the fact that 'believing Philip' is identified with 'receiving the word of God' (Acts 8:14). These considerations indicate that the Samaritans' faith was real.

If it be said that Simon also believed but his faith proved at least short-lived if genuine at all, I ask: what does this prove? Simon is clearly not a model Samaritan believer and is not portrayed as a typical case in Samaria.

[21]Leaving aside Acts 19:1 for the moment the term *mathētes* always means 'Christian' if it is without further definition, whether it comes as 'a certain disciple' (Acts 9:10; 16:1; 21:16), or as 'a disciple' (Acts 9:26), or as in the 21 occasions when 'the disciples' means 'the Christians', or as in the one occasion when we have reference to an 'early disciple' (Acts 21:16), or when the phrase is 'the disciples of the Lord' (Acts 9:1). On the only occasion when it is Paul's disciples that are referred to this is made clear by the genitive 'his'; thus Acts 9:25 refers to 'his' (Paul's) disciples.

In Acts 19:1 we have reference to 'some disciples'. In the light of the usage of Acts and without further definition this must refer to some Christians. They may be different in some way, but the difference does not lie in their being called *mathētes*. The absence of the article ('the') is entirely non-significant. Luke is not saying Paul met '*the* disciples', as though they had been previously mentioned. John 4:1 is another instance where reference is made to disciples of Jesus but the disciples are not specified and therefore the article is omitted. In Acts 19:1 *tinas mathētas* is the plural form of *tis mathētes* found in Acts 9:10; 16:1; 21:16, where it means 'a Christian' in each case.

Similarly in Luke's Gospel the various occasions where disciples *other* than the disciples of Jesus are mentioned there is a genitive (as in Acts 9:25; Luke 5:30, 33; 7:18–19; 11:1. The wording of Luke 5:33 'the disciples of John' is precisely the expression *not* used in Acts 19:1.

[22]Haenchen's viewpoint (from his own standpoint of radical criticism) is similar to the one proposed. 'These men must – as μαθηται – be Christians' he says. But it is an 'incomplete Christianity' until the Spirit is received (Haenchen, *op. cit*, pp. 556–557). Bruce also says that μαθηται refers, 'Presumably to disciples of Christ, in accordance with the meaning elsewhere of μαθητης thus used absolutely' (Bruce, *The Acts of the Apostles, Greek Text* [London: Tyndale Press, 1951], p. 353).

High-church Anglicans – with their distinctive view of confirmation – also tend to view this passage along lines similar to Lloyd-Jones (a fact that Lloyd-Jones made use of in *John*, Sermon 1083). For Knowling, Acts 8:15 refers to nothing less 'than a bestowal of that divine indwelling which makes the Christian the temple of God'. The Samaritans are not *full* Christians before that time. (See R. J. Knowling, 'The Acts of the Apostles', *The Expositor's Greek Testament*, vol. 2 (ed. W. Robertson Nicholl), p. 216.

[23]So F. D. Bruner, *A Theology of the Holy Spirit* (1971), pp. 207–214. Bruner concedes in a footnote (n. 59, p. 208) that Paul's question could imply that it would be possible to believe in Jesus and yet not receive the Spirit. He thinks the remainder of the narrative corrects this possible false impression. His view is linked with the assumption that regeneration takes place through baptism. That the Ephesian disciples were not initially Christians is also maintained by J. R. W. Stott, *(Baptism and Fullness*, pp. 34–36).

[24]F. F. Bruce seems to take this view. He regards it as 'anomalous' that a true believer should not have received the Spirit (*Commentary on the Book of Acts: The English Text* [London: Marshall, Morgan and Scott, 1954], pp. 386–387).

[25]J. I. Packer, *Keep in Step with the Spirit*, p. 89; J. R. Lumby, *The Acts of the Apostles* (1885), pp. 331–333.

[26]See above, pp. 110–114.

[27]Thus Simon Tugwell, despite his sympathy to charismatic experience, speaks of his 'rejection of the doctrine of the baptism in the Spirit' and of the 'reification of a particular kind of experience'. 'It is not', he says, 'a matter of an "experience" looking for a name' (*Did You Receive the Spirit?* [London: Darton, Longman and Todd, 1979, revised edition], pp. 7–8).

[28]See above, pp. 26–27.

[29]Donald MacLeod, 'The Sealing of the Spirit', *Reformation Today*, no. 48 (March–April 1979), p. 19.

[30]See F. D. Bruner, *A Theology of the Holy Spirit* (London: Hodder and Stoughton, 1971), p. 37.

[31]*Ibid.*, p. 39.

[32]See above, p. 32.

[33]There is a variant reading concerning the tense. Is it 'is in you' or 'will be in you'? I do not think the sense is greatly affected. The word *en* with the plural is better translated 'among' than 'in'.

[34]It is important to note that *three* prepositions are used in John 14:16–17. The idea is not that the Spirit had been *with* them but would henceforth be *in* them. This is surely John's well-known habit of varying his terminology (see in detail L. Morris, *Studies in the Fourth Gospel* [London: Paternoster, 1969], ch. 5, pp. 293–319, 'Variation – A Feature of Johannine Style').

M. M. B. Turner rightly argues that to distinguish the Spirit's work from outside and His work from within is virtually meaningless. In the Old Testament background the Spirit may be 'on' Moses but 'in' Daniel. (See further, 'Spirit Endowment in Luke–Acts', *Vox Evangelica*, vol. 12, 1981, p. 48.)

[35]Thus Anne Mather asserts: 'Among the questions raised about the charismatic movement by its critics, probably the most serious concerns the possible implication of a first-class and a second-class Christianity' ('Talking Points: The Charismatic Movement', *Themelios*, vol. 9, no. 3 [April 1984]), p. 20.

[36]T. A. Smail, *Reflected Glory* (Grand Rapids: Eerdmans, 1975), ch. 10.

[37]*Ibid.*, p. 30.

[38]A starting-point in tackling the matter would be Peter Donovan's *Interpreting Religious Experience* (London: Sheldon, 1979)].

[39]This approach to Romans 8:15 (following RSV) is found in C. K. Barrett, *Reading Through Romans* (Philadelphia: Fortress, 1977), p. 43; J. R. W. Stott, *Men Made New: An Exposition of Romans 5–8* (London: IVF, 1966), p. 93. M. Black also takes much the same view but relates it to baptism (*Romans: New Century Bible* [London: Marshall, Morgan and Scott, 1973], pp. 118–119). H. W. Schmidt explicitly makes the point that *elabete* is to be taken with *eis phobon* (*Der Brief des Paulus an die Römer: Theologischer Handkommentar zum Neuen Testament* [Berlin: Evangelische Verlaganstalt, 1963], p. 141).

[40]D. M. Lloyd-Jones, *The Gospel of John*; (sound recording [Barcombe Mills, East Sussex: Martyn Lloyd-Jones Recordings Trust, 1983]), sermon 1099.

[41]See J. H. Alexander, *More Than Notion* (London: Fauconberg Press, 1965, reprinted 1967). Foreword by D. M. Lloyd-Jones. It is not easy to quote a representative passage illustrating the assertions above, but an introspective atmosphere permeates the book as a whole. It is almost entirely concerned with 'impressions', 'fears', 'evidences' (*i.e.* subjective marks evidencing one's salvation); the 'recesses of the heart', the expression of deep feelings. I have no objection to any of this but there can be no doubt that an over-interest in such matters leads to introspection and needless doubt.

[42]His interpretation would have been stronger, I believe, had he noticed the exact parallelism between Romans 7:7–12 and Romans 7:13–25 which I may explain diagramatically below :

1) Question	What then shall we say? That the law is sin? (Verse 7a)	Did that which is good, then, bring death to me? (Verse 13).
2) Reply	By no means!	By no means!
3) Proposition	However, if it had not been for the law I had not known sin. (Verse 7c)	It was sin working . . . that sin might be shown to be sin. (Verse 13c)
4) Development	Verses 8–11	Verses 14–24. (Verse 25a intrusive).
5) Conclusion	So the law . . . (Verse 12)	So then I of myself serve the law but . . . (Verse 25)

Such a schema reveals that Romans 7:7–12 and Romans 7:13–25 go over the same ground twice, confirming Lloyd-Jones's view. It would also have confirmed his conviction that no special significance is to be seen in the change of tense. The change of sub-section is not at verse 14 but at verse 13.

[43]D. M. Lloyd-Jones, *The Puritans* (Edinburgh: Banner of Truth, 1987), p. 350.
[44]*Ibid.*, p. 366
[45]D. J. Lull sees Galatians 3 in much the same way in *The Spirit in Galatia* (Chico, California: Scholars Press, 1980), ch. 3, pp. 53–95.

Keep in Step with the Spirit

J. I. PACKER

Understanding the Spirit is a crucial task for
Christian theology at all times; honouring the
Spirit is a crucial task in Christian discipleship
today.

Is the church in danger of overemphasizing or
quenching the Spirit?
What are today's acts of the Holy Spirit?
Is charismatic life something new or unique?
Are modern spiritual gifts the same as those of the
New Testament?

Dr Packer considers these questions in the light of
Scripture and Christian history, and issues a
radical challenge to personal and corporate
revival.

'. . . this is a helpful, timely book which has much
to teach the Church today.'
Christian Weekly Newspapers

302 pages   Large paperback

Inter-Varsity Press